"OFTEN HUMOROUS, AND OCCASIONALLY HEARTRENDING."
—*Booklist*

"Losee engagingly relates the challenges and rewards of doing his duty for forty-five years in [this] spirited, episodic memoir."
— *The Cleveland Plain Dealer*

"Losee may be rustic, but he's no crude sawbones. . . . [He] manages to convey his respect for the practice of medicine while at the same time displaying a candor that is all too rare in the world of doctors. DOC will have you wishing that this no-nonsense, no-frills country doctor were your personal physician."
— *American Bookseller*

"Losee gives the reader an insight into the strains and the joys of doctoring in a small town. [His] book brings the ranchers, miners, fly fishermen, and townspeople he's met to life as he recalls nearly a half century of life in Madison County."
— *The Missoulian*

"[A] colorful narrative, which promises to appeal to a wide audience."
— *The Daily Inter Lake*

"Doc Losee gives the reader vivid images of people, places, and incidents, and threaded carefully through each are glimpses of human qualities that enable the reader to see both the awesome and the everyday in his career as a country doctor. The stories are told by a storyteller with passion, humor, and honesty."
    —LINDA SHADIOW, Professor
Northern Arizona University

"A giant of a story by a giant of a man. I enjoyed it immensely."
    —JOHN A. FEAGIN JR., M.D.
Duke University Medical Center

"This is a fascinating book about rural medicine practiced with endless work, courage, conviction, devotion, and individualism. Ron Losee's vignettes of Montana medicine in the raw should be required reading for young people thinking about a career in medicine, medical students, and especially post-graduate residents in orthopedic surgery. This man is a doctor for all doctors to follow. If one-tenth of the medical profession followed the principles of Dr. Losee, there would be no health crisis in America."
    —WAYNE O. SOUTHWICK, M.D.
Professor Emeritus, Orthopedics & Rehabilitation
Yale University School of Medicine

DOC

*Then and Now with a
Montana Physician*

R. E. Losee, M.D.

IVY BOOKS • NEW YORK

Ivy Books
Published by Ballantine Books
Copyright © 1994 by Ronald E. Losee

Library of Congress Catalog Card Number: 95-94966

ISBN: 0-8041-1415-3

This edition published by arrangement with Lyons & Burford, Publishers.

Manufactured in the United States of America

First Ballantine Books Edition: March 1996

10 9 8 7 6 5 4 3 2 1

I dedicate this work with all my heart
and with all my soul
to my wife,
OLIVE TATRO LOSEE,
and to my daughter,
REBECCA LOSEE ASHENHURST,
and to my son,
RONALD JONATHAN LOSEE,
and to my three grandchildren
—Rebecca's JOSHUA, AMBER, and DEIRDRE.

I love my family and all my in-laws, and although
my book is not their story it remains as a reference
to Papa's and Grandpa's time and manners. As
wonderful as it has been to have been called "Doc"
by the people, nothing supersedes Becky's and her
Kit's "Poppa," Jon's and his Cathy's "Pop," and the
grandchildren's veneration with "Grandpa,"
and Olive's "Grandpa!"

Contents

PART 3   BONES, JOINTS, AND KNEES

PART 4   NOW

PART 1

Somewhere West

Somewhere West

JOIN OLIVE, OUR two-year-old daughter Becky, and me, Ron Losee, as we depart, in August 1949 from No. 2 Shad Row in Middle Haddam, Connecticut, in our 1942 Ford Army Jeep (Serial Number: GPW 28810). We depart for "Somewhere Out West." It was time to go to work. Ma, Olive's mother, kept reminding me that I was still studying at the grand old age of twenty-nine. And she was right; it was time for her son-in-law to become practical, to earn a living, to take care of his family. We'd finished a Senior Internship in surgery at the Royal Victoria Hospital in Montreal. We'd saved what we thought was enough to get started, perhaps a little over a hundred dollars. Olive augmented this sum a bit by ironing clothes at a dollar a basket for neighborhood wives while, in preparation for departure, we paused at her sister Julie's 1734 cottage in Middle Haddam. She did this to pay for the Jeep overhaul and in anticipation of dire coming needs. Julie found the old junk Studebaker trunk that we then bolted to the rear of the Jeep. In preparation for the emigration and from scraps, we encased the area behind the open-sided front seats of the Jeep out of plywood scraps. We made a forward entrance to this construction that opened between the two front seats. We fixed screened window slots on the top side-edges of the contraption for Becky to peer out when she stood in her padded cell while we careened along at forty miles-per-hour. We painted the addition red to contrast with the blue Jeep. The conventional removable canvas top remained.

It was packed with old blankets; tire irons, tire patches,

3

jack, shovel, and ax strapped to the side; canned milk for Becky; duffel bags; and all we owned. There it is, stuffed with stuff! We even forced a scoured card table between the trunk and rear. Hit the foot pedal on the driver's side to clang the Bermuda carriage bell. Hit it again! With this, a couple of *Aw-oo-gahs*, and lots of hand-waving, we departed.

We synchronously crossed the Hudson River in the same westerly direction as the freight train of empty coal cars was crossing, to our north, over the neighboring cantilevered Poughkeepsie Bridge on its way to the Pennsylvania Coal Mines.

Going back to the 1930s, up the river twenty-five miles lies Upper Red Hook. It consisted of half a mile's length of the Albany Post Road, lined with a double row of houses, yet separating the Dutch Reformed Church and the two-room schoolhouse at the north end. An eighteenth-century red-sandstone milepost in front of the school bore the engraved marker: 107 MILES TO N YORK. The little school with its high-pitched come-to-order bell inspired the pupils toward the pursuit of excellence in a patriotic and secular way. Whereas the church, with its moaning, doomsday toll bell, its bell that boomed above Gothic windows overlooking the garden of the dead, gathered the children together to remind them of their mortality.

Henrietta Fraliegh, the schoolteacher, taught us the Constitution, how to darn our socks, and how to play chess.

Dominie French taught us adolescents the brotherhood of man, forgiveness, mercy, kindness, generosity, and the quintessential Golden Rule. In harmony with a strong pacifist movement in the thirties he furnished us boys with a copy of *The Horror of It*. After reviewing the book's pictures of flies covering the blown-apart faces of dead soldiers and dozens of other horrors, we lost our juvenile enthusiasm for war. Aside from this, he conveyed the idea that the privilege of living obliged us to pay our dues to Our Maker, and one possible way could be a life of service to mankind. Because of this, I can vividly remember the moment, at the age of thirteen, I vowed to become a doctor. I think I had just read Paul De Kruif's *Microbe Hunters*.

Grandmother, one night, reported to her country-doctor husband (a doctor's son, himself) that their grandson was going to be a doctor. This was in their living room/office, with the pill cabinet in one corner, topped by the brass microscope that would later fail me, and Granddad's leather chair in another. He got up from his chair and stepped to the fireplace. He stooped and knocked out a wet and burnt wattle of rank "Afrikander" pipe tobacco against the sunflower andiron, and snickered, "The damned little fool!" I knew enough to hear approval in those words, but it would be years until I understood their many truths.

We continue on our Jeep ride to "Somewhere West," now on the west side of the Hudson and looking back toward Connecticut; we recall a scene in pathology class at the Yale Medical School in New Haven in 1942. The sophomore class was sitting in two rows facing a doorway over which was inscribed HIC LOCUS EST UBI MORS GAUDET SUCCURRERE VITAE, which I think translates to "This place is where death gives comfort to life." The elevator door in the back of the room opened. Our classmate, sitting in the center of the front row, hastily took his last puff of a cigarette and smudged it out under his foot. The small, wiry, black-eyed, leather-faced, pongee-shirted, and bow-tied Dean-of-All walked around the front and faced and glared down at our seated classmate in the center. "Have you noticed the age of our custodian?" Silence. Continued drilling and piercing countenance. "You should know that he must clean up your mess. You knew that when you soiled this hallowed floor. No. Don't lean over." And, he meant, "Don't you dare touch your mess." He retreated and disappeared into the elevator. There was trouble this morning in the hallowed room. The elevator door opened again. He appeared again, this time carrying a broom and dustpan. The student sat there with feet wide apart, all the while imagining dismissal from school. The flattened cigarette butt still nestled there in its ashes. Winternitz leaned way over in a truly kyphotic manner, grabbing the broom just above the bristles, making sure that his effort was permanently implanted within each brain present in that holy room, on that holy day, forever! I don't remember the pathology lesson of the day.

At the autopsy table in front of us, Professor Winternitz had removed a diseased heart with what I thought to have been an excessively long and large knife. With his left hand dripping blood and holding the heart, he waved the knife in his right hand, approached Tony Stone, whom he called "The Rock," and suggested, "I suppose, at this moment, you are imagining that it is *my* heart that *you* are holding in *your* hand, Mr. Rock."

After the autopsy the class retired to the lab tables, each member to peer for countless hours into the microscope. Looking through it, I saw myriad individual rings of pulmonary cells finally bordered by strips of pleural cells like acres of sunflowers butted against a stone wall. My view was only two-dimensional. I questioned: How can this incomprehensible organization exist? Why does the wall stop here? How is it proportioned to the whole? What commands the pleura to contain the lung, the lung to contain the bronchi? Instantly I realized that I was observing but an iota of the structure of the whole organism, including the brain, and that I had to include the thought of the explosion of a galaxy upon the union of two microscopic gametes, whether human, animal, or plant. I proudly admit that these observations gave me a reverence for life.

It's 1949 again and we continued jeeping over the narrow two-lane road through the Water Gap. At the end of the day we bedded down in a farmer's cornfield in "Hex-Barned Pennsylvania Dutch Country." Becky slept in her Jeep house while Olive and I slept on blankets spread on the grass.

The following day, upon arrival in steaming Washington, D.C., we sought refuge at the apartment of Dr. John and Elizabeth Silensky. We slept on the hard, hot floor of their apartment that night. Denver, where we had become acquainted, was never this hot. John, my orthopaedic friend, and I spent the next morning at the Georgetown University Hospital where he was finishing his training. I assisted him that morning while he performed bilateral high tibial osteotomies to correct a severely bowlegged child. John was kind to invite me to help him operate, and in those days there was no thought to the contrary. Assisting as a visiting doctor is no longer a random decision of the surgeon who operates; instead today it has become a matter of *administration* approval.

Our visit with the Silenskys suggests our days at the Denver General Hospital.

My first internship, in Denver, followed my graduation from medical school in 1944. I had spent two summers at my father's place in North Las Vegas, Nevada, and wanted more of "The West." Denver General Hospital accepted my application and responded on stationery headed with a sketch of Denver's City and County Building, which Olive and I naively thought was a picture of the Denver General Hospital. It was very attractive and impressive. We studied the picture and imagined the surgical wing and the medical wing. We flourished the picture about, proudly showing classmates our fortune. It was even more impressive than Boston's Massachusetts General!

We arrived in Denver at the Rio Grande Railroad Station. We light-heartedly walked out of the station hand-in-hand, cantilevered by our bags. We were thrilled to start living beneath the Rocky Mountains, and happy to have ten dollars in our pockets. We boarded the trolley car, which soon turned, heading southward down Broadway. With the impairment of our baggage we stood up front where we could talk with the motorman. We looked east to see the Colorado State Capitol on our left, and then with a second look to the west, we confirmed to each other that, "Yes, there it is, right across from the Capitol. There it is, the Denver General Hospital!" And to the motorman, "Where do we get off? Here?"

"Yeah, if y' want *The City-County Building*," the motorman obliged.

"No. We want to get off here at the Denver General Hospital."

"Y' don't wanna get off here. Denver General's on down a few blocks."

And what we thought was the beautiful "Denver General Hospital" passed by.

We got off later, walked a block to the west, and stood facing the front entrance to the old brick building. With its huge brick stack in the rear, it looked like a tool factory in New Britain, Connecticut. Olive cried.

Now, thinking back about the Denver General Hospital as we saw it that day in 1944, Olive and I had walked inside a "politically devised wretched people tank," a social horror of the day very much resembling the present social horror of homelessness. There was exceptionally poor supervision by an almost nonexistent medical staff. The excuse was that there was a war on. I'm sorry to think there were plenty of doctors in private practice in Denver at the time who were too busy to do their duty. The doctors assigned to service patients at the Denver General Hospital then were a bunch of green, untrained interns. We worked a service (e.g., pediatrics, anesthesia, etc.), the best we could for four weeks and then changed to another. The night before starting the anesthesia service we would read in a panic about the four stages of ether anesthesia. This was our only instruction. Then, for the next morning, noon, and night, for four more weeks, we presided, sitting on a stool at the head of the operating table, armed with a can of ether in our right hand and a gauze-covered sieve-cup held with our left. We covered the face of and nearly choked the surgical patient about to have his rupture fixed by a greenhorn from Chicago who had served one year as an intern, during which time he had spent only four weeks learning surgery! He was now proclaimed the "surgical resident." There was no trained supervising surgeon in the operating room for "routine stuff," like herniorrhaphies, appendectomies, or the suturing of perforated stomachs. Thank God for the excellent professional nursing staff.

Our ten dollars was gone in a day or two and Olive found work at Montgomery Ward on Broadway for seventeen dollars a week. We were paid fifteen a month to intern. (Good hospitals like the Massachusetts General in those days paid naught.) Twice a month we were paid another fifteen if we rode the Denver Police ambulance all night. With this total income we were in clover. Once a month we ate out on the town!

Officer Mike Carrol chauffeured me my first night on duty as a police surgeon in the only white city ambulance, made by General Motors Cadillac. The protocol was to race to the scene and return as quickly as possible to be on-the-ready for the next emergency. My first ambulance case was that of a man who committed suicide in his garage. The man had killed himself by directing the muzzle of a twelve-gauge shotgun against his umbilicus and then pulling the trigger. The crumpled, warm corpse lay supine, with escaping intestinal gas forming bubbles of blood and stool that exuded from his blown-apart shirt front. Mike and I loaded the cadaver on the stretcher, shoved it into the back of the ambulance, and took off at eighty miles an hour to deposit the body within the small city morgue in back of the hospital. We received another call on our way. There was a quick reverse on the street and a run to Fifteenth Street, where we loaded a second patient destined for the Denver General Hospital. I accompanied the living and the dead in the back of the ambulance. The living, now recovered from an epileptic seizure, looked out and screamed, "We're going too Goddamned fast," and tried to open the door I was guarding. Mike saw this in the rear-view mirror, slammed on the brakes, and patient, corpse, and doctor were pasted against the partition. Officer Carrol knew exactly what to do in that situation! Only once more on this trip did I reposition the cadaver on the stretcher from which it had toppled as we rounded a street corner "too God-damned fast." On arrival we escorted the patient to the emergency room for "Greenhorn Care." Again, the nurses saved the day at the Denver General Hospital. Then, and only then, did we attempt to deposit the cadaver at the morgue.

On another police ambulance occasion that year, Officer Frank Tanko and I picked up the body of a man who had succumbed to a head-on collision with a trolley car. The man's head had been flattened and converted into the shape and size of a medium pizza. On another day, while riding on East Colfax Avenue, Tanko asked, "Doc, do you know how I'd like to die?"

I answered, "No," then wondered, now what's coming?

"I'd like to hit a trolley car—head on!"

At the moment, we were trailing the right rear of a trolley clanging westward. Ahead, and it seemed hardly a block away, was another trolley approaching us on the other track.

Tanko double-clutched, shifted down, fully accelerated, turned on the siren, passed the ongoing trolley on its right, then crossed the way to the left side of the street while missing the oncoming monster of steel by only yards.

Continuing our trip to "Somewhere West" in 1949, three days out of Washington, D.C., we parked in front of my mother's little house in Sarasota, Florida. Mother had fractured her hip and we had detoured our westward journey to help her convalesce. The surgeon set her hip and fixed it with a nail developed by the great surgeon from Boston, Smith-Peterson, a few years previously. This tri-flanged nail was driven from the side of the thigh below the hip, through the angle of the hip, up its neck, across the re-aligned fracture site, and into the head of the femur to hold the fractured ends together until they healed. The operation eliminated the need for traction and casts and enabled the victim to sit and to use crutches during the healing period. In spite of the wonderful nail, a consequential percentage of "nailed hips" either failed to unite or progressed to aseptic necrosis, implying a devitalized femoral head without infection.

Mother's hip united but it lost some blood supply and flattened enough to "speak with the weather" in ensuing years. It didn't cripple her.

The sweltering hot August in Sarasota passed and it was by now mid-September and we were anxious to continue our search for a place to settle. Mother was well enough to be alone again. We left Sarasota with a very small teardrop trailer coupled to our Jeep, and by two nights later had reached Biloxi, Mississippi. At this point in our trip, we were far south of Fort Knox, Kentucky, where Olive and I had spent two years while I was in service.

During the war, the army enlisted medical students in its Specialized Training Program. At the conclusion of the program the participant was discharged and then re-enlisted as a first lieutenant medical officer. While I was serving in Fort Knox, my discharge document from the A.S.T. program permitted me to purchase a war-surplus army Jeep, our first vehicle. Olive proudly drove around in our Jeep number GPW 28810. The colonel who saw me driving my personal Jeep was pissed. He ordered me to paint it another color or keep it off the post.

Our daughter Rebecca was born in the Kentucky Baptist Hospital in Louisville during my assignment at Fort Knox.

It was my first duty. I naively replied to the major's inquiry that I was more interested in surgery than in medicine. He then assigned me to examine the groins and anuses of all the soldiers passing through the Fort's separation center. Lieutenant Longacre was given the same high honor.

The first platoon of men entered the room and formed two lines. I carefully palpated each inguinal ring for a bulge and the scrotum for a hydrocele or tumor. To examine the anus I walked behind the rank, had each soldier bend over and spread his gluteals. There were no rectal gloves nor an anoscope available for proper inspection. By the time I had even looked at five men, another twenty were crowding the door. My immediate assessment was that the procedure was a hypocritical farce. At my present age I would tell the general and secretary of defense to go to hell and I would enjoy the brig before I would do that again.

Christmas Day we examined one thousand and five hundred dischargees. To hold down the backlog of examinees, I soon learned to face two men, and with my palms up, put two of my right-hand fingers up the inguinal canals of the man on my right while applying two of my left to the man on my left. With smart military sidesteps past two men at a time, I passed along the lineup. I then walked by the rear of the rank, swishing the spotlight up the clefts of spread butts. This rapid maneuver gave time for another move at the chessboard, withdrawn from the table drawer, between assemblies. Longacre was not a chess player. Around the tenth or twentieth day, while seated in his tilted chair against the wall, waiting for the next group, he clasped his face between his locked fingers and screamed that he was going blind. Hysterically blind, they took him away. Longacre had seen one asshole too many.

On our way Somewhere West we enjoyed a mint julep at the Court of the Three Sisters in New Orleans where the waiter served Miss Becky her very own treat with a deep bow. After camping in a cottonfield the next night, it took us three days to cross Texas. But, on our way we clanged the Bermuda bell as we drove through the emptied streets of Fort Worth early in the morning. After spending a hairy overnight in the Garden of the Gods with hoodlums shooting while circling our outfit, we halted at the home of friends in Denver to catch up on our laundry.

We left the army in June 1947 for a second go-around at the Denver General Hospital. At the beginning, I was drafted to run the emergency room because I was "experienced"—I had done this before. We each worked a twelve-hour shift alone. There were two rooms across a large hallway with seven fixed white-granite-coated examining tables, not gurneys, in each room. We'd work our way down the row of seven, sewing lacerations, starting intravenous drips, ducking psychotic thrusts, diagnosing appendicitis, mountain sickness, asthmas, clap, flea bites, cancer of the rectum, birth, and death. Here's a fool who put his penis in a ring and couldn't remove it from the near gangrenous organ. Work one room, then run across the hall to minister to those of the other sex in the other room. "Who's first?" She is a little girl whose father put a firecracker in her mouth. She is a total innocent with little wet eyes sadly looking up above a blackened, bloody mouth. God, why? Where is she now?

A young black lady waited for me at the fifth table on the female side. She was unable to talk. In the mad rush, I diagnosed an hysteria, and hypnotized her (I learned how to do this in the army); she talked, and left gratified. She returned the next day with a diptheritic membrane. I nearly killed her with my magic, my obscene shamanism, I learned. She survived.

I used this time in the emergency room to search my inclinations—medicine or surgery? I liked surgery, applied for a residency at Yale, and was turned down there but accepted at the Royal Victoria Hospital in Montreal.

Now, no longer in the emergency room but on the obstetric floor, Bill, the ob-gyn resident, taught us obstetrical forceps skill by rotating occiput-posterior-presenting babies back again so we, the lowly interns, could master the forceps technique. I cringe remembering those lessons. No harm was done. Amazingly, the angels must have smiled on young, enthusiastic hearts not yet endowed with sober judgment.

The surgical resident might have let us remove an appendix or two. It's fortunate he kept the scalpel for himself. Rotating interns should assist. They are not surgeons. It was appalling that there was only the occasional accomplished surgeon supervising. During this second internship in 1947–48 at the Denver General Hospital, the new interns used nitrous oxide and Pentothal instead of ether to render anesthesia. This unsupervised use of the above agents by an untrained intern caused the death of a young man being operated on for a simple fractured patella. There was no one available who *even knew* how to help the young intern save his patient in that anesthetic crisis.

The best service that year was the Resident John Silensky, who was trained by Arthur Steindler at Iowa University. Dr. Silensky capably did his duty in orthopaedics. He enthusiastically taught us principles he learned at Iowa. He taught as if we all wanted to be orthopaedists and when we were working with him I think we all did want that. He was a real doctor, dedicated and concerned about his charges. He'd look at the X-rays of an indigent elderly woman who was admitted with a femoral fracture of the neck that had been neglected for a month. He would say, "What are we supposed to do now? It's a little late. The head's off the neck!" He commandeered proper help when needed.

During my second session at the Denver General Hospital, police ambulance service was part of the internship. The first night on duty I was assigned to accompany a new intern at the police station and was to ride with him. While waiting in the police surgeon's office, the intern asked, "Not much really happens here, does it?"

I responded, "Wait and see."

There wasn't much waiting. We rode seventy miles an hour to Five Points. Our patient was an adolescent lying on his back on the sidewalk. A knife handle was sticking out of the left side of his chest and was moving reciprocally with each irregular and failing heartbeat. We placed him, supine, in the ambulance like this, and both of us rode in the back with him. We looked at each other. The intern asked me, "What the hell do we do with the knife?"

"Take it out, what else?"

We took the knife out of his chest. There was nothing else we could do in those days. Cardiac surgery was just being thought of then, but there was none available yet at the Denver General Hospital.

The kid died. No time for the morgue. A rush to Larimer

Street and we picked up another victim. This man survived an oblique eighteen-inch-long knife slash down his back. The living and the dead were delivered.

We picked up a baby that appeared very recently dead in an hysterical household. I had the child in my lap on the front seat of the ambulance as Officer Fithian raced through town. We didn't know the mouth-to-mouth resuscitation technique then. I took off the tube of my stethoscope and was sucking on it to aspirate the infant's pharynx. It was to no avail. I was concerned about the possibility of catching diphtheria when we reached the emergency room, but when we got the child under the light, we saw she had been garroted. The ring around the neck was plain!

Again, we were called to an impoverished section near the railroad tracks and entered a shack. The place did have a flush toilet in the rear. The patient was a middle-aged, emaciated man in tattered overalls. In death he was rigid, on his knees, bent over the toilet bowl with a remaining intact thick column of clotted blood formed between the lips of his limpid, opened mouth and connected to the bottom of the bowl.

I could hear my granddad saying, "The damned little fool!"

Resuming our 1949 adventure, after a day's visit and finishing our laundering in Denver, we turned west again at Fort Collins, Colorado. We were aiming for Lander, Wyoming, where my father's friend Dr. Paul Holtz was practicing.

My parents divorced in 1938 and Dad married Bette. Since divorce didn't fare well in Upper Red Hook, New York, during its Calvinistic heyday, the sinning couple migrated to North Las Vegas, rented the Kyle Ranch, and boarded other "sinning couples" establishing their six weeks' residency requirement. Dr. Holtz (flight surgeon at McLaren Field) and his family sublet there. In 1939 I rubbed my ankle raw horseback riding in the desert in back of Dad's place. Dr. Holtz saved my life. He treated my blood poisoning with sulfathiazole, which made me puke! Years later he asked me, a new M.D., to come to Lander, Wyoming, where he had settled after the war.

We had been driving all day. The Caché la Poudre River, a clear thirty-foot-wide, rock-strewn stream, was on our left. It was a long, slow haul around one rattlesnake in the road and up to Cameron Pass. If we were lucky, we could find a campsite in lonely Walden, on the other side. We weren't lucky. The sky darkened. Snow fell. We reached the top. We started to descend the western side. Lonely. Lonely. There were neither stars nor cars to be seen. We looked down a long, snowy embankment on the left. A man frantically waved us down with his flashlight. A logger had rolled his truck down to the bottom and was "layin' down there." We parked GPW 28810 & Co. We couldn't see the wreck through the snowflakes. The man and I slid our butts all the way down the bank to the wrecked truck. The logger had been thrown free but had fractured his tibia.

"I need a fiah," was his shivering and hypothermic request.

We wired the floor mat of his truck around his broken leg and started the big upward haul. We slipped, we strained, we farted, and I, this easterner retching in the high altitude, puked with the mighty effort to get him to the top. Olive poured lots of sweet coffee down his throat. We stuck the man, bloody and muddy, between the freshly laundered blankets in our trailer and waited for the arrival of the ambulance service from Fort Collins, which eventually happened. If there were no wrecks involving the ambulance on the way back, I'm sure he recovered.

The forest ranger gave a hand, then gave us a bed in his log house two miles down the road, and his wife fed us elk steaks and hot cakes for breakfast.

The trailer had become a mud hole. Vast, empty Wyoming plains lay before us the next day. The Sweetwater River trickled east from South Pass. The Wind River Range loomed to the west. Becky became shocky in the afternoon.

(Two years later we realized she didn't have the enzymes to handle elk meat.) We made Lander that night.

The Holtz Family sheltered and pampered us for three or four days. I "doctored" with Paul. Olive helped Thelma. We played bridge at night. Dr. Holtz kindly asked me to join his practice. I declined; I wanted to solo it. With our last fifteen dollars we departed amidst an early October snowstorm.

Across the Continental Divide, over the western slope of the Wind River Range, into a white Green River Valley. Snow from the north mercilessly beat the Jeep's riders. The card table on the windward side helped, but we had to let little Becky wet her pants rather than freeze by unbundling her. We used a hunk of the fifteen remaining dollars for a room with a kerosene stove in Kemmerer, Wyoming, that night.

Montpelier, Utah, was a pretty town. How does one start a practice here? They didn't teach me how to start a practice at Yale! We'd decided to head for Longview, Washington, where Uncle Darb and Aunt Ags would grubstake us. We desperately wanted to settle down.

If there had been any experience that had best prepared me for what lay ahead, it was the previous year that we had spent at the Royal Victoria Hospital in Montreal.

(Flashing back a year.) We were scheduled to arrive, ready for duty, on the morning of the first day of July 1948. All of our worldly possessions were piled in the Jeep as we approached the Canadian border from the Northeastern Kingdom of Vermont. Olive was driving because I had a bellyache from eating peanuts the day before. By morning we arrived at the hospital and were directed to store the trailer in the parking area not too far away from the private parking area of the Ross, the private pavilion of the hospital that serviced affluent Montrealers. We neatly parked the trailer next to a Jaguar. I had to get going, bellyache and all! The chief resident, Charles Ripstein, poked my abdomen and thought my appendix was quieting and I would be spared a laparotomy for the time being.

Mount Royal overlooks Montreal and the north shore of the Saint Lawrence River. The Royal Victoria Hospital lies at the southeast foot of the mountain and overlooks the city, the river, and more immediately, McGill University just across Spruce Street. From my window in the intern quarters, the city, the Sun Life tower (the tallest building then), the wheat elevators and docks along the river, and the long, multiply-trussed, up-river Victoria Bridge all confronted the wooded plains to the south, to the States. Olive and Little Becky were imprisoned in the Carpentiers' apartment on Le Duc Street in Ville Saint Laurent, a suburb.

I was assigned to Howard Dawson's surgical team of Sandy MacIntosh and Stewart Baxter. Dawson leaned toward oncology, MacIntosh was the chest surgeon, and Baxter was master of thyroid surgery and children's surgical and fracture problems. This was no Denver General Hospital, this was an orderly, organized, and proper teaching institution. There were weekly grand rounds and fracture rounds conducted in an amphitheater. (The Canadian general surgeons handled fractures, but not urological or gynecological problems.) Visiting dignitaries from Toronto, England, Boston, and New York lectured. There were four surgical teams, each serviced by an assistant resident and two interns. Patients were admitted to the service on alternate days. The interns examined them and their blood and urine; then they wrote up the histories and physical examinations. Volumes and volumes! Interns administered all intravenous solutions and surgical dressings. All special studies, family contacts, X-rays, consultation arrangements, progress notes, interdepartment errands were expedited. The interns were up half the night with their patients. The interns assisted at all operations upon their assigned patients and were instructed in performing progressively complex operations on the public patients. A senior intern would become proficient in performing appendectomies, hernia repairs, and hemorrhoidectomies, but he might be permitted to do one cholecystectomy, radical breast resection, partial gastrectomy, or thyroidectomy during the latter part of his junior term. They let me remove a lady's gall bladder, and I did a good job.

This was the year that introduced me to the complexities of ill-performed biliary surgery, the tragedy of a post-gastrectomy failure of a duodenal closure, the disaster of injury to the recurrent laryngeal nerve, and inadvertent excision of the parathyroid gland in thyroidectomies, as well as the horrors of portal-vein hypertension (causing intractable hemorrhage), and esophageal stenosis (narrowing) from cancer. The surgical list might include colostomies for bowel obstructions, colectomies for uncontrolled ulcerative colitis of the large intestine, abdominal-peroneal resections of the rectum for cancer, radical mastectomies for breast cancer, choleduodenostomies for biliary problems, gastrectomies, thyroidectomies, and subdiaphragmatic abscess drainage.

The last third of the year I served with Gavin Miller, the chief surgeon. He did his subtotal gastrectomies (partial stomach removals) for intractable ulcers in an hour. The great Frank Lahey from Boston watched our team one day. He wore spectacles with lower-half lenses only. He tipped his head back to inspect Miller's intestinal clamps, approved them, and stuck them in his pocket.

The year enabled me to practice by December 1949. It was marvelous for me. It was rough on Olive, who was stuck in French-speaking Ville Saint Laurent, with her man home late and pooped on alternate nights and gone the next morning at six.

Having completed my Montreal internship at the end of June 1949, we continue our journey, now traveling west of Wyoming in October of that year. Empty beer and soda cans looked tempting to us on the side of the U.S. highway outside of Mountain Home, Idaho. Olive, to this day, reminds me that I was too damned proud to pick them up and turn them in for money in the next town, Boise. We continued, Blue Mountain Range to our left. We parked and slept

in a wheat field near Pendleton, Oregon, after passing a
barn whose entire side bore the painted advertisement, MAIL
POUCH TOBACCO. The next day, at four o'clock, in Hood
River, Oregon, we ran out of cash. But we had sixty cents
worth of good United States postage stamps. Although the
post office would not redeem their product, the Texaco garage man accepted them for gas, and I know gave us more!

It was midnight as we approached the bridge in Portland
that crossed the Columbia River. Our map read, "Fifteen
cents toll." But there were no cars crossing in the night and
there was no toll-master to collect what we hadn't.

As we sloped off the Washington State side of the
bridge—*Bang, flobbada, flobbada, flobbada!* That was the
toll that fate ordained that wicked night! Hammer, hammer,
hammer in the wet bar pit for an hour. Olive never bitched
as I fixed the flat tire.

We arrived in Longview in the middle of the night and
in an instant one of life's little theatrical sets changed from
a cold, wet, open-sided, bumping Jeep to a warm, lighted
kitchen. There was my aunt, who used to squeeze me at
age five, laughing and welcoming us, and her husband, serious Uncle Darb, full of questions. We had come from the
Atlantic to the Pacific in a roundabout way. If we were to
settle in the West, it was high time to get serious, and here
was a reprieve and an assistance.

The next morning Jeep GPW 28810 and its tag-along
was not on the street. Uncle Darb had gotten it towed away,
decommissioning it for the time being. He deemed it wise
and professional to sell us his 1935 Chrysler Coupe for
$500.00 that he loaned us, interest free, for ten years. I pre-
ferred the Jeep, but November and December approached.

I gathered two hundred and fifty bucks, an economic
windfall, less train fare, for a two weeks' locum-tenens job
with Dr. Holtz in Lander again while Olive and Becky
stayed in Longview. I turned thirty. It was high time to
make a living!

Before leaving the Northwest we investigated Oregon
towns. In Corvallis, I stopped to inquire with the local phy-

sician about a prospective practice. We were sitting side by side on a couch in his office when he leaned toward me and asked, "How many roads lead into this town?" I wasn't sure, but Corvallis wasn't very large then, so I answered, "Four, I guess." He expounded, "Yes, that's right. There are four roads that lead into this town. There's one from the north. There's one from the south. There's one from the east and there's one from the west. There are four roads in and there are four roads out. Good-bye, young man!"

At Willamina, Oregon, I was invited to a Kiwanis Club lunch, then escorted up the road to the chiropractor's office. I was shown his colorful assortment of examining gowns and assured that they cheered the ill. We then entered a dark, slate-covered room with the opposite wall sprouting hydrants, valves, pressure gauges, and hoses. I knew it was his "colonic irrigation room." It was hard for me to believe that a customer would walk (barefooted?) in that dark room in a colored nightshirt and let the professor grease the anus, insert the hose, and turn on the hydrant. I imagined the stench, the sound of wet farts, and the groans from belly cramps and tenesmus. Does this irrigation bring forth some pathological rectal orgasm that would addict the duped person who would ever return? I remembered that back in Montreal I had seen a patient suffer a near fatality from peritonitis caused by a "colonic irrigation." After showing me his "diagnostic machine," where he "tuned in to the pancreas" to "diagnose" diabetes, he pathetically retreated and sat in the corner, wept, and offered to sell me his shop for $30,000. Having just purchased gas with postage stamps, I was in no condition to buy. I was appalled at the cruelty of the people who had educated him at the time, and we left Willamina, depressed.

The Northwest, we determined, was not for us. We preferred the physiognomy of the Rocky Mountains and the Western Plains, the "Cowboy and Indian Country." The Northwest was more settled and had an Eastern semblance from which we had chosen to escape. We pressed on in the Chrysler Coupe.

Now grubstaked by my relatives, we had accumulated a black medical bag containing a stethoscope, four artery forceps, surgical scissors, a scalpel with a package of No. 23 blades (a Royal Victoria Hospital favorite, a blade with less curvature on its belly and a useful point at its tip), a hypodermic set, some bandages, and a minute supply of what I thought were essential pills. We also had five hundred dollars in hand, borrowed from Uncle Darb.

We set out toward the east, over Mullen and MacDonald Passes in the northern Rockies, and on we drove to Helena, Montana, where the brother of my Dartmouth College roommate was practicing medicine. We stopped at Buddy and Mary Little's place. Buddy had heard that a doctor was wanted in a little cow town called Ennis, Montana, and to entice a doctor to practice there, the citizens were building a combined office and residence. "Let's go to Ennis," we said. And we did.

As we entered Ennis at dusk, on the left side of the road at town's edge was a building framework that was to be the new clinic and physician's residence. We passed by, rounded a left-hand curve to the east, and viewed the display of the main street of Ennis below and the entire north-south stretch of the Madison Range beyond. The conifer foliage and the snow made these mountains appear singularly black and white. We passed through town and climbed the bench land and five miles of alluvial fan that led to Jack Creek where it emerged from the mountain range. Here we were entertained by the building committee hosted by Bill and Lois Bry at their dude ranch. We ate illegally harvested elk for supper by the smoky fireplace in a sod-roofed log house. Olive and I were thoroughly studied by the committee. I was interested in neither a clinic building nor a residence, but suggested to the town fathers (and mother— Alice Orr) that they change their plan and make a little hospital out of their effort. They all thought this to be an excellent idea, and Olive and I agreed to return to live in Ennis.

Three days later, after sundown, November 29, 1949, our family of three stopped at the Sportsman's Lodge across the road from the hospital site for supper. Otis and Laura Crooker fed us a steak that night. I wanted to pay, but Otis said, "We'll get you later." I examined the hand of their helper, Mr. Pistol Kraft, in the dining room of the Lodge and felt of some use. We were rebuked when we reached the Bry home at eight o'clock that night.

"Where've you been? You've got house calls to make!"

From that time onward I never went to sleep in Ennis, Montana, without a phone call to awaken me, until the mid-sixties when Dr. Gene Wilkins came to Ennis to live.

My guide that cold, black night was Bill Hill, the lame poacher, who had shot the elk upon which we feasted at our initial visit. The first house call was to a ranch in the valley on the outskirts of Jeffers, Ennis' smaller, sibling town on the east side of the Madison River. The crossroad, which was Jeffers, had a small Episcopal church and a smaller Masonic hall kitty-cornered from Helen Wonder's post office. Our destination, a ranch house, was a mile to the southeast at the foot of a two-hundred-foot glacial terrace. We were greeted at the kitchen door by three men, the old rancher and his two middle-aged sons. They escorted me to the back bedroom. The room had only the double bed, a chair, and perhaps a small stand. The light source was a bare sixty-watt electric light bulb hanging from a cord at the middle of the ceiling. The patient was an old woman suffering with a strangulated femoral hernia. The gut had been stuck in the sack protruding from her right groin for hours. All eyes were upon me, the proclaimed professional, about to "doctor" in the Madison Valley. I manipulated the bulging mass. There was no budging the contents of the protrusion back into its abdominal abode. I ordered the foot of the bed elevated and snow brought in from outside. I packed the snow around the mass. I retrieved the hypodermic set, purchased in Portland, from my black bag, loaded it with morphia that Buddy Little had furnished, and injected. Still, the trapped intestine could not be squeezed proximally into the abdominal cavity. There was a lot of squeezing, silence, and intense onlooking of the old husband and his two sons.

Nothing gave way and I turned to tell the audience, "Sometimes we have to operate a strangulated hernia like this."

"Nobody operates on Ma," the old rancher said.

Ma didn't want an operation either!

Suddenly a little squish of intestine squirted under my hand and in a short while I had the gut back in the abdomen where it belonged. The gut had not lost its blood supply. I devised an old-fashioned yarn truss for the old lady and begged exit. An hour had passed and we had more house calls to make.

"How much do we owe you, Doc?"

I'd passed their test! The word "Doc," to me, sounded better than "Mr. President."

Now what's this about "How much?" I was a green, thirty-six-year-old boy-doctor. This had never happened to me before. If money had been mentioned at Yale, we would have been expelled by nightfall. In Upper Red Hook, New York, I picked strawberries as a youngster for three cents a quart and it took all day to pick forty or fifty quarts.

This isn't strawberry-picking. I'm a professional. But let's not be extortionary, I thought.

"That will be three dollars."

No one smiled. One of the men reached deep in his pocket, brought forth the money, and counted it. I pocketed the three silver dollars and have kept them in my bureau drawer, yet to this day, to remind me of those folks and my initiation to the Madison Valley.

PART 2

Madison Medicine

Moving In

ENNIS, MONTANA, IS but a dot on the map. It's a hundred and twenty miles south of Helena, Montana's state capital. It's nearly that far from both Butte, to the northwest, and Bozeman, to the northeast. Ennis lies at the north end of the seventy-five-mile-long and eight-mile-wide Madison River Valley. The valley is bounded at its east by the Madison Range of the Rocky Mountains and at its west by the Tobacco Root Range. As we first approached the valley's northern boundary, over Norris Hill, Olive remarked that all she could see was brown. Five years later her sister Julie, crossing Norris Hill, exclaimed, "Jesus, this looks like Jerusalem." When I first crossed Norris Hill at night, I noted only one lonely red light-emitting diode coming from somewhere down there. It was the only artificial light peeping out from the vast valley. When we reached Ennis, ten miles farther on, the diode turned into Otis Crooker's red, hundred-watt electric lightbulb on top of his Sportsman's Lodge. His motel served the traveler about to descend the alluvial edge bounding the western edge of Ennis.

William Ennis, the town's founder, and his family reportedly settled in the Madison Valley in 1866, arriving from Missouri. His granddaughter, Winifred Jeffers, rented us her new log house built on the site of the original Ennis homestead. Fire destroyed the old two-storied home in 1917. The new log house, finished in 1949, faced Main Street at the end of a long and crumbling concrete walk shaded by cottonwood trees. The agreed rent was fifty-five dollars to be promptly paid on the first day of the month. (This prompt-payment bit wasn't what I was about to experience in my forthcoming practice of medicine in rural Montana!) Were we tardy in our obligation, after the second or third day of the month, we unfailingly heard the staccato, "Rent's due!" from our landlady. I never did try "Fee's due" with my patients.

The end of the crumbling concrete walk abuts another crumbling concrete sidewalk bounding the north side of Main Street. To the left, through the dust, with a few pickup trucks parked diagonally on both sides of the street, we can see the *entire* east half of town contained within a block. Beyond, the outline of the Madison Range is always higher than the dust-cloud—that is, until a band of sheep passes through town. To the right, the west, this half of Ennis terminates with the square, two-storied, dingy grade school that faces Main Street from the elevated alluvial till. This is the complete town scene. Dogs—the town bums—run from between the buildings, snarl from the back of pickup trucks, and mount each other, male or female, in front of the citizenry and children, anywhere, anytime. Listen to the heehaw of Lyle Thompson's donkey, disturbed by a dog as he grazes along Poop Creek, so called because of its distinctive odor, redolent of human sepsis that it has gathered while meandering past privies on its way to the Wide Missouri. But Poop Creek's aroma is diluted with the smell of fat vapors that seep through the stucco beneath the asphalt roofing of the Ennis Cafe and mix with the humors of a fresh flop from Miss Tits, Fay Jeffers' cow. If you take a deep breath, you can just get a hint of the skunk that Heinie Rakeman can't dislodge from under the drugstore at our left. This town has not been cursed yet with ordinances, politics, and taxes. It's not even a hundred years old. Folks are too busy living, too busy playing pan at Oscar's Bar, too busy gathering at the post office across the street, too busy gossiping while leaning on Winifred Jeffers' fence right here under the cottonwood tree on our left—all too busy to bother about odors, sepsis, fallen and scattered cottonwood branches, or building repairs. Who

needs a street-cleaning machine when Jesso Baker, cursed
with age and a speech defect, arises at four o'clock in the
morning to sweep the sidewalk in front of the three bars?
For this, Jesso, who pronounces "beer" as "bee-oh," re-
ceives a free one now and then. There's provision for a
town fire crew, however; Howard Barnett drives the tin-can
fire truck. It's Ennis' first, a 1941 Ford pickup sporting a
two-hundred-gallon water-tank and a pump balanced on the
front bumper. Charley Bauer, the fire chief, and his friends
organized this acquisition in 1947.

At its western end Main Street ascends a grade while
curving northward heading toward Butte and Helena. Its
eastern end curves south, immediately bridging the Madison River leading to Idaho, Wyoming, and Yellowstone
Park.

On the east end of town the farmers' co-op faces Waller
Angle's hardware store. On the south side of the street
stands Julie Erdie's bar. Back toward the center of town is
Hal Pasley's Chevrolet garage. Fred Nelson's Ford garage
is across the street. Olive and I patronized General Motors
and Ford. These two corporations and the government succeeded in devouring any capital we acquired over the next
generation.

Across the street from our crumbling walks is Oscar's
Bar. Oscar himself could be seen standing in the doorway,
leaning against the jamb when there were no customers. He
spent nearly two years leaning for reportedly cheating in a
gambling operation within.

"Prosecutorial" discretion was the accepted, blessed practice of the day. The state's attorney general allegedly enjoyed the gambling in Ennis. The county attorney denied
himself "saloon-heaven" in Ennis. He discretely refrained
from bar-hopping in Ennis, abstaining from, no doubt, certain embarrassments, confrontations, and professional en-
tanglements. But he liked Ennis the way it was.

It was Oscar who taught me a cardinal application of the
golden rule when selecting the proper consultant for my patient. Oscar developed a chronic hoarseness. I looked down

his larynx as he sat on the folding chair in the backroom office of our log house. I examined his vocal cords with my laryngeal reflector. I either gagged him too much to see anything, or saw nothing, or saw something and I didn't know what I saw. I referred him to the otolaryngologist in Bozeman, the only specialist in the city at the time. The hearsay was that he gave Oscar a shot of penicillin. But Oscar had an intelligent premonition and knew damned well that the administered penicillin shot was crap. He returned to his bar for a day or two. Then, in silent desperation he walked out of his bar, turned to the west, continued all alone, out of town, and hitch-hiked to the railroad station eighty miles away. He took the train to the Mayo Clinic where he was laryngectomized for a malignancy. His speaking days had ended but his life was spared for many years. My lesson from that moment was to pick the consultant for my patients whom I would choose for myself and then to continue to worry about my selection until the problem had been resolved.

The post office was the center of town activity in those days. Winifred Jeffers owned it, ran it, rented it to the government, and ruled it as the postmistress. "The Stage," an oversized metal box on wheels, delivered the daily mail. Upon arrival to Ennis, "The Stage" backed up to the lofty, roofless post-office stoop, obstructing Main Street long enough for the driver to hurl the mail sacks and parcels upon it. "The mail's in!" And it would be all strewn about, with professional authority, in the dust, in the occasional rain, or in the snow, to be retrieved by Winifred and placed in little brass-framed windowed cubicles at her own proper timing. It was impossible for me just to pick up my mail. There was always another citizen in the post office who had some symptom (cramps or some other irregularity) to report.

We had a movie house in town, The Madisonian, owned by Mr. and Mrs. Erie. Mrs. Erie vigilantly kept track of the age of the children. After our son Jon arrived and then grew enough to accompany his sister Becky to the movie house, he asked his mother for "tiptoe money." "Tiptoe money" consisted of a few pennies for Jon because *he wanted to pay too*, even though children under six could get in free. He had to stand on his tiptoes to render his pennies to Mrs. Erie, who presided in the little windowed box at the theater's entrance. On the epochal day when Jon became six years old, he ran back across the street to our house to tell his mother that "tiptoe money" didn't work any more and that Mrs. Erie wouldn't let him in until he produced "real money," fifteen cents. Mr. Erie, the tall, lean, and elderly ex-sheriff of Madison County, sat at the back of the movie house and used his flashlight to maintain order amongst the attending teenagers. Moms with babes went upstairs to the tiny "crying room."

There was another bar in town, the Silver Dollar. It's previous proprietor, Larry Dunn, didn't want to tear down the two-foot-wide cottonwood tree occupying the spot where he wished to build his icehouse in back of the bar. He built around it. The tree still stands in the middle of the old icehouse room attached to the back of the bar. Tar paper around the trunk protruding through the roof pretty well kept the wet out of the place.

I am told that in prohibition days the icehouse was rarely used for ice. Instead, its *sawdust* was used to hide jugs of contraband. Kept out of sight under the bar, there was one sole bottle available. A shot glass, water glasses, and a pitcher of water were in sight. There were no mixed drinks in those days in Ennis. A man would stand up to the bar for his drink. The bartender retrieved the bottle from beneath. The customer would pour into the shot glass, until not quite full, then dump that into his own drinking glass and use water as a chaser. The price was twenty-five cents. When Hugh Wakefield, the banker, stood to have his drink, customarily other men who had been sitting in the shadows of the room would gather to immediately stand alongside the banker and silently let the bartender fill their shot glasses at the same time. The banker paid the round.

Poop Creek crossed beneath Main Street at the base of

the hill below the school. After perfuming its way by the Ennis Cafe it passed just west of our log house. Poop Creek was off limits to our kids. Our water source, seventy feet away from it, offered Epicurean-class drinking water.

The dentist's upstairs office was next door on our side of the street. Olive once witnessed our five-year-old Jonathan pumping the dentist's chair to raise Dr. Best himself ceiling high. Becky tells me today he would always fill the children's cupped hands with mercury when they visited. The youngsters marveled at the antics of the neurotoxin as they poured the heavy, silvery metal from hand to hand. They haven't twitched yet from the exposure. Instead, they tell of pedaling the foot-powered dental drill while visiting the grand old man.

Finally, to complete our tour of Ennis, think of the town as it sits in the lap of the entire north-south expanse of the Madison Range, five miles away. In summer, the dark- and black-green conifer foliage covers the base of the range and contrasts with the gray, rocky tips. In winter the black contrasts with the snow. There is a lot of cold weather in Ennis. Snow has capped the range, in random years, even in July and August.

Upon our arrival at Ennis, the Bry family generously hosted us for a couple of weeks. A week before Christmas 1949, we moved into the log house. We moved in with nothing but a doctor's bag, a card table, an army cot, and our clothes. Mrs. Orr, proprietor of the Bear Creek Ranch and enthusiastic member of the new hospital board, loaned us a chair, a two-seat cowhide-covered bench, and a home-made desk. The landlady furnished the electric stove. We brought the refrigerator and mattress from Bozeman. The first morning in town we woke up to the donkeys' heehawing down main street and Miss Tit's mooing and plopping outside our bedroom window. Subsequently we always woke up to the telephone ringing, which, too often, was followed by, "It's five o'clock. Aren't you up yet?"

The closed-in front porch led into the living area which was divided, partially, to identify a kitchen area in the rear.

Two small rooms sandwiching a smaller bathroom completed the arrangement. We furnished the office in the little rear room with an army cot for examining patients, two folding chairs, and the card table. The total medical equipment was in the bag, stored on the floor under the card table.

Mrs. William Clark, short, cheerful, and concerned, brought her three-year-old grandson to the house and we ushered her into the back room with the card table and two folding chairs. I examined the boy and he had a cold. The grandmother sat in the folding chair across from me at the card table while the boy was on the army cot, under the window. I had spent fifteen minutes with the two when the ugly truth devastated me. This boy has a common cold! In an instant I recalled medical rounds in the wards at New Haven Hospital with Professor Blake commanding the entourage. I recalled the professor leaning over the nude upper half of the patient percussing the chest with adroit little taps all the while maintaining the most serious, humorless countenance. I recalled the professor's astute diagnosis of an incurable illness at the time. Returning, in spirit, to my place across the card table, I realized I could name the illness but could not cure it, and somewhere along the line a great hypocrisy had entwined its thorny fibers into the great gauze of medical education! The truth is slow to reveal itself to some of us. For me, it took time, humor, practiced honesty, and above all, the sympathetic understanding of my patients to finish an inadequate teaching job begun by my proud professors and to instruct me that the word "doctor" means "teacher" and not "God."

I played my proper role as physician and informed Mrs. Clark that little Jerry had but a harmless cold, and advised her to put him to bed, to force fluids, and to give him a baby aspirin! Years later we learned aspirin could have killed a child suffering with Reye's Syndrome, an unheard of entity in 1950. I quickly distrusted "playing the role as a physician" because it interfered with my personal ability to communicate with and think about my patients. Because of this I soon felt free to challenge accepted practices. Using common sense I emphasized that fever was the natural way to fight bacterial invasions into children's systems. I reserved the use of aspirin to ward off febrile convulsion. It wasn't long before a few patients quit me to go to Bozeman because I did not generously prescribe. I chuckle now as I recall Tana Rakeman, the druggist's wife, anxiously remarking to me, after my first month of practice, "Doctor, you don't write very many prescriptions, do you?"

My father and stepmother came for Christmas. Somebody lent us a bed for them to use on our back porch that served as the spare room. Dad and I built a lab bench we installed in the ten-by-ten rear office. It was quite a lab! It was totally unfurnished and since the doctor seemed to be the last to be paid, I had no idea how long it would remain that way. Luckily, with meager proceeds in hand, we all left town for a day away, drove up Pipe-stone Pass over the Continental Divide, and down into the Silver Bow Valley, to Butte, Montana, "The Richest Hill on Earth." There, we patronized Dan Harrington's surgical supply house and returned to Ennis with a bag full of reagents. These enabled us to analyze urine, to count blood cells with the new chamber, and titrate gastric acidity with the new pipette. There was money enough left over for Christmas presents or a blood pressure cuff. It was Christmas! The blood pressure apparatus succumbed to affairs of the holiday and I had to continue to estimate the systolic pressure on my patients with my fingers. No one stroked-out that month.

On the exact midcentury's New Year's afternoon the county judge sat across the card table in my ten-by-ten rear-office chambers. Thereupon, I patiently felt the holiday slip past as I was forced to listen politely to the old boy discuss in painfully precise terms, his insomnia at night and his somnolence at the bench.

In the meantime an elderly couple was waiting their turn in the living area. They were being hosted by Olive and my parents. The gentleman needed the removal of a few sutures from his gums, which were placed there during recent tooth extractions. His wife talked to Olive and my parents without cessation all the while I was captured by the judge. She explored the bedroom and even studied Olive's undergarments. When I finally faced the couple, having escorted the judge out the front door, the wife recited, to all, my life's history. She had already, in three weeks, gathered this biography from the neighborhood. In the true spirit of marital responsibility, she desired the confirmation of its accuracy, all the time double-checking on my surgical qualification to remove a suture or two from her husband's jaw. She then repeated, over the next fleeting holiday hour, her own intimate medical history in all detail, stressing the uterine pathology. At the conclusion of the afternoon of January 1, 1950, my stepmother dubbed her "Mrs. Hysterectomy."

My parents departed the first week of the year.

This log house immediately became the medical center of an area the size of Rhode Island. Within a week the word was out and the testing began. Within a month or two there were twenty patients, many with families, to be doctored in a day. Try to imagine the scene: Olive was now six months pregnant with Jon. Three small rooms including our bedroom immediately became as public as a French pissoir. Even our bedroom! We put patients on our bed. Over it we hammered a nail into a log to support a liter bottle of saline for an intravenous drip. We devised Wangensteen suction with corks and tubes fitted to gallon cider jugs which were then attached to the reclining patient's nasal-gastric suction.

Once, when I myself was ill and confined to my own bed, I opened my eyes and saw with rigid disbelief a grown, fifty-one-year-old man casually entering our bedroom, approaching our bed, turning 180 degrees, dropping his pants and drawers, bending over, spreading the cheeks of his hairy ass, while uttering a muffled request for a hemorrhoidal examination. In our bedroom!

Our kitchen too was no longer our private domain. The pressure cooker became a steaming sterilizer. Crusty white plaster of Paris smeared the floor. Soiled bandages filled the trash can. The smell of ether, used to set a limb, permeated the house.

We would enter our living area first thing in the morning and see coughing kids spray their snot on our three-year-old, then we'd turn to extract the grandmother who had sunken too low in the soft seat. The rest of the family sat on the floor while the father generously offered, "Take your time Doc, finish your breakfast."

They watch as we try to finish our breakfast cereal while the phone rings simultaneously with their kids screaming to poop, and I emphasize, *to poop in a hurry*! As the kid is led to the bathroom, the front door opens to admit an old herder tracking in manure and pulling down his collar to point to the necrotic carbuncle on the back of his seborrheic neck. At that moment a new neighbor, a young, thoughtful wife, bounds across the threshold of our back door to pass us, still at our table. We watch her circulate among the patients with a plate of homemade doughnuts that are vaporized by the time she returns to our table. The carbuncle-man takes two. Olive and Becky share the last one.

The practice of medicine in Ennis began in earnest. What was the legality of all this? There was none. Morality was refreshingly far more consequential than legality in that time and in that place. The prudence of the day was, "A doctor was needed in the Madison Valley." Peers of my friend Dr. Buddy Little of Helena were Drs. Otto Kline and "Monk" Cashmore who represented the State Medical Society. This group realized the above prudence and besought the state licensing board's verbal approval to permit me to practice prior to the examination, which was scheduled to be offered in April 1950. No official ever spoke to me about this. No written temporary document was furnished. Prudence, not raw law, ruled in those delicious days! From the day I saw my first patient on December 10, 1949, until my license arrived in the mail in May 1950, no one, *not one soul*, ever asked to see my medical license, nor my medical diploma. They didn't give a damn! They tested me in their own way. They tested both Olive and myself at church, at every card party, at Julie Erdie's, Oscar Clark's, and Larry Dunn's bars, at the Women's Club, the Lion's Club, the Commercial Club, at the Ennis Cafe, in Sport Keller's barber shop, and at every hour over the telephone's party lines. The state's medical examination was nothing compared to the community's inquest. Their gossip tended to establish and maintain a decent social behavior; it continued, and when we comfortably accepted it we could happily call Ennis home.

Start-Up

YOU CAN SAY that a rural general practice of medicine starts with the first home delivery. Shall we thank our friend who made this tale possible? She is Jean Hansen, for years and years our secretary, who has shared so many of these reminiscences. Our kids grew up together. Jean gave birth to her Charlotte two months before Olive had our Jonathan. Listen Charlotte, this is your story too.

Even today, in my Ennis office in the Madison Valley Hospital, there is, "for old-time's-sake," a wall full of ancient medical school texts. Why? I suppose as a novice doctor I believed it might be a bit impressive to have a bunch of textbooks on display.

The thought makes me laugh. In our log house with my first patients facing me, as we consulted across the card table, there were times when I desperately needed a textbook to impart an answer. Take down a medical book from the shelf and open the pages on the card table? No way! That would be like exposing my privates right there! For the first month of practice, when that need arose, I excused myself to use the book, in secret, in another room. It wasn't long before that deception died a deserving death. Too many questions in too rapid a sequence meant too many trips away from the card table with the patient thinking, "Does he have kidney trouble?" The hell with it. Get the damned book down and let's look it up together!

I kept those old, well-used books. Through the years the old dusty books shelved on my office wall came to resemble an old beloved tree. They offer, if not shade, a sense of academic nostalgia. Another book beside my favorite, A. K. Henry's *Extensile Exposures*, showed such loss of tread. It was *Williams Obstetrics*.

Williams Obstetrics reached my desk at the beginning of the six-week maternity course during our senior year at medical school. To graduate from the fourth and last year at the Yale School of Medicine in 1944, members of the senior class had to successfully pass the National Board of Medical Examiners' Part II test which included obstetrics. I studied obstetrics the month before, the day before, all the night before and kept right on studying until I *had* to put the book down to take the test. I had reviewed four questions appearing on the test the *morning* of the exam. In spite of that academic bonanza, I earned *only* the critical seventy-five percent passing grade. The entirety of my preparation for the obstetrical world consisted of a total of six weeks of obstetrics in medical school with a grand total of five accouchements observed in New Haven Hospital and six weeks more of unsupervised "experience" in Denver General Hospital. This was the armamentarium provided for the obstetrical battles to come in the Rockies of Montana.

Even after my arrival, and as late as March 1950, the expectant mothers of Ennis arranged to have their babies in Butte or Bozeman. Each mother declared her personal obstetrician to be the best, if not in the world, then in the Northwest.

Ennis is connected to the outside world by the Norris Hill, a two-lane highway that twists over a pass of rolling hills separating the Madison River from its tributary, Warm Springs Creek. But on this day in March 1950, the road over the Norris Hill was obstructed by snowdrifts. Jean Hansen sensed an obstetrical urgency, when promptly she and her husband, Gil, set off to go to Bozeman that day. The Hansens were unaware of the hill's winter activity until they plowed onward into a huge swirling snowdrift. Gil shoveled snow in a whirligig frenzy until they realized, horrified, that there was no way out of the valley. They had to retreat to Ennis in terror to draft the untested services of the person who had barely passed obstetrics at Yale and who had *never* delivered a baby in practice before.

After the urgent call for obstetrical help that morning, I read through *Williams Obstetrics* as rapidly as the near-dying describe their lives' experiences passing by—all in an instant. *Williams Obstetrics* devoted a few pages to home deliveries. One striking illustration in the book was that of the "Home Delivery Set-up." It revealed two straight-backed chairs placed side by side, three feet apart, with the chair backs right against the side of a double-bed mattress. It showed newspapers on the floor and on the seats of the chairs. The *idea* was to have the mother lie across the middle of the double bed, place the crotch of each knee over the top of each chair, and then put each foot on the seat beyond. In this way, the obstetrician could handily operate while sitting on a round piano stool positioned between the lady's abducted thighs. From there, the operator could work while facing the portal of infant origin.

Retaining the picture of the chairs so arranged, Olive, seven months pregnant with Jonathan, and I, doctor's bag in hand, went to the Hansens. At the time they were living in a cellarlike home that would eventually become the basement garage beneath the first floor of the house.

The husband boiled water. Olive did everything to assist. But *Williams Obstetrics* left out the detail that most beds sag a bit in the middle. The sag of the bed made the piano stool too damned high. The backs of the chairs then wedged into the popliteal area of the mother's knees sufficient to paralyze both the peroneal and the posterior nerves supplying the lower leg and foot. Protective toweling over the tops of the chairs was of worthless comfort. The chairs were soon kicked over while two legs waved and kicked, desperately searching for some firm foundation for the counter-push. At the height of the delivery I looked up at the high cellar window across from my station between the chairs on the piano stool and saw a small audience of neighborhood children and their dogs. They had heard the obstetrical news and, blessed with healthy inquisitive minds, these youngsters were now peeking down into the cellar in the annoying manner of circling and stinging deer flies, but I was far too occupied to swat at them. Newspapers scattered, the kitchen steamed, the piano stool tipped backward, the operator worked on his knees, and a beautiful little Charlotte entered the world with the umbilical cord wrapped three times around her neck. I must have read what to do about that in *Williams Obstetrics*. It worked!

The state medical licensing examination was on April 5, 1950. But there was no time to study for it. People were in our log house with their bellyaches, hemorrhoids, and ingrown toenails morning, noon, and night. Three-year-old Becky toddled among patients waiting in our living room and patients wandering to the kitchen for coffee or for milk for their babies. One day would give us a dehydrated and vomiting alcoholic lady on our bed, another day, a man in shock, kicked by a horse. House calls were day and night, night and day, in the dead of the winter, from the Missouri Flats on the Continental Divide to Pony in the Tobacco Root Range, a hundred miles apart. Study? Study, how? Study, for what?

Somehow, I was among the group of us who took our exam that April in the Montana legislative chamber with the huge Charley Russell painting behind the speaker's pulpit. I didn't need the bright brass spittoon on the floor by my "legislating" desk. I passed. I'm number 2433.

I lost my first patient the night I returned from taking my exam. Parham Hacker's horse rolled on Erick Maybee. He was thirty-five years old, and the weight of the upside down horse forced the pommel of the saddle into his liver. He was dying in one of Otis Crooker's cabins, with a systolic blood pressure of forty, when I returned from Helena that night. I remember frantically hand-cranking my grandfather's old centrifuge to separate blood cells to cross-match and transfuse. We got him as far as the rickety old elevator in the Bozeman Deaconess Hospital where he died on the way to the operating room. I think his widow received ten thousand dollars compensation in those days.

On April 25, 1950, our son Jonathan sent urgent messages to Olive. Jonathan was ready to be born. Dr. Buddy Little in Helena, one hundred and twenty miles away, was Olive's doctor and our friend. It's a hell of a long way to Helena and it looked like snow. Olive's water burst on the way and she will never forgive me for driving *slowly* alongside a huge Northern Pacific steam engine so that I could watch it pull its long string of freight cars up the pass between Townsend and Helena. We reached Buddy's and he dished up fried eggs dusted over with garlic salt and parsley for a late breakfast for all except Olive. By four o'clock in the afternoon Buddy was sitting at the foot of the obstetrical table while I was standing at supine Olive's left side. I could look down from above and see the back of the little one's head, the nape of the neck, back, bum, and kicking legs when Buddy looked under and proclaimed to six people in the room, "It's a boy! He's hung like a bull!" Olive still reminds us that Buddy's declaration didn't dignify the moment! Now we had *two* kids for the public to admire and cough over as they invaded our log house night and day!

Olive's twenty-eighth birthday was on June 13, 1950. That morning little three-year-old Becky was running around the log house waiting to be fed and washed. One-month-old Jonathan, naked on the kitchen table, was being washed and diapered. Relatives, Uncle Darb and Aunt Ags, were sitting on the brand new couch waiting for the birthday celebration to begin. Grandma Moore down the street was slowly dying from a malignancy and I started a transfusion in her home. Another lady had slashed her wrist. I was suturing that lady in her home while Olive ran back and forth helping with the transfusion. A young man from the Bear Creek Ranch had fractured both his shoulders. We put him on the army cot in the living room with both of his arms plastered in hanging casts. By then, plops of white plaster smudged the kitchen table, baby Jonathan, the kitchen floor and living-room scatter rug, and couch (at $30 a month). By night we diagnosed that Doris Wonder had an acute appendicitis. We examined Doris on our bed. Her father, Denny Wonder, who was the state predatory-animal control officer exclaimed to another villager that I was the "best surgeon in the Northwest!" Jesus, what embarrassment a young doctor must endure! So, "the best surgeon in the Northwest" had to take Doris' appendix out of her abdomen!

We set off to Dave Rossiter's hospital, thirty-five miles away in Sheridan, in the neighboring valley. Denny took Doris in his car and Uncle Darb came along with me in my car so we could return right away.

An hour later we were in the upstairs closet of the Ruby Valley Hospital, with Doris, supine on a homemade operating table, an automobile lamp shining down on her belly button, an assistant doctor giving anesthesia, and Dr. Dave Rossiter, my lifelong friend-to-be across the table helping me operate. My uncle was leaning below and parallel to the peaked roof of the closet, enjoying a full and perfect, if not stable, view of the appendectomy.

We returned to Ennis in the middle of the night. Olive, exhausted from running from house to house all day and night caring for the house-bound patients, was in tears because she couldn't nurse her baby. The milk was gone. Agnes tended the young man on the cot all this time. In private she confided to me that the patient had to urinate but had no free hand to hold his pissing organ. She had tried to force him to sweat it out rather than to pee it out. Yes, the miserable soul was patiently lying there blanketed (three wool ones) on a summer's night! We set him on the pot, nearly in shock, now relieved by a prolonged and weak trickle leaking from the stretched and nearly paralyzed bladder.

Poor Olive had no birthday cake that year.

The Madison Valley Hospital opened with great urgency in late August of 1950. The roof was on, windows were in, and yes, there was finally water coming from the faucet. A couple of flush toilets worked. There were no beds yet. Bud Angle, a young man in his early twenties, was sitting on his idling brand-new motorcycle in front of his father's, Pop Angle's, hardware store. His older sister, Win, wanted to try it out and the two of them were mounted in tandem with Win at the controls. She accidentally twisted the handle to full-throttle. The motorcycle shot across Main Street only to crash head-on into the co-op. Bud smashed his head against the concrete wall. Win missed the wall and crashed through the front plate-glass window. Bud lay on the sidewalk in a coma and Win, crumpled inside, was badly lacerated. All able-bodied and available citizens pitched in. The hospital at that instant was declared open, ready or not! The Angle siblings were transported to the new facility.

Ladies started organizing. Food had to be prepared three times a day. Olive was drafted to nurse and to cook for three days without relief. Beds were commandeered from the Sportsman's Lodge across the street from the hospital. Someone donated a very large rubber plant. As I looked at its leaves I wondered whether or not they might be used as hemostatic compresses or would they, during the night, burst into a meat-eating mutation. We placed Win in the southwest room. We put Bud in the single-bed room meant for terminal patients. With all this action going on, a tourist stood impatiently in the hall amidst the pandemonium asking Olive if he could please bring his wife in, because she was so sick. Olive queried, "Is she having a baby?"

He said, "No. I think she has food poisoning."

Olive welcomed, "Sure. Bring her in. Our hospital isn't open yet. We'll put her on an army cot until we can get a proper bed." Olive put the lady on an army cot in the southeast room. Volunteers held her intravenous bottle until a hat rack could be borrowed.

Bud was in terrible trouble with his head injury. We had to quickly transport him to Montana's only neurosurgeon, in Great Falls. Charley Raper, the undertaker and coroner, had the only ambulance in the county, his hearse. Ordinarily, Raper drove the dead to their graves at a stiflingly somber snail's pace but he, the man of the dead, "hearsed" the living at deadly speed. Tires have exploded on the Continental Divide during his ambulance services. That night the good neurosurgeon decompressed Bud's calvaria, enabling him to survive the effects of the cerebral edema caused in his wreck.

I moved my scanty equipment from the back room of our log house to the hospital. This gave our children a bedroom of their own. Within a couple of weeks patients started to arrive at the hospital rather than the log house. But as long as we doctored in Ennis they never quit making that "handy office call" at the house when the last movie, across the street, was over.

I was busy seeing patients in my office in the hospital one day when George Little interrupted my work. He had dire need for a vehicle to take his wife to Dr. Hill in Whitehall about sixty miles away. Dr. Hill was "her doctor" and there was an extreme urgency (gynecological) to see him.

There was only one thing to do. I assured him, "Go ahead, George, take our old Chrysler Coupe. Take it! Hurry up! Get going!"

"Thanks, Doc," and they took off for Whitehall while I turned back to my other patients, relieved that I didn't have to attend a gynecological emergency with no anesthetist, with no operating table, with no NOTHING!

I saw the 1935 Chrysler Coupe one other time, but not in Ennis. I saw it completely disabled in Alex Parsnick's garage in Harrison, Montana, twenty-five miles north. The coupe died on the Norris Hill. In times of jeopardy it seems that speed becomes a somewhat perilous comfort. George drove that '35 Chrysler Coupe hell-bent to save his wife's life only to burn its main bearings to the configuration of metallic slag on the Norris Hill. I never did know how he was able to transport her from the breakdown site to White-hall. Alex, proprietor of Parsnick's Garage in Harrison (halfway to Whitehall from Ennis), called me to say that he would give me fifty dollars for the dead Chrysler. Over and over and over again I had been counseled *to always trade in town.* I had to trade. I was desperate. I had a house call to make out there immediately. I needed wheels! I asked Hal Pasley and Fred Nelson to come right up to the hospi-tal. Hal sold Chevys. Fred sold Fords. I was going to buy. Both came up right away. They were there in the little wait-ing room sitting side by side, both ready to deal. I needed a two-door. It didn't matter to me, Ford or Chevy.

We used silver dollars in Montana. They were like America used to be, genuine, reliable, and as solid as a dol-lar. With a silver dollar in your pocket you knew you had a meal; you felt its authority.

There was nothing like tossing a silver dollar to settle an issue. We were talking cars for only a very few minutes when I tired of it. I proposed a toss. I would buy from the winner this time. I would buy from the loser the next time I needed a car. Hal called "heads," but Fred won. Olive and I had a new Ford two-door. Later I learned, when it came Hal's turn to deal, the trade-in value of my used two-door Ford wasn't so hot.

The Hatch

The First Operation on a Summer's Night in the Madison Valley Hospital in 1951

IN THE NINETEEN-FIFTIES Ennis advertised its great resource, recreational trout fishing, with one-foot square white signs placed at the side of the three roads entering town. The signs read, 400 PEOPLE AND 400,000 TROUT. As we've read, Ennis borders the west side of the Madison River about a hundred miles north of its source in Yellowstone Park. (As a boy I remember seeing a photograph of President Hoover fishing in the Madison River. The photo was printed in a Sunday edition of the *New York Herald Tribune*, which I found scattered about on the floor of my granddad's combined living room/doctor's office in Upper Red Hook, New York.)

Presently, during any July evening, while Olive and I occupy our screened-in patio overlooking the western channel of the Madison River, we watch thousands of newly hatched caddis flies silently form a dancing cluster of busy, zigzagging winged dots that hover about the roof corner or protruding gutter pipe. They do this without touching, repelling each other like the north poles of a thousand magnets. Once in a while a few of them "take five" and land on the screen to rest. Then, one by one they will take off again and join the flying bug society.

On one July's summer night in 1951, before dark, I had diagnosed an acute appendicitis on Dorothy Stratton, a woman in her late twenties. All arrangements and mighty preparations had been made. We had only to wait for Dave Rossiter to arrive from over the hill in Sheridan to give the anesthetic. By dark, Dave was splashing ether over the up-

side down and gauze-covered sieve he'd placed over Dorothy's upturned face as he sat at the head of the rickety
operating table. The eighty-dollar top-heavy surgical
lamp—Fernie Hubbard's gift to the hospital—was beaming
down over my left shoulder, lighting a medium pizza–sized
area over her abdomen. I was standing by Dorothy's right
side as she lay there. Olive passed instruments and re-
tracted. Billy Piper circulated. The rectangular operating
room was of adequate size and paralleled the north hall of
the hospital. Across the narrower width of the room facing
east were five regular-sized windows that overlooked the
valley and the Madison Range in the background. When we
operated during the wee hours we were greeted by the sun
rising over the "Beehive," a promontory of the range. I
liked that. I missed that "contact with God" in other institutions. A scrub sink installed against the wall of a seven-
by-eight-foot alcove joining the southeast corner of the
room let us prepare for surgery. The scrub sink had a "no
touch" faucet, just like uptown! Sometimes the pressure of
the water would make it splash all over our scrub suits. I'd
try to remember to throw a splash of iodine in the sink, as
a germicide. Other times the water would scald. In the winter, more than likely, it would be ice cold and impossible to
make a lather. Later we also put an autoclave—earned by
the community by holding cake sales, card parties, and
other functions—in this same alcove. On this particular
evening we had sterilized our surgical drapes and instruments with community-donated home pressure cookers.
Madeline Flowers, our first resident nurse, claims we
burned out twenty of these cookers before we got our autoclave.

"Let's get at it, Ron. It's getting late, I want to go home;
I've got a big day tomorrow," urged Dr. Rossiter.

With the proper dignity of a self-important surgically
trained young doctor (partially trained, let us remember!)
the abdomen was prepped with tincture of green soap followed by tincture of iodine. A sudden twist on my part at
that moment, to pick up a sponge, precariously tilted the

top-heavy lamp. Billy Piper, the circulating nurse, caught it and prevented its crashing across the operating field. Had it crashed, there were five inlaid ceiling lights in the room that would have continued to function, but we would have lost our essential spotlight. Olive passed the towels that were then clamped to the belly; using secondhand clamps we had acquired during a trip to Butte. The towels now covered the abdomen, leaving a rectangular open space for the surgical approach. Now the vertical "right rectus" incision could be made. A lady anesthetist arrived from Whitehall, late, and this relieved Dr. Rossiter. Dave now stood by with a hemostat awkwardly pinched in his right hand. Dave had accidentally shot off his middle and ring fingers with his ten-gauge shotgun while hunting ducks from a boat on the Lower Madison River in 1939. He could tie bleeding arteries with instruments very well. (Dave had taught Olive to tie trout flies to the leader using his impaired right hand. Olive subsequently used her right hand to tie flies in the same pincer fashion that Dave had shown her. She could not tie otherwise.)

We incised the skin, split the rectus muscle, and carefully incised the peritoneal membrane without nicking an intestine. The proximal end of the large gut, the caecum with its red-hot erect finger, the appendix, was delivered between the white towels and was well lighted with the tipsy eighty-dollar operating lamp.

A very small flying bug landed on the towel beside the caecum.

"It's a summer night, no problem," I hoped.

"Give me a sponge please, Olive."

I placed the sponge over the winged bug, pressed it while twisting to extinguish its life in the underlying towel. Another bug landed on the towel on the opposite side of the caecum. Then another! Now I called for a towel to cover a countable number. As I placed the towel over the drape, I had to release my hold on the caecum. For a moment it remained exposed like a small shiny breast, but with its attached appendix replacing the nipple. While attending to the bugs on the towel, three or four, maybe six bugs proudly marched over the caecum. Before I could capture them, bugs, guts, and all disappeared, with a sucking slurp, back to home base within the abdominal cavity.

This presented a bit of a crisis. Before retrieving more bugs from the operating site it was paramount that their source was discovered and eliminated. A look on high at the top-heavy lamp revealed a vortex of whirling caddis flies, seemingly the size of locusts. The miniature tornado whirred immediately above our operating field.

I had *never* had the proper instruction for this eventuality, even in all my postgraduate years of work. I spat out four consecutive orders:

"Put out the lights!"

"Put 'em on again, quick. I can't see a damned thing!"

"They're still there. Give me another towel."

"Get the DDT, Billy; get it quick."

Billy Piper ran out of the room and returned (without undertaking the proper antisepsis protocol) with a DDT spray. Billy sprayed and sprayed. (I prayed and prayed.) Now *dying* caddis flies came descending in terminal convulsions, fluttering and spinning from on high to *rain* upon our operating field!

"Stop!"

"Get the electric fan, quick!"

Again Billy returned in a flash and without protocol. This time she carried a big framed-in General Electric four-bladed fan that twisted from side to side while operating from a fixed position on a table. But Billy was too short to be effective.

"Get a stool. Get something to stand on. Quick!"

For the third time Billy came back. This time she improvised by fetching an old Flexible Flyer sled she knew was lying alongside the back door. I nervously wondered if she had retrieved a few tetanus bacilli on the bottom of her shoe covers on this trip outside.

Billy stood on the sled placed underneath the top-heavy surgical lamp. For the rest of the operation she valiantly held the fan by its base and at its automatic command she oscillated reciprocally with it. The blowing fan turned the swirling cone of locusts to a *horizontal* vortex of bug life that ceased to contaminate our operating field. We had no subsequent caddis-fly visitors upon our exposed gut that summer night. We successfully completed Dorothy's appendectomy. And though she now has a few minute, encysted caddis-fly cadavers contained within her omentum, Dorothy has never suffered a symptom nor a sequel. We rescreened our five operating-room windows with a proper prophylactic fine mesh and mastered the caddis-fly handicap.

On February 5, 1954, I wrote in my journal: "Dorothy's appendectomy scar is stretching. Dorothy's first baby is due in March. She said it was three years ago when we took her appendix out."

Temptation

WE SURVIVED THAT first abdominal operation in the Madison Valley Hospital, carried out at night beneath a hoard of locusts. An ensuing, more rational appendectomy operation in our little hospital is part of a larger story that exemplifies the country doctor involved in family care. This particular family taught me in return.

My junior surgical residency at Montreal qualified me to remove an inflamed appendix perhaps a little more than most of the general practitioners who had only trained for a year after graduation from medical school. These generalists routinely did abdominal operations in the neighboring cities of Helena, Bozeman, or Butte. Practicing in Ennis, I was the doctor and I was supposed to take care of the people. Such care included delivering babies, setting broken bones, and doing surgical operations. I was licensed to practice medicine and surgery. The people of Ennis had built their hospital. The people expected their doctor to perform.

My first contact with the McLean family was in the spring of 1950. Our hospital was not finished yet. I had performed two previous home deliveries. My third took place when Mrs. McLean had her child in her parents' home just west of the crossroads in McAllister, seven miles north of Ennis. Marie Paugh, Wilma McLean's mother, boiled the water and Pat, Wilma's father, retired appropriately. Wilma had symptoms of preeclampsia. Her blood pressure had become elevated during the terminal part of her pregnancy and I worried that she might develop eclampsia with its threat of convulsions and possible fatality. I had not even a pair of obstetrical long gloves in the event of a hemorrhage. It was a primitive night of terror for me, but all concluded well. The family could not think of a name for the boy child, a typical oversight, I was to learn. "Jimmy" sounded right to me and "Jimmy" it stayed. Because of her preeclamptic symptoms, and fearing a repeated and dangerous threat, I said I would not deliver Wilma again if she became heavy. (I would refer her to the one obstetrician specialist we had in Butte.) She didn't conceive again.

In 1951 the McLean house burned down. Wilma threw Jimmy out of the window, onto the ground, then emerged from the house carrying her six-year-old daughter, Carol. I treated Carol for smoke inhalation and she recovered. Jimmy, however, was severely burned on both legs and over his abdomen. We worried about his outcome and Jimmy, and the rest of us also, suffered with each painful dressing change. He healed.

Carol had rheumatic fever in 1952 and recovered without

a sequel. Then there were earaches, an earlier feeding problem with little Jimmy, and both children had measles. On February 8, 1954, Wilma McLean drove sixteen miles over the treacherous Norris Hill to Ennis with Carol, now nine years old. Carol had been vomiting for twenty-four hours. She could not straighten up. Her abdomen was rigid all over. It was not quite as hard as a board; not a bowel sound could be heard. The skin was a bit more sensitive over the right lower quadrant when the applicator stick was brushed over the abdomen. These were signs of peritoneal irritation, of appendicitis. She had eaten peanuts forty-eight hours before.

I had a superstitious feeling that eating peanuts could cause appendicitis. I personally had experienced appendiceal symptoms after eating more than a dozen peanuts. After my own appendectomy I had no further similar symptom; nor did I again note an intake limit, other than my general capacity for peanut consumption.

Carol's white blood count was 15,000 and her temperature was 101.4°. Her urine analysis was normal.

I wondered: Appendicitis, ruptured appendix with peritonitis? Meckle's diverticulitis? I worried: If I operated for an acute appendicitis, could I handle alternative abdominal pathology?

My conclusion was that I had to open this child's abdomen immediately.

At this stage our little hospital bursts into a furious uproar. Olive is to hold off other patients in the office. Fanny Merica, my office helper with absolutely no nursing training, is to set up the intravenous, to enable me to start dehydrated Carol on parenteral fluids. Mrs. Phillips, our boss nurse at the time, takes command of the operating room. However, since our little hospital was so small, there was no appropriate storage room for extra beds and equipment. Where has this stuff been for the past week or two? In the operating room, where else? Mrs. Phillips becomes the mover and then washes down the ceiling, walls, and floor.

My jobs? The instruments must be picked, many more

than needed, from towel clamps to the last piece of 0000 silk (a fine thread popular at the time) needed to close the skin. Check the suction apparatus; it may be needed by the anesthetist to clear her airway. Is the sterilizer started? Is there Penrose drain material in the sterilizer in the event we have to drain pus? Look up the proper pre-anesthetic medication that I had copied from Dr. Wilkinson's orders. (He was the anesthesiologist at the Royal Victoria Hospital.) We'll give Carol morphia, grain ¼8, and atropine, grain ½00. We will start her anesthesia with divinyl ether. Has the date for the divinyl ether expired? Do we have enough regular ether? It is daylight, thankfully, so we won't have to call the Montana Power. It's hell when the lights go out when we operate at night. The power company is most cooperative. Then, I call Dr. Rossiter in Sheridan, to assist me, and Dr. Seidensticker to pour ether. Rossiter is thirty miles away and Big John Seidensticker has a practice ten miles beyond in Twin Bridges.

I beg them, "How soon can you come, boys?"

Are the batteries fresh in the laryngoscope? Don't forget the intestinal clamps in case it is a Meckle's diverticulitis. Is our cider-jug Wangensteen suction all here? Did Dave bring it back from Sheridan? He borrowed it for one of his patients. If Carol gets an abdominal abscess after the operation, it will be tough, but I'll have to be able to locate it and drain it! And, let's get the antibiotic going. Cultures are still impossible in Ennis! It takes a week to get reports of cultures when they are sent to Butte.

All the parties were gathered. It was time to operate. Big John Seidensticker poured ether. Dave assisted, standing across the table from me. Olive scrubbed and passed instruments and Bea Phillips circulated. The operation was straight-forward enough. The appendix was perforated. The intestines were bathed in pus. Three Penrose drains were inserted, one in the right lumbar gutter, one in the pelvis, and one beneath the subcutaneous fat. A glassful of pus exuded on the dressings over the next twenty-four hours. I had Carol lie on her stomach to promote better drainage for the next two days. Dr. MacLaughlin, the Great Falls pathologist to whom the appendix was delivered, reported it to have perforated in a multiple sievelike manner.

Day by day I waited for the fever. I waited for the abscess to develop, the intestinal obstruction to follow—but it never did! She vomited three or four times after the operation, then spent most of her time reading comic books. Carol survived.

Just two weeks after Carol's appendicitis attack, her mother Wilma came to the office complaining of gas with vomiting spells. Wilma had an intolerance to cabbage and other foods, a complaint associated with gallbladder disease. Fanny, my able and nontrained X-ray technician, obtained a couple of fine films of Wilma's gallbladder. I counted eight marble-sized negative shadows in the same. These were gallstones. I was taught by Dr. Wilkie in the Royal Vic that excision of the gallbladder was advised when gallstones were discovered. I also vividly remembered the anatomical variations, the difficulty in exposure, the deadly complications of a lost cystic artery or a severed hepatic duct. I respected the ramifications of gallbladder surgery. I was disgusted when previously I accompanied another patient to the city, to Bozeman (at her request), and assisted an incompetent general practitioner in removing her gallbladder. But, now with Wilma diagnosed in my office, I was tempted. I asked her, "Wilma, you fellows have had enough, haven't you?"

"Yes, I should say so," she whispered.

"Well, I guess you're going to have to put up with *just a little bit more*."

"Does it have to come out, Doctor?"

"Yes, Wilma."

"Can you do it here?"

It's probably the daily experience of every believer to have the devil, *the very devil himself* present a luscious temptation. These were my thoughts:

"Dave and Big John could come over to assist me. We'd

need two assistants for a gallbladder removal. Janet Mac-
Kenzie from Whitehall could give anesthesia. Wilma has
big stones. There are probably none in her common bile
duct. Wilma isn't too damned fat; that would make the operation easier. I'd start doing gallbladders! The first one is
the hump. Midge Hardy should have her gallbladder out.
She carries a huge stone! Wilmer Davidson needs his out.
It's not my first. They let me do *one* at the Royal Vic. I've
seen variety after variety of gallbladder pathology in the
operating room. We could sure use the surgical fee."

Then countered the small inner voice, "Remember when
they had to remove a rib to get at the biliary tract after
three previous surgeries? Have you ever taken a rib out?
That would be easy if I had to. If I got the rib out, could
our local anesthetist safely continue? Has she ever given
anesthesia for a chest operation? Our operating-room light
would not afford proper vision for such in-depth surgery!
Remember, many excellent American surgeons consider biliary surgery to be the most difficult of abdominal operations. Do we have a portable X-ray in order to make a
cholecystogram on the table? No. Even though the stones
look large on her X-ray, there could still be small ones
stuck in her common duct. It would be a catastrophe if one
of these was left in at the time of operation. To avoid this
we would need to do a cholecystogram during the operation
to find out and we do not have the equipment for such a
test here. A bungled first gallbladder operation means repeated operations, and at times an eventual fatality. Actually, I asked myself, just how many gallbladder operations
have you done? One! Would you want to take out your
own gallbladder if it were feasible? No? Is this being decent to even *consider* doing a gallbladder operation in
Ennis on Wilma? Appendectomy, yes! Gallbladder, NO!"

I answered: "No, Wilma."

And I referred her to a competent surgeon.

Wilma had her surgery and even though her gallstones
were the size of marbles, one of them had lodged in her

common bile duct. The duct had to be opened and explored and the stone removed. Good light and special instruments and equipment had been required. I realized a bit sadly, "No place for such surgery in our little hospital, yet."

In the fall of 1992 a man stopped at my office and asked my secretary if he could visit during hours. He said he wanted to see the person who gave him his name. Jimmy was now forty-two. We shared a lot of smiles. We talked of his parents, his dad who lives and his mother Wilma, who passed on years ago. We talked about his old burns, his sister and his grandma Marie, who helped me deliver him and who is now in our nursing home. He told me he likes his name!

Whiteout

WHEN DAVE ROSSITER was studying radiology in St. Louis, Dr. John Seidensticker of Twin Bridges, Montana, covered his practice. Twin Bridges was only ten miles west of Sheridan where the Ruby met the Jefferson River. We both missed Dave. One evening before suppertime in February 1954 John called me. It was at the end of a busy day and I had been looking forward to supper with Olive and the kids. But it was not to be.

The voice over the phone coming from the Sheridan Hospital pleaded, "Ron, I need you. Can you come right away? I have a lady in labor and she won't deliver. We may have to do a section."

"Sure, I'll be right over," was the only response a doctor could offer. I sat for a moment in my office with my feet on the windowsill, contemplating supper. Out of that window I was already seeing one hell of a Montana midwinter snowstorm blowing over the highway. It was a blizzard. I called Olive to tell her what was happening and left immediately for the wild ride over the Virginia City Hill.

By 1954, the State of Montana had paved the dirt road from Ennis, over the pass, to Virginia City where it joined the previously paved highway from Virginia City to Sheridan. The new road turned westward a couple of miles south of Ennis toward the pass. Here, the road crossed the West Side Irrigation Canal, then started a six-percent incline over a fill, then gouged its way through a cut in the glacial terrace. The banks of the cut were twenty feet above the road. When I reached the cut, the snow had filled it from bank to bank. There was no alternative but to return. Back at the office I believed, after a call to John Seidensticker telling him of the impossibility, I would be exonerated and would be able to skip right home and be with my loved ones. But, Seidensticker maintained that *I must know that there was another route* from Ennis to Sheridan! I knew that very well, it was the route that went over the Norris Hill and up the Jefferson Valley. But *it was a hundred miles from place to place by that route*, an extra sixty-five miles of a Montana winter blizzard! By then it was seven o'clock at night and black as soot.

"Okay John," I said, "I'll go the other way."

I had never experienced a Montana whiteout before. All was well until I arrived at the base of the Norris Hill eight miles down the road. It became impossible to drive more than five miles an hour. Even with the brights on, the road was invisible. I had to drive by the side of the road where I could see weeds sticking out of the snow. Continuously sweeping past the windshield, the snow created the unsettling illusion that the road was stationary and the car was twisting. When all reference points were lost, *reflex* applied the brakes. I thought the car had stopped but according to the weeds it was still going. A bigger squeeze on the brake pedal would work. Vertigo and nausea were in vicious command of the passage up the pass. On what I thought was the summit of the Norris Hill there was a vision of stationary black instead of the blinding white snow.

"Jesus!" I shouted to no one. I had seen black all right. It was a Black Angus steer, the first of a herd that formed a solid black obstruction on the road.

No matter, I could go no faster than they. I kept thinking of the spacious voids on the left-hand edge of the road on the downhill side of the pass. These long and steep embankments have subsequently claimed more than one life. I made it to Harrison, twenty-five miles from Ennis. Harrison was easy to recognize. It consisted of a quarter mile of western buildings, false fronts and all, on the right side of the road as I was going north. They never built on the other side of the road; those on the right side had an unobstructed view of the Tobacco Root Range (in good weather!). All I could see was the big two-storied schoolhouse and then the lights of Duffy's Bar. The snow quit. On to Sappington! I flew over the railroad crossing in Whitehall. I passed the lights of the Silver Star Bar, then survived the zigzag of the treacherous Ironrod bridge. I passed Byers' round barn and the Blue Anchor Bar in Twin. Only ten more miles to go. At last I reached the cottonwood trees in front of the Sheridan Hospital. At last I had arrived. Only not quite in time! The baby was being born as I entered the hospital at midnight and with it came the dreaded post-partum hemorrhage. John liked obstetrics. I hated obstetrics. I would puke with nervousness after every one of my deliveries. Hemorrhage was the worst nightmare for me, but this bleeding didn't seem to bother John.

He said, "Ron, I'll handle it here." (He was upstairs in the operating-room closet.) "You type and cross-match her for some blood."

This wasn't my bailiwick either. Shirley, the boss nurse of the Sheridan Hospital, was too busy helping Seidensticker to help me find lab equipment.

I fussed, "Where is the microscope? Oh, here it is.

What? This! Only a brass tube! A prewar Japanese tube with a cloudy lens perched on a rusty ratchet gadget."

I drew the blood sample from the donor, made the dilution, and added the typing serum.

Trying to type the blood looking through the brass tube, I thought, "Jesus, can I see through this rusty scope if these cells clump?" (There could be a fatality if the blood was improperly examined and then administered.)

The same agony took place with the cross-matching of the blood, but the donor's blood was type O and better than none for the patient if John couldn't tampon the flow. He did. A transfusion wasn't needed. All was well with the mother and girl child. (A quarter of a century later I made a patellar stabilizing operation on the knee of the baby born that night.)

The crisis was over. Just as I began with relief to consider my return home, I heard Dr. Seidensticker's casual request: "Ron, would you take a look at this fellow here? I thought he had a hot belly around suppertime. He was pretty sick then and I had his folks keep him here until we were done."

Back to yon Nipponese magnifier for a white count! The cells looked like dirty salt crystals, but the count and the rigid and tender belly forced the need for an immediate appendectomy. This had to be done in the surgical closet upstairs in the hospital, the "∧"-shaped room with the Oldsmobile headlamp.

The smartest thing I ever did as an untried doctor in Ennis, Montana, was to declare, loudly and clearly, to my colleagues Dave Rossiter and John Seidensticker, at our first professional meeting in December 1949, that I didn't know how to give anesthesia (pour ether). This was so very honest, especially when considered in the light of today's methods. On the other hand, I employed a little "truth economizing" because I *had* given ethylene at Yale and I *had* poured ether and I *had*, even, used endotracheal anesthesia for thoracoplasties in the good old Denver General

Hospital. In this case, John *could have* poured the ether, but he preferred to operate on his patient with the hot appendix.

Seidensticker announced, "We'll get old Dr. Dwyer"—an elderly and semiretired physician who lived in Sheridan, whom I had not yet met.

The old doc had trudged across the wintry street from his home to the hospital, changed into a white gown, worn thin from washings and time, climbed the steep, narrow stairway with a right-angle turn halfway up, and entered the operating room. Now, with Big John in command, the room seemed to be *just* sufficiently large enough to work within—that is as long as the massive man remained bent forward as he worked over the operating table. The old anesthetist sat at the head of the table on a stool so low that all I could see of him was his pink head, his bent elbows at each side, and his hands holding the ether mask over the boy's face. The Oldsmobile lamp was scorching my left shoulder.

John worked away and delivered the caecal pouch, with its inflamed appendix attached, out of the wound. The pouch now became a little hill of shiny gut which lay below and to the right of the belly button. We surrounded it with the customary small sterile muslin handtowels. It took a long time to do this. At least to me, it seemed to take a long time. I was thinking of the one-hundred-mile drive home. John had so very much to talk about. He talked about the hunting trip he had taken with his father, a hunting trip to Africa. Operating activities kept reminding him of fascinating hunting stories.

There was an unusual activity at the head of the table. Out of my right eye I saw more than the head of the anesthetist. I saw very wide eyes looking down at the head of the supine patient. Instead of holding the ether mask to the boy's face, the old doctor's panicky arms and hands were flapping six or seven inches above it.

The boy had become over-etherized. No one seemed to be doing anything. It was the copilot's turn. In those days all we knew to do in such an emergency was to "administer" artificial respiration. Did I ever "administer" that on that particular night!

I leaped upon the operating table and with my knees astride the boy at pelvis level, my hands pushed his ribs in a straight-armed fashion. Sterile technique be damned! My ass squashed his appendix and caecum against the surrounding toweling and who knows what else it contaminated every time I reared back to have another go at squeezing his chest. It worked. The boy started gasping again and recovered. As we finished the operation, all that could be seen at the head of the table was the pink head of the master, now again pouring ether at a lesser volume-per-minute. The job was done. The boy recovered from his acute appendicitis without further trouble.

When we finished, I suppose we had coffee in the backroom kitchen of the hospital. The drive home was tranquil. The winter dawn in Montana will keep a person awake. This time the big pink sky silhouetted the Bridger and Madison Ranges as I drove home. The bar lights in Harrison were off by then. They probably were turned off after two o'clock, the legal closing time for the Montana bars. Back at Winifred Jeffers' log house at eight o'clock in the morning. Sun was just up by then. I climbed the two or three front steps, passed through the porch, and opened the main door to the living room of the house. Olive was still asleep *on the floor*. The kids had been ill all night with scarlet fever and were asleep on the couch. Olive was exhausted. There hadn't been much "togetherness" during that family crisis. Olive, also, has her stories to tell!

"Men Will Never Know the Meaning of the Word, *Relief*"

THE FIRST YOUNG man to be born in the new five-bed Madison Valley Hospital, September 5, 1950, was Mr. Ward Jackson of Norris, Montana. Johnnie, his mother, delivered him on an unfinished door supported by two sawhorses, which we set up in the little room between the southeast "two-bed ward" and a short hall leading to an east window overlooking Madison Range. Architect Montgomery Orr had designed the room to be the kitchen for the doctor's home. In it and above a proposed kitchen sink was a high double window that likewise faced the mountains. But with the modification from an intended residence to a hospital we converted the little kitchen into both the delivery room and the newborn nursery.

Young Ward Jackson spent his newborn hospitalization time in the top left-hand drawer withdrawn from the hallway cupboard. The drawer was nicely upholstered with a pillow, cotton flannel sheets, and towels. We kept him warm by hanging a mechanic's drop light over him. The improvised bed inspired the hospital board to vote to authorize an incubator, our first major improvement. Dr. Little, hearing of our plight, convinced Saint Peter's Hospital in Helena to give us a wreck of an operating table equipped with ill-fitting stirrups. Proud of this acquisition, our Madison Valley Hospital now had an advanced medical technical apparatus—old Saint Pete's discard! Ed Maynard drove Olive and me to Helena in his half-ton truck to retrieve the monster for the new obstetric facility. Three years later we obtained a bed-pan flusher. The only available space for it was on the east hall's wall, dangerously close to the entrance to the delivery room.

My ten-by-ten-foot doctor's office adjoined the twelve-by-twelve hospital entrance and waiting room, north of it, both rooms facing west. My dialless telephone perched on a ten-dollar desk with cubbyholes. A chair was positioned by the desk so the seated doctor could face the patient. I kept my granddad's *Gray's Anatomy* and his dad's *Wilson's Anatomy* with my other medical school books in a small corner bookcase. The office had one window to the west that faced Montana's State Highway 1. During exhausting times I could sit in my chair with my feet either on the desk or on the windowsill contemplating the world out there. The next room north of my office was an eight-by-ten-foot examining room. My father and I had built an examining table to replace the army cot while we were seeing patients in the log house. We moved it to my examining room in the hospital and put it against the north wall.

There was one standard-sized window that brightened the room from the west. I was able to do a right-handed gynecological examination while looking out the window where I could see an occasional car pass fifty or sixty feet away.

One day when the new hospital had just opened and the builders were still at work, there was so much medical activity in progress that we hadn't thought of the amenity of providing at least a lower half-curtain on the window. Most civilized toilets have such a facility but our very private examining room did not. I don't even remember if we subsequently made the improvement. One afternoon I was carefully trying to bimanually palpate a lady's uterus when my eyes wandered to the floor, to the ceiling, to the person, to the north wall, to the window—to the wind—Oh, Jesus! My eyes met the piercing eyes of a young painter, whose head was framed by the undraped window. The head remained centered, needing to understand what it was seeing. After a long minute the head realized that it ought not to be peering within, and slowly lowered itself out of sight.

During night deliveries, exhausted, I would lie on that

hard examining table and listen to each groan from the laboring mother that echoed down the short hallway. Sleep was futile. After five or six contractions I sprung off the table to check my patient again. Then back I rushed to my office to open *Williams Obstetrics*, to try to anticipate, and to try to prepare for some horrible possibility that seemed imminent with each laboring cry. And then, at last, the baby would be born.

But the placenta! The birthing wasn't over until the placenta was out and inspected. Very early on in my experience, a placenta retained. The usual oxytoxic drug and uterine manipulation failed to stop the bleeding. Did I massage the uterus too much? The hemorrhage was as if a kitchen tap had been turned on. I didn't have time to read *Williams Obstetrics* then, but knew the leaking barrel of blood had to be plugged before the blood could be replaced. There was not time for one man to arrange and administer a transfusion while blood was gushing forth. It would have taken an hour to commandeer and type a donor, to cross-match, to draw the blood from the donor, and finally to administer it to the hemorrhaging mother. It became imperative to manually remove the placenta. I had never even seen that done. I had, however, acquired long gloves from Harrington's Surgical Supply in Butte for such an event.

I had been taught how fragile the uterine wall could be, and when reaching up the pelvis, elbow deep, to staunch the flood of blood, I was certain that I had poked through the uterine wall and *was palpating liver*! After removing the retained placenta my arm was still upriver and the back of my hand was packing rolls of gauze against the emptied uterine wall. No one had told me that the contracting uterus would nearly paralyze my entire arm. I hardly had the strength to push and pack the immense amount of gauze needed to pack the cavity. And what if the packing would not stop the hemorrhage? The relief was intense when the hemorrhage was arrested, but blood now had to be replaced. Olive had to drive in the middle of the night to meet the highway patrolman carrying a couple of bottles of blood from Bozeman.

That nightmare inaugurated the "Blood Sister Program." Thereafter, early in pregnancy, we cross-matched the blood of each expectant mother with the blood of one of her friends who volunteered to be available at the hospital all through the confinement. The program now provided that at least *one* pint of blood would be on hand for such a crisis. There were eleven other obstetrical hemorrhages in my general practitioner days. I must have done something amiss. Eleven very white mothers, but all pinked up again. Mrs. Hossack, at the height of the manual extraction of her retained placenta, while lying supine on the table, curled her neck and head forward so that she could address me and said, "Doctor, what you need is a long-handled spoon!"

I soon *unlearned* the pain management protocol of repeated doses of 50 milligrams of Demerol taught to me at Yale. Babies became toxic by such nonsense. I immediately nullified the insanity of denying the babies the breast for twenty-four hours, a stupid practice of the time. We were taught that pumping the chest, with the patient prone, was the proper way to perform artificial respiration. We never heard of mouth-to-mouth resuscitation. In 1953 I put my mouth to the mouth of one little baby who wouldn't spontaneously take her first breath. I expanded her lungs in this way; she gave her first cry. I had heard about this technique as a folklore. Vurnie Kaye Barnett lives today and there was no hesitation to perform mouth-to-mouth resuscitation after that.

One day in 1993, as I was leaving the hospital, I saw two elderly ladies enter. They had come to visit a close relative. I thought I recognized a face. Yes, one was Florence, a lady who, many years ago, nearly hemorrhaged to death from a duodenal ulcer. This happened because she had tried to lose weight and had dieted too vigorously, using the method recommended by some popular periodical. She had also frac-

tured her hip twenty years previously and I had the
privilege of pinning it for her. As I looked at her companion I recognized the other, younger gray-haired lady to be
Carol, her daughter.

I gave Carol a squeeze to say hello and recalled the night
she broke her rib.

Forty years before, she was my obstetrical patient and at
the time we bartered services. Her husband was to make
me a Thom's pelvimeter as total payment for my obstetrical
service (seventy-five dollars then). I was worried about the
size of her pelvis and wanted a pelvimetry. Neither Butte
nor Bozeman had such a device to my knowledge at the
time. To make the pelvimeter, her husband drilled hundreds
of three-eighth-inch-wide holes, one centimeter apart, in a
two-foot-square sheet of lead. We used this to make a
proper pelvimetric study of Carol's pelvis and, having done
so, deemed her safe for a vaginal delivery. She obliged by
coming in to the hospital on the evening of our wedding
anniversary, February 5th. Buddy and Mary Little had come
to Ennis to help us celebrate. It was late in the evening and
Dr. and Mrs. Little were about to leave for Helena. Facing
another delivery alone, I suggested, "Bud, let's look at
Carol before you go. Let's see how far along she is."

Dr. Little examined Carol in the hospital and said that
she hadn't started labor yet and probably wouldn't deliver
until morning. He and Mary then left. Carol was terrified.
The baby was not going to get here until morning?!

Within a half an hour Carol disproved that prognosis. We
got her into the little room just in time and she pushed so
hard that she cracked a rib. Her son, Gary, was the new
person.

My Scottish grandmother who resided in Upper Red
Hook, New York, during my childhood had a small autographed picture of Sir James Y. Simpson in her study. My
grandmother had been a close friend of the famous surgeon's niece; hence the autograph. The great man had pio-
neered the use of chloroform for anesthesia, had used it on

Queen Victoria, and had been criticized by the clergy for so doing. "Women were supposed to bear children in pain." He also invented a proper obstetrical forceps.

The suction cup now used in its place was before my day. I had a pair of Simpson forceps. I still have the old bearded fellow's autographed picture in my office. This will introduce another obstetric account of the 1950s that happened in the Madison Valley. I was again privileged to name the child at the conclusion of the birth.

I share this private tale with you as I remember the incident. This personal story can only be recognized by the heroine, Olive, and myself. The husband is deceased. The story exemplifies the misery of back-country motherhood in the midcentury. We'll call our patient Mrs. See. She suffered with what I thought was an iatrogenic doctor-caused gynecological problem resulting from a previous diagnostic curettage (scraping) done elsewhere. This apparently caused a scarring of the cervical canal with subsequent stenosis (narrowing). Did this initiate sterility? Did this produce her presenting fever from intrauterine infection? A simple dilation of Mrs. See's cervical canal remedied the infection and to the pleasure of this world the lady became "in the family way."

The dilation had hardly been accomplished when our landlady, the postmistress, went after Mr. See out of the post office as far as the sidewalk and questioned, "I hear Mrs. See is in the hospital. What's the matter with her?" Olive overheard the perfect response:

"She had her ears pierced, Winifred."

"Oh," said W.

Because of the scarred and what I considered narrowed cervical outlet, I was anxious about the forthcoming delivery. I questioned whether or not the cervix would dilate properly at birth. I consulted with my obstetrician classmate at Yale. Probably my concern was foolish.

Labor started and Mrs. See was admitted to the southeast room of the Madison Valley Hospital. We placed her in the bed by the window where she could look at the Madison

Range. There was no problem at all with the full dilation of the cervix, the first stage of labor. I had conjured up that nightmare and had stayed awake, worrying, many nights for nothing. However, after full dilation of the cervix, the next stage of labor quit progressing. Again, here we were alone to battle the worrisome complication in the isolated Madison Valley. I took her to the X-ray room for a Thom's pelvimetry. Pelvimetry indicated sufficient size of the pelvis to permit passage, but the baby wouldn't come. It wasn't twisted; it just wouldn't advance and her suffering was impressive. I called my friend Dr. Rossiter in the Ruby Valley to come and help. I called Janet McKenzie, the anesthetist, to rush here from Whitehall, sixty miles away. Janet arrived in an hour, but Dave, who was closer to Ennis, hadn't arrived yet. I called him again and he had mistakenly thought he was only on "standby." He left and arrived in record time. With both assistants now present, we placed Mrs. See on St. Pete Hospital's discarded operating table in the little kitchen-nursery-delivery room. Janet was ready to pour ether at the head of the table while I applied Sir James Yance Simpson's obstetrical forceps.

I may have talked aloud to myself saying, "Slip the LEFT blade with the LEFT hand alongside the LEFT side of the baby's head. Then apply the right blade. *Apply without force!*"

The handles of the forceps fell together and fit properly. I continued, "Now, slowly pull down. Now slowly pull, curving upward, *but do all this during her contraction.*"

With that, *only the table* and not the baby moved. Mr. See, who was at the scene standing to my right and at the mother's side, swore as he watched the table move from the traction applied to his immediate family.

To this day I cannot imagine the mother's distress and terror of the moment, and to this day, the somber implication of that moment fills my soul with dread. To have remedied a "failed-forceps" would have necessitated an operation, very risky in the Madison Valley Hospital in the mid-twentieth century.

Dave and I agreed that one more easy attempt had to be tried before operating. The "easy attempt," with a little more table sliding, brought forth, unscathed, precious Miss See. The relief! The relief! The relief! (Mother, Father, Doctors, Nurses!)

Nearly but not quite every delivery caused me to vomit from nervousness after it was over. Bea Clark had a pretty tough delivery with Ray-Ray the first go-around. She was now in the southeast room to have her second child.

I sat on the edge of her bed and suggested, "Bea, do you want to try having this baby under hypnosis? They say it works and can be painless. If you do want to try this, just give in. Then start thinking that you *want* to become hypnotized and that there *won't* be any pain to it. Just think sleep."

Mrs. Etchemendy was in the bed parallel to Bea's and was next to the window to the east where you could look out at the Beehive peak in the Madison Range. Mrs. Orr used to say that it reminded her of God when she looked out of that window. Bea's bed was against the west wall. Fixed in this wall was a closet door with a nice round brass doorknob. The doorknob was a little higher than the bed height. It was perfectly placed for her to study it.

Bea agreed to be hypnotized and we went right at it. I instructed her to stare at the doorknob and to listen to me and implicitly do and *believe* what I said, and to relax and to think of nothing but sleep. Bea turned out to be a good hypnotism subject. The mumbo-jumbo that I suggested she say aloud to herself when a contraction—we no longer called a contraction a pain—occurred was "Doorknob, Doorknob, take the pain." It was to be said slowly, seriously, and with reverence.

Labor started. Bea quietly whispered, "Doorknob, Doorknob, take the pain."

This worked wonders and Bea continued. I began to wish I had focused on some object other than that damned doorknob we used as the vehicle for the hypnotic litany.

With progress the litany became, "Doorknob, Dear Doorknob, take the pain."

Time passed. The contractions hardened and lengthened. Bea, now, quite earnestly spoke, "Doorknob, Dear Doorknob, I *implore* thee: Take the pain!'

Then, true to her faith, she continued as if in church with, "Doorknob, I beseech thee, Doorknob, Dear Doorknob: Take the pain."

Bea had another boy. This delivery, Bea said, was a painless experience. During the event, her roommate, Mrs. Etchemendy, seemed to look at me with unmistakable suspicion. With its result, Mrs. Etchemendy seemed as amazed as myself. All I could think of was the deification of the doorknob.

On Saturday, July 18th, in the summer of 1953, with a Yale Medical student externing with us, Olive was both nursing at the hospital and cooking at home not only for our two kids but also for my father and stepmother who were visiting. At about eleven in the morning, in my office in the hospital, I picked up the phone as I was sitting between the west window and my ten-dollar desk. The voice came from the Centennial Valley, a hundred miles south of Ennis. The voice continued with, "My wife's having a baby. Can you come, quick? You're a doctor, aren't you?"

The rule of country doctoring at the time was: "Anybody, anything, any place, any time, anywhere, anyhow, no matter what, do it. It's your duty!"

"Sure, I'll come. I've never been to the Centennial Valley. It's a long way from here. I don't see how I can make it in time to deliver the baby. Tell me how to get there and I'll leave right away."

The whole family decided to go with me on this call. The medical student to learn, Olive to nurse, and the old parents came along just for the show! It *was* a long way from Ennis. We drove forty miles up the Madison River. We crossed the Continental Divide over Raynolds Pass on a two-track dirt road with dusty grass in its center and came to the rectangular, random-windowed, white clapboard Sherwood post office and museum at the head of Henry's Lake. We turned west here to pass Henry's Lake on our south, then to cross the Divide again over Red Rock Pass on another dirt road leading from the Snake River drainage to the Jefferson River drainage. We rounded some hills after passing through Alaska Basin and reached our patient's homestead that was planted at the foot of a large sage-covered, arid hill. It was an unpainted twenty-foot-square, one-storied, four-sided, and pointed-roofed house. It sported a single window on each of the two opposite sides of the house. The front door, with a single window by its side, faced the length of the Centennial Valley. The view from the open door included the Upper Red Rock Lakes in the middle ground with the Centennial Range of mountains looming to the left. No other dwellings were visible within the extensive view. The home itself was surrounded by an outhouse, a root cellar, and log barns and animal shelters that seemed more elaborate than the house. Within the house there was one small, main room with a couple of dusty, overstuffed chairs and a gas-operated refrigerator half-filled with a dried up rack of elk ribs. To the left, as we entered, was a cubby-sized bedroom containing a spotlessly clean double bed now occupied by the mother with the new little person who, of course, had preceded the doctor. There was no major problem other than the need for a minor obstetrical repair operation. This was done on the kitchen table in the remaining rear room. It was a happy day as Olive and I left the happy family and walked down the front steps to the dry Montana grassy yard. To the west, looking up the fifty-mile mountain valley, we watched the Canada geese flying and honking to the trumpeter swan on the lake below. Feeding in the marsh, in the foreground, was one old bull moose. This was a far cry from New Haven!

A year or more later the same mother came to the now-established Madison Valley Hospital to have her second baby. She was comfortably bedded in the same southeast room that hosted our first tourist patient. Meanwhile the outpatient department was very busy that morning. The phone rang in my office. It was Dr. John Seidensticker, calling from the Ruby Valley Hospital in Sheridan, describing a patient about to burst his appendix.

"You've got to hurry, Ron," Seidensticker urged. "His abdomen is rigid. I'm afraid he's leaking now!"

"But I can't, John. I've got a mother in here with a baby coming."

John responded, "Is she in labor!"

"She's quit for the time being, John," I answered, "but she can start up again at any minute."

"Bring her over here. We've got to operate quick."

I went from the phone in my office to the southeast room in the hospital. Yes, the good lady was resting quietly and not contracting. I told her of Doctor Seidensticker's request and his patient's plight. I emphasized the dangerous situation in the other valley while asking her if she would be willing to transfer there. I could then help the doctor with his operation and if her baby came we could deliver it over there. She agreed in the usual neighborly demeanor of the day. Our thirty-five-mile trip across the Virginia City Pass was of no account. John Seidensticker and I operated on the young man. We knew that we had saved his life and we felt quite proud of our profession and our menial capabilities.

But, Mother Nature decreed that our obliging transferee commence a very slow and a very painfully prolonged birthing process. There was no way I could leave her in the Sheridan Hospital nor safely return with her to the Madison Valley Hospital and to my complaining patients, so we stayed put. Olive kept phoning to remind me of the urgencies that kept occurring there, episode by episode. The babe wasn't born all that day, nor even that following night.

Dr. Seidensticker had obligations to his own practice in Twin Bridges and couldn't help. My friend Dave Rossiter was right next door and it was comforting to know that he *was* there if we had to do a cesarean section. I had Dave consult and examine the mother, but he didn't sympathize with his anxious colleague, and all he would say after his exam was that she wasn't in labor yet. Finally, the next day, the baby was born in the upstairs operating-room closet under the aura of the Oldsmobile operating-room light, and all was well. That is, all was well until the father arrived at the Ruby Valley Hospital. He had lost the whereabouts of his wife. He expressed no delight over the blessed event. Instead, he throttled all his energy at being pissssssed off at me. He informed me with all the authority of the law that I had crossed the county line with his woman!

A few more beers and all was well. A new person had come to stay. They say that the grief and pain of child-bearing is soon forgotten by the mothers; not by me! And I'm cocksure, not forgotten by that most unselfish and ac-commodating mother who helped us save a boy's life.

I end the chapter with Mrs. Smitty Overstreet's procla-mation to me at the moment of the birth of her second son, Reid. She gave an extended sigh and avowed, "Doc, men will never know the meaning of the word, *relief*!"

The Bronchial Casts

MONTANA POWER COMPANY manages a small hydroelectric plant a few miles south of Ennis. The dam and power plant are reached by a twisting dirt road running along the Mad-ison River as it flows through a deep canyon. The employ-ees' houses are a few hundred yards *below* the dam and the thought of an earthquake to those who live there and look up at the canyon walls must be like that of lightning: "Just keep your suspenders twisted and it won't strike you," as my neighbor, Don Thexton, tells me. It was impressive to sit in the plant at night with the operator working in a room of dials and indicators that hummed with the background noise of steadily whining generators. As the needle on one of the dials sharply moved, the operator said, "See that?" It was easy to see. He added, "That's one of the Milwaukee's electric locomotives generating juice as it comes down Pipestone Pass from Butte."

There used to be a boarding house below the dam that rested on a rock wall built up from the south side of the river. One night in the early fifties it caught fire, and Olive and I drove our Jeep there to help fight the fire. We arrived before the Ennis firetruck did and had a memorable time fighting the fire with a garden hose. We put it in one window and shot the water toward the ceiling and it would put out the fire in that room long enough for Ron and his brother Ralph Northway to retrieve some articles. Their mother, Aggie, cooked at the boarding house and their father, Bill, worked for the company. The town fire truck arrived in time to observe the holocaust. While we watched the climaxing balloon of the fire, the volunteers were busy lowering the intake hose into the river. There was plenty of water to pump, but the pump wouldn't work that night. After the fire had turned the building to embers we took Ron Northway back to the hospital office. In the light of my office, he was curiously squeezing his nares shut while breathing through the left side of his nose from a site halfway up to his eye. While fighting the fire, falling glass nearly cut off his nose. The tape Olive had applied there had loosened. The hissing escaping air made large, bloody bubbles in the process. Olive and I sewed the hole shut even though we couldn't put out the fire.

Occasional professional jobs for the Montana Power Company taught me, as a young doctor, about corporate medicine. I remember spending the best part of a day with an ill patient who resided in the old boarding house below the dam before it burned. My expenses for the work were probably fifteen or twenty dollars for materials used. I was paid thirteen dollars gross for the work by the euphemistically labeled Chief Surgeon of the Company, Dr. "J. Du P." out of Seattle. How much he charged the power company and for what each month, I'll never know. I only know I never saw him look at a patient. He just raked it in! We men in the Madison Valley had our own provincial terms for entrepreneuring extortionists like that. We called them "assholes." If that was corporate medicine, it was not for me; I soon ended that relationship.

One spring, in the late afternoon, I was called to the chief operator's house in the canyon below the dam. The access to the home was over a swinging foot-bridge. The teenage daughter was acutely ill with a membranous pharyngitis that was so toxic she was having cardiac symptoms. She didn't have a diphtheritic membrane resembling those I had seen in the pesthouse in Denver, but she certainly had a "Quinsy sore throat." Her pharynx, tonsils, and even her palate were afire with inflammation and splotched with plaques of exudate. I loaded the patient in the front seat of our Ford and transported her to the Madison Valley Hospital thirteen miles back, while worrying every minute about her chances of survival.

Immediately upon my arrival at the hospital I was confronted by a family who had rushed in from Harrison twenty-five miles away. They presented their infant who was choking to death.

As an intern at Denver General in 1944 I had been obliged to care for youngsters with diphtheria. Yet, two decades before the Denver experience, in our village in Upper Red Hook, New York, I remember the community horror at the multiple deaths among the children of the Ezra Bathrick family, deaths from diphtheria. At the time, my doctor granddad immunized the grade-school kids in the village (and myself in his living room–office) with "toxin-antitoxin." As a little fellow, I felt pretty smart to throw the name of that prophylaxis around. No wonder my little classmate Johnny Katrulya poked me in the puss every day for the first two months of my school career.

Diphtheria, in addition to its tendency to release fatal cardiac toxins, obstructs the upper respiratory tract by forming, in the acute inflammatory process, a gray-yellow membrane in the throat. But now, as an uninitiated, thirty-two-year-old doctor, I knew that to save these young patients from choking to death, it would be necessary to intubate the trachea or to make a tracheotomy (a hole in the windpipe) below the obstructed area. The horrendous problem in those primitive days was that there were neither master otolaryngologists nor master anesthetists available to serve those choking kids. There remained a scarcity of these specialists at the end of the war. In the Denver General Hospital tracheotomies had to be done in the best way possible by rank beginners. The intern would watch the resident, one year his senior, perform the tracheotomy. I saw two of these performed in Denver. One tracheotomy saved the child and the other did not. The child died choking to death not only from the obstructing membrane but from the obstructing blood and prolonged lack of oxygen during the operation. The tracheotomy was probably done too late. It was with this memory in the back of my mind that I confronted the baby now at hand in Ennis. But, before I turned to the baby's problem, I quickly obtained culture, ordered antibiotic, and put the young lady under an oxygen tube so that I could get on with the emergency. She did recover.

It was obvious that the infant had severe obstructive pulmonary disease, that a tracheotomy was imminent, and that I would be obliged to do one for the first time whether I wanted to or not. I called the ear, nose, and throat specialist in Butte and beside telling me to get at it, he added, "It's easy to do." I put the phone down and sure as hell didn't think it was going to be "easy to do."

Into the operating room with the little one! Luckily and with some previous forethought I had purchased from Dan Harrington, the proprietor of the surgical supply store in Butte, three sizes of tracheotomy tubes for a hundred dollars. This had been a priority purchase early in my practice. A tracheal hook came with the set. The child was supine on the old operating table. The eighty-dollar surgical lamp was turned on and Olive and the nurses gathered to help me sweat this one out. The infant was so ill that local infiltration with Novocain was no problem. It seemed as if the trachea was so deep beneath the skin that it lay against the backbone. By digging into the trachea with the tracheal hook, I could pull it forward to where I could get at it and cut a slit in it so that I could insert the tube into the infant's windpipe. With a small suction tube inserted down the tracheotomy tube I was able to gently suck out a complete hyaline cast that had plugged the right bronchial tree. This cast came from below and was pulled out through the tracheotomy tube. I retrieved another cast from the other bronchus. I had recovered two small rubbery trees of thickened mucus, each about an inch and one-half or two inches high. I had never even heard of such a thing but I immediately knew the cast had broken off at the end of each inch of the rubbery tree and that there *had* to be residual bronchial obstruction distally. And, there was. The obstructive symptoms persisted even with the now-completed tracheotomy. Steam and frequent cleaning of the tube did little. I had even, in my urgency, put the INSIDE tracheal tube in the windpipe instead of the OUTSIDE tube. We now had to clean it with moistened pipe cleaners. That, however, wasn't our problem. The problem progressed to a respiratory failure, general hyperthermic sepsis, and even to symptoms of meningitis by early morning. My good old pediatric friend Dr. Buzz Moore was kind enough to drive a hundred and twenty miles down to Ennis from Helena and arrived to help me by midafternoon. We worked, administering the best we knew, with intravenous and subcutaneous fluids and the antibiotics of the day. At seven in the evening Buzz suggested we go to the Sportsman's Cafe for food and I said, "Not yet, Buzz. She is about to go." Buzz thought that I was clairvoyant because the child perished within the half-hour. Bless the parents of the infant. The father begged Olive not to throw the little one in the trash. He'd not experienced this horror before and, in grief, didn't know what was about to happen. Olive gave hugs and assurances and made sure the undertaker was engaged to provide slim comfort to those good folks. Exhausted, we wept from the loss of the child.

The Bell

Brrrring.

"This is Losee."

"This is Brown."

"What's the trouble?"

"Our baby is vomiting."

"How long?"

"Three or four hours. What shall we do?"

"Has the baby any fever?"

"I don't think so." (He shouts, "Dixie, has the baby any fever?")

"No."

"How old is your baby?"

"Two months, you remember."

"Yes." (I delivered the baby—I should have known!) (Now what to ask? They live forty-five miles away.)

"Is there diarrhea?"

"Dixie, is there any diarrhea?"

"No."

"Don't feed the baby. Watch it."

"Shall I bring it up?"

"I don't think so."

"Okay, we'll watch it."

Watch it they did. And three hours later they drove from Three Forks to Ennis, forty-five miles in thirty-five minutes. The baby was cyanosed (pasty-blue) and was vomiting. It had a White-Wolfe-Parkinson Syndrome, and thanks to a recent article in the *J.A.M.A.* I was prepared. The treatment, digitalis, worked, and the baby lived until he was accidentally killed as a young man. After that phone call, when in doubt I always said, "Bring it up!"

Or the ringing of The Bell at night:
I'm dreaming.
Brrrrinnnng.
The dream pops.
The Reach!
The tipping over of the bedside lamp!
The rehearsal of saying "Hello, Hello," but not directed into the phone, in order to check how much phlegm is in the throat; then finally,
"HELLO." (A little too loud.)
"Were you sleeping, Doc?"
"Yeah. Whooze this?"
"John." (With a silent pause expecting immediate recognition, but no such luck.)
"John Carpenter."
"Oh yes, John, what's the trouble?"
"Can you come over? Effie's bleeding again."
"Okay John, I'll be right over." "Right over" means a trip to Indian Creek twenty-five miles up the Madison.

Or, this is a common one in Ennis, Montana:
Brrrrinnnng.
"*Roar . . . buzz . . . roar . . . buzz*" (This means that the U.S. Forest Service line is calling, or, more likely, Pony, Montana, forty miles from Ennis. The telephone lines roar and buzz a lot there.)
"Hello."
"*Roar . . . buzz . . . pffftt* Dr. Losee, *buzz*?"
"Yes" (in a loud voice), and I think, "Damnation, am I

going to have to yell? Here I am in the office and the partition between the office and the waiting room is paper thin. There are people out there in the waiting room, eager to listen to this."

"*Roar . . . buzz*, I can't hear you. *BUZZ Ssñap.*"

"Hello."

"Dr. Losee, can you hear me? This is Nell, the Harrison Operator."

"Yeah, Nell, I can hear you."

"I can't hear you. Talk louder. I'll relay the message."

"Okay," spoken in a loud voice. (Talking now ceases in the waiting room as the patients stop to listen attentively.)

"*Roar . . . buzz*, Mrs. Johnson is sick. They want to know what to do."

"Where is she sick?"

"*Buzz . . . roar*, Where is she sick?" (Repeated by the Harrison operator.)

"They think it is a *BUZZZZ, ROAR, BUZZZZZZZ.*"

"What?"

"Dr. Losee, can you hear me?"

"Yes. What did you say?"

"They think it's a miscarriage. What should they do?"

"Save the tissue."

"*Buzz*. What? *Buzz . . . roar*, You'll have to talk louder, Dr. Losee. I can't hear you."

"Save the tissue: the clots." (In a loud voice—with complete and utter silence in the waiting room—at this stage Olive bursts into the office complaining, "Do you have to talk so loud?")

I wave her away with my hand.

"They want to know what tissue? *Buzzzz.*"

"The blood that comes from the vagina." (Luckily, these people know about such things, this being cattle country.)

Nell relays, "*Buzz . . . roar*, the blood that comes from the vagina," and asks me, "*Buzz . . . buzz . . .* what will they put it in? *Buzz . . . buzz.*"

"A teaspoon of salt in a quart of water."

"A what? Oh! In the vagina?"

"Tell them to bring her up."

"Okay, Dr. Losee. *Buzzzzzzz.*"

(Silence.)

"They're afraid ... *buzz* ... to move her."

"Okay." (In utter desperation.) "I'll be down."

"*Buzzzz.* Thank you, Doctor."

It's suppertime in the office at the end of a full day; *Brrrrinnnng*, rings the phone on my desk.

I pick it up on the first ring.

"Hello."

"This is Lucy, Doc." (Lucy Nelson, the telephone operator on shift.) "Jonathan is asking for Papa. Here he is!"

"Papa, Mama says, 'Supper's ready.' Come home, quick."

"Okay Jon, I'll be right there."

Sometimes a party-line conversation is a wonder to behold.

Brrrrinnnng.

"Hello."

"This is Gerrard. It's time. Squee is having pains every ten minutes. Shall we leave?"

"Yes, Gerry. Come on down. We'll be ready for you."

"Doctor." (Third party. Who? What? Why?)

"Yes. Is that you, Gerry?"

"No. Who is it?"

"It's me, Hetty. Gerry, can you get through the snowdrifts? We can come and get you with our tractor."

"No thanks, Hetty. We'll make it okay."

"If there's anything you want, just let us know."

Gerry and Squee arrived. Squee took the bed in the southeast room of the hospital where she could look out at the Madison Range to the east. She threw her mink coat over the foot of the bed to keep her feet warm and in due course delivered her fifth child, the first boy, whom they named Summer III. Happy times!

* * *

Brrrrinnnng.

From my bed, in the night, and before I could say, "Hello."

"Doc, what'll I do? Kurfiss' guts are on the floor."

Talk about a rapid awakening! I hollered back, "Jesus Christ, Penny! Did you say 'guts'? Did you say, 'guts on the floor'?"

"Yes, Doc, they're on the floor."

This was nurse Penny Clark speaking. Penny was one of the children who had peeked in the cellar window during Charlotte Hansen's birth several years before.

I answered Penny, "Pick 'em up in a sterile towel. But, Penny, be sure you soak the towels well in saline. Just open a new bottle."

Penny was serious; she asked, "What'll I do until you get here?"

I answered, "Just put them on his belly. They're slippery. You might have to keep them from sliding back down on the floor. I'll be right there. Holler to one of the patients to get up and call Madeline for anesthesia." (Madeline O'Neill was our boss nurse and anesthetist.)

Mr. Kurfiss had been operated on in Bozeman and sent home to our hospital to recover. His wound dehisced. Madeline quickly came and put him asleep. Olive scrubbed and I sewed his burst belly with wire sutures just like a turkey. He healed. Tough old buggers of the Madison Valley!

There were times when the ringing was intolerable and I wouldn't respond at the jump. But it would only keep on ringing anyway if I didn't. For me, nine-to-one, the bell was the noise of trouble or fear.

A Rattlesnake or Two

IN THE SUMMER of 1955 Subby Italia from Wethersfield, Connecticut, and Gary Fry from Miles City, Montana, both third-year medical students at Yale, had come to spend some time learning about the practice of medicine in the boonies. One night in August, Olive and I left home and rode over the Virginia City Hill to spend an evening with Dave Rossiter and his wife, Bertha. We were enjoying socializing with our friends and having a few drinks when, as was to be expected, the phone rang. It was Subby, calling from Ennis for help because a woman had been bitten by a rattlesnake.

I put down the phone and told Dave about the lady with the snakebite and he laughed. He indicated that a rattlesnake bite was no more serious than a chigger bite. He didn't mention any cases that he had had, however. The phone rang again and Subby begged us to return to Ennis. We left, much to the disgust of Dave. He thought we were silly to become nervous over a snakebite. But, did he understand?—Perhaps.

The patient had been gathering eggs in her henhouse in Pony, Montana, when she felt a sting on the back of her right middle finger as she picked an egg out of the nest. It was dark; she was somewhat deaf and didn't hear any rattling. However, she suspected the sting might be a rattlesnake bite. Immediately her husband found a prairie rattlesnake in her henhouse and killed it. Then in the light they saw fang marks.

When we arrived at the hospital, Subby met us; the terrified patient had been placed in a bed in the hospital hall.

I looked at the first aid rendered to her hand and, not aloud, but sarcastically thought, "Now here, ladies and gentlemen, is a dilly to admire!" There had been great slashing of her finger by her husband's jackknife. The bloodied fingers of her bitten right hand were swollen twice the size of those on her left. The arm and forearm were so tightly swollen she couldn't bend the elbow and had to keep it nearly extended. The skin was so firm, shiny, and tightly stretched, I worried her circulation would be compromised, but there was still feeling in her fingers. Compartment compression syndrome was not in my treatment repertoire in 1955. I thought decompressing the tissues would be a good idea but didn't have the guts to do it. The swelling included the entire right side of her thorax, breast, and rib cage down to the belt line. The skin of her chest was pitted like the outside of an orange and was a watery pale-blue color. I had never seen edema of the chest wall before. Her subjective sense of weakness and "dying feeling" were very worrisome.

We elevated her arm, applied cold packs, gave antitetanus and gas gangrene shots, antibiotics, and morphia.

Heinie Rakeman, our druggist, had rattlesnake antivenin on hand for the last five years, but the day before, he had dispensed his entire stock to Phil Yeckel whose horse had been snakebitten. No antivenin in Ennis!

I telephoned Butte. None in Butte! None in Helena. There was none in Bozeman, either, but the sheriff's office found a source in Livingston about eighty miles from Ennis. Olive left Ennis. She passed a rattler on the highway by the old Red Bridge in the canyon halfway to Bozeman when she met the highway patrolman there. He had raced from Livingston. Olive rolled down the window and refused to get out of the car to receive the package because of the snake she had just passed. The patrolman laughingly obliged by passing the antivenin out of his open window.

While waiting for the serum, I made some calls. None of

my immediate doctor friends had treated a snakebite. I called Dr. Holtz in Lander, Wyoming. He told me, "They all swell like a house, but I never lost a patient with rattlesnake bite." He assured me he had treated his patients with snakebite in the same way as I was doing.

The good lady survived. There was remnant finger stiffness the last time I saw her, a few weeks after. She had subsequent nightmares. I might be in error, but my old notes describe a ten-dollar charge for services rendered that night plus another three for the subsequent call. Checking my old books, I conclude, "Bad crops that year. They couldn't pay it."

Another favorite patient, Rita Cornack, a struggling widow in Norris, each time when leaving my office after I'd checked her boy Alvin, used to tell me, "Charge it to the dust, Doc. Let it settle with the rain."

Not all snakebites are that horrendous. I treated Dave Moe in 1956 for a rattlesnake bite. Dave worked in the canyon at the Montana Power Hydroelectric Plant. I had treated him for a minor fracture of his right wrist and had him in a cast. He and his friends saw a rattlesnake along the road from the plant by Meadow Lake. Let a rattlesnake live? In Montana? Dave knew exactly what to do and he demonstrated his skill to his friends. He grabbed the snake to snap its neck. The cast was too heavy. The snake was too quick. And it got him in the back of his finger. There was very little swelling. I split his cast. Heinie Rakeman had antivenin on hand that day. All was well.

Our friend Audrey Powell didn't need my treatment for snakebite. She used Montana prophylaxis. Her husband Wilbur was Gerry Gerrard's foreman at the Bar-7 Ranch up Wigwam Creek, a few miles south of Ennis. Audrey saw the rattler out of the window—which was directly over her kitchen sink—in her garden. She grabbed Wilbur's shotgun, crawled up in the sink with it, opened the window, stuck the muzzle out, aimed, fired, and blew the snake apart. The gun's recoil caused her backend to hit the faucet, turn it on, and burn her bum with hot water. Later when she showed me the pink spot, I smarted, "Audrey, don't you have any *Bag-Balm* at your place?" (Richard Avedon immortalized Wilbur in his book *In the American West.*)

Dr. Rossiter's Diagnosis

DR. DAVE ROSSITER quit work in Sheridan for two years, studied radiology in St. Louis, returned to practice, and came to Ennis to consult weekly. One fall Tuesday, we both were among our scattered X-ray films in my office, when I heard the Canada geese honking, migrating from the North. I tore out of the back door of the hospital, grabbed my shotgun out of my car parked there, and took a missing shot at them as they went over. I thought I heard a simultaneous shot from the front of the hospital. Instantly Dave and I were studying X-ray films again as if nothing happened. Dave asked me, "I heard a shotgun go off in the back of the hospital."

"I heard one go off in front," I countered.

"That was me," said Dave.

"That was me, out back," said I.

"What would the boys in Bellevue think of that?" ended Dave. (He meant the doctors working in Bellevue Hospital, N.Y.C.)

On another occasion, in walked the last patient of the day, Mr. A. B. Critchfield of Pony, Montana. His complaints were simple enough. He had attacks of substernal pain, of random onset, accompanied by sweating. (Pain beneath the brisket with sweating is a classical sign of coronary artery occlusion.)

"Does the pain radiate down the left arm?"

"No."

"Do you have swollen ankles?" (That would indicate dropsy, a sign of a heart that fails to pump efficiently.)

"No."

"Hold on here," I think, "not all substernal pain is heart disease," and continue, "Is it relieved by sitting?"

"Yes."

(I hadn't weighed the reason for that question yet—nor the answer.)

"Is it coliclike? Does it well up and cramp and then die down?" (I was thinking of gallstone passage.)

"No."

"Do you have trouble swallowing?"

"No."

"Do certain foods bother you?"

"No."

"Do you have heartburn, a burning in the pit of your stomach during or after eating?"

"No."

"Has anyone X-rayed you?"

"No."

"Is your urine brown, like Coca-Cola?" (I was thinking of obstructive liver disease, whereby backed-up pigments are excreted by the kidneys.)

"No."

"Do you have a chronic cough?"

"No."

"Did you ever cough up blood?"

"No."

And it continued. "No, no, and no."

"STOP!" I thought. "Now we are getting nowhere. Let's let Mr. Critchfield start all over and tell me his problem again, this time in his own way and in his own words."

The pain was there. He perspired during an attack. The pain was relieved by beating on his chest while he leaned forward. I thought, "I'm thirty-four years old now and I've never heard *that* before!"

Sometimes he regurgitated coffee. Sometimes after he swallowed his coffee he felt as if the coffee went around a corner just before it dumped into the stomach. I had never heard of that symptom either. But now we were getting somewhere. It made me think of a lower esophageal lesion. I recalled other patients I had seen with esophageal problems.

Cloe Paugh, who lives in Ennis and is our elderly hospital-board accountant friend, suffered with regurgitation of liquids with her diaphragmatic hernia. Mack Bates had substernal pain that radiated down his left arm, resembling coronary artery disease, but his symptoms were from a diaphragmatic hernia. A French patient in the Montreal Royal Victoria Hospital had her substernal pain relieved when she sat up. She had a diaphragmatic hernia. Shad Hobbs, who lives by the lake (Meadow or Ennis Lake north of town), had none of these symptoms with his diaphragmatic hernia.

But, I was convinced that Mr. Critchfield had a diaphragmatic hernia, or hiatal hernia as it is sometimes called, and wanted to prove it.

Mr. Critchfield returned the next Tuesday when Dave Rossiter could see him. When we finished our X-ray and fluoroscopic examination of Mr. Critchfield's esophagus and stomach, Dave coldly said there was no hiatal hernia. I didn't see one, either, as I watched Dave fluoroscope him. Dave took the X-ray pictures of the lower esophagus after Mr. Critchfield swallowed and while he was holding his breath and straining as if going to stool. (This was done to make the top part of the stomach protrude upward, through the hiatus in the diaphragm, if it was herniating.) Mr. Critchfield remained undiagnosed.

My confidence was low. What the hell was I supposed to say? "You have nothing wrong with you. You just have a pain that is not explained, is unnatural, and was not there before."

He surely knew that, without a doctor bill to add to it. Yes, my confidence was low.

"Mr. Critchfield?"

"Yes."

"Would you please come back next week when Dr. Rossiter comes so we can X-ray you again? For free?"

He was a grand patient. He returned again, with an empty stomach. This time we gave him two Alka-Seltzer tablets in warm barium water. (The barium water makes a white shadow on the developed X-ray film.) This time Dave showed me, "Here it is!"

The upright view demonstrated a beautiful air-contrast picture of the fundus of the stomach and lower esophagus, and we found, for our friend, the hiatal hernia with gastric rugae (wrinkles) protruding through the diaphragm into the lower part of the chest cavity. Dr. Rossiter left. Mr. Critchfield was now at the chair beside my deck.

Mr. Critchfield continued with the reasonable question, "What medicine will cure it?"

About this time I lit a cigarette, went to my little blackboard, erased it, and drew two sketches. The first picture was that of his type of hernia, a diaphragmatic hernia. The second picture was the more common inguinal hernia, the ruptured kind.

"Can you cure a rupture with medicine?" I asked.

"No." He knew.

"That's right. Your hernia through the diaphragm is like a groin rupture. It has to be operated on to get rid of it."

We both thought, Montana style, "Who the hell wants to be operated on?"

We discussed how often he had the distress. Maybe only once every week or two. Could he raise the head of his bed? Could he watch overeating? Did the beating of his chest help? Yes, after a time, after a good burp came up. If coffee was a problem, would quitting coffee be too much for him? Would he take Tums at bedtime? Had aspiration of stomach contents awakened him? No. Then, the key question I finally asked Mr. Critchfield was: "Are the symptoms worth going through a big operation?"

He chose not to have an operation. I treated him "conservatively," meaning I did nothing. I hope the advice I gave helped him.

Frtfrtfrtfrtfrtfrt

The Story of Ice Anesthesia

BESIDE PRACTICING RADIOLOGY upon his return from St. Louis, Dr. Rossiter continued his general practice in the mid-1950s. Late one afternoon, he called me and asked me to come over to the Sheridan Hospital at eight o'clock the next morning to help him with an amputation. His patient had diabetic gangrene and he wished to make an above-knee amputation. He told me that he was going to use ice anesthesia.

I begged him not to use it.

"Damn it, Ronny," he said, "they're doing it in St. Louis."

Instantly, I conjured up a forthcoming bad scene.

He was the boss. It was his case.

I said I'd be over and that I wanted to bring over Uncle Darb's father's amputation saw.

(Uncle Darb, my father's younger sister Agnes' husband, was born in Dumfries, Scotland, and grew up in South Africa where his father was a general practitioner. During medical school days, my uncle gave me his father's surgical kit which contained an amputation saw. I thought it was time to do honor to the ancient instrument.)

Dave replied, "All right, Ron, bring your uncle's saw, then."

Dr. Rossiter had started the Sheridan Hospital upon his return from the China-Burma-India Theater at the end of the war. (He, too, has written up this amputation experience

in his book *Pick and Shovel Doctor*.) His partner in his pre-
medical mining days was Frank Spuhler. Mr. Spuhler's
wife, Shirley, at the time of this tale, ran the Ruby Valley
Hospital in Sheridan. The hospital was the Spuhler home. It
was on the north side of Mill Street and a block or two
from the center of the village. It was a story-and-a-half
high. It was a pitched-roof building that was fronted with
one or two cottonwood trees. A trestle was built on the
right-hand side of the building as seen from the street. The
trestle extended up a fifteen or twenty degree angle from
the ground to an upstairs door. The floor of the ramp consisted of two parallel twelve-inch-wide planks, and there
was a makeshift railing to go with it. Part of this ramp operation was a homemade gurney. The gurney top was an
ironing board. Two bicycle wheels on the back and two
crazy wheels (each attached to a free moving turntable on
a vertical axis) on the front furnished its mobility. We
would load the (sometimes obese) patient on the gurney.
Then, with a mighty surge, we would jettison the victim up
the ramp and through the door to the upper story of the
hospital.

There was a closet under the pitched-roof "L" portion of
the upper story that functioned as the Sheridan Hospital
operating-room suite. There was a skylight in this room and
we would try to plan our elective operations between 11 AM
and 1 PM, at which time the sun would pass over. We had
a better and more direct light to operate during those hours.
Otherwise we would have to use an old Oldsmobile automobile headlight to work with. It was hot light. Damned
hot!

When I arrived the next morning there was water leaking
over the sill of the front door. I thought, "Damn it, he's using ice anesthesia."

I surmised that Dave was going to operate in the front
room instead of the usual upstairs closet. He had been talking about changing the area of the surgery. I looked at the
water again and realized that *they were actually going to try*

to freeze the leg! I opened the door to see water, old sopped newspapers, and partly melted ice chips covering the entire floor.

Dave, perturbed because I was ten minutes late, hollered, "Where the hell have you been? You're late. We're running out of ice!"

The patient was prepped. Shirley, the boss nurse, gowned us. Dave started to cut. He started with the attitude of the surgeon about to make the *coup de maître*. This was an underhand reach beneath the lower thigh of the limb to be amputated, scalpel in hand, looking at the sharp edge of the scalpel, and ready to make a circumferential, sweeping incision to the bone! It was used in the pre-anesthesia days to speed the horrendous process. I always wondered why this pose was still necessary now nearly one hundred years after the use of ether. "Tradition, tradition!" Although Dave didn't make a huge incision, there was enough of a cut to cause an emotional response by the patient that could have been heard in Ennis!

The ice had not done the job, of course.

I didn't say, "I told you so."

There was enough excitement in the room without that further irritant.

"Okay, Shirley, you might as well set up the spinal set." The advanced-aged lady then was assisted to sit and to lean forward, now with a compress hastily applied to the proposed amputation site. Dave tried to insert a long needle in her back to administer spinal anesthesia. Her spinal column, instead of being segmented, resembled a tube of bone because of aging and degenerative osteoarthritic changes. After five or six attempts, Dave thought that he found an entrance to the spinal canal and he injected the anesthetic solution.

Then came the "wait to see if the spinal worked" interval.

The table was tilted to cause the solution to rise along the spinal cord, but the effect of the anesthesia only reached midleg level, not the required crotch height.

There was much testing of the level of anesthesia by pricking and pricking, hoping that maybe the pricking itself would cause the anesthetic level to rise high enough to cut the leg off above the knee! Finally Dave quit that effort.

"Okay, Shirley, get the ether."

Dave now left his place as *le maître*, went to the head of the table, and placed the sieve with the gauze cover over the lady's face. The patient was now supine. Dave poured ether. The aroma of ether permeated the house, everywhere, even as far as the kitchen. Today, I wonder why we never had an ether fire, but then, we weren't dumb enough to have struck a match with the ether can open. The patient snored away. Shirley took over the ether can and continued pouring. Dave put on a new pair of sterile gloves and prepared for the coup. He had the soft tissue divided and the arteries ligated and the bone cleared and ready for the saw.

"Okay, Ronny, let's see you fire away with your Scotch uncle's amputation saw."

I was to have the honor of actually sawing the femur in two. With all the authority of a young country doctor I made a vigorous pass across the femur with the saw and, *Ffrrttffrrttffrrttffrrttffrrttffrrttffrrttffrrtt* is the best way I know to approximate the sound that resonated against the big femur bone.

I could hear it. I could feel the vibration at the very first, but at the end of the *ffrrttffrrtt* there was no more vibration.

Every one of the teeth of that Gaelic instrument had broken off the stock and the chips were now lying in the muscle.

My first instinct was to keep right on sawing with the toothless instrument, only to do it faster and with more force in the hope that, as in a sexual act, something might happen. But it didn't. Maybe if I sawed faster it might burn its way through the femur.

"Okay, Shirley," Dave ordered, "go down to Walter's store and get a hacksaw. I'll pour ether."

I spent time trying to recover tiny triangles of metal on the proximal side of the wound. It didn't matter if there were particles on the distal side because it would be discarded—if we could ever get the son-of-a-bitch off! Shirley returned with one of those little hacksaws without the bow but with the replaceable obtuse triangular blades. It took time to boil it up. Its teeth held and the gangrenous extremity was separated successfully from its source and the patient was grateful to get rid of the rot.

Dave asked a friend of his to bury the leg because he was too busy catching up with his patients. They all had to be seen at one time now that the morning had nearly passed in a surgical exercise.

That was the last we heard on the subject of the leg until later that fall. The good Sheriff Brook traveled one day from Virginia City northwest down Alder Gulch to the Ruby Valley, past The Robber's Roost, to Sheridan, and then directly to Dr. Rossiter's office. He deposited, on the floor, a long, cylindrical object wrapped in canvas or a similar water-repellent material. Sheriff Brook needed a little medical advice from Dave, even though he was not the medical examiner. Madison County had no such forensic luxury. Usually such matters were quickly dispensed by the coroner (who usually was the undertaker), with a "natural cause" conclusion. The contents of this package was, however, in an unusual category. It was a human leg, in a fetid and deteriorated condition, no doubt. The sheriff observed that the femur had been sawed off and possibly a doctor had done it. Dave recognized it to be Emma's gangrenous leg and asked the sheriff, "Lloyd, where the hell did it come from?"

"Some boys had been hunting up California Creek." (This was in the Tobacco Root Mountains east of town.) "They found it and brought it back on one of their horses. You should have seen the kids' eyes!" Sheriff explained.

Dave didn't take long to figure it out. His friend who had taken charge of the disposal of the leg had an airplane. It was a damn sight more fun to take a ride in his airplane than to dig a hole.

"I Wish You Hadn't"

(Teaching Can Be Dangerous)

WHY IS IT that young apprentices trust their mentors to the point of absurdity? I think my most embarrassing instance of this was at the Cedar Creek Training Area at Fort Knox, Kentucky, in 1946 or 1947 during my army-doctor days. This was a small outpost with steep walls of stratified limestone which rose perhaps two or three hundred feet from the valley floor. The terrain was wooded and beautiful to behold in the Kentucky springtime when red bud and white dogwood bloomed. The camp consisted of a few shops and dormitories, a dining hall, a command building, and a small dispensary, my bailiwick. My duty was to hold sick call each morning and to be on hand in the event of a catastrophe. Sick call consisted of hangovers, colds, and minor ailments. As medical officer, I arranged for the entire cadre to be outfitted with low-quarter shoes, much to the annoyance of the bureaucracy.

One sick call an older cadre member came in with sciatica. My hours at Cedar Creek Camp had been so unoccupied that I was able to read a lot of medical literature. An article in *The New England Journal of Medicine* suggested a way to diagnose a protruding nucleus pulposis (intervertebral disk) in a patient suffering with sciatic pain. The way to do this was to put a blood pressure cuff *around the patient's neck and to inflate it*! If inflation made the pain come, the patient had a ruptured disk. A very simple test, indeed!

I believed the buggers! They wrote it in *The New England Journal of Medicine*!

I tried it.

The effect was immediate and spectacular. The complete cerebral anoxia resulted in an immediate syncope and convulsion that was rapidly resolved with the release of the cuff.

"Whew! Jesus Christ! What was that?" the soldier, sweaty and piqued, whispered up from the dispensary floor.

"You passed out," was about all any jack-ass-doctor-who-would-do-such-a-stupid-thing could reply.

Two years later, I watched the surgeon-in-chief, Professor Gavin Miller, at the Royal Victoria Hospital operating and commanding an aura of esteem and near-reverence among his young assistants for his masterful and meticulously rapid surgical techniques. In one of his lesser spectacular techniques he had no hesitation in removing testicles and spermatic cords to facilitate the adequate repair of a direct inguinal hernia. He taught this as he leaned from side to side working the tissues with such dexterity. And at the conclusion of the operation there was no doubt that the direct hernia would be sealed for all time.

I swallowed the idea. I was an easy believer. Then came the day, three or four years later, in Madison County, Montana, when I had the chance to try out the old boy's dogma. The patient was an old-timer, seventy-five years old, and he had bilateral inguinal hernias. For some reason or other that I can't remember, the operation was done in the Sheridan Hospital in the little upstairs closet with the skylight, probably at eleven o'clock in the morning when the sun was passing overhead. The old boy granted permission for castration to obtain a good, solid, and permanent repair.

Dr. Vern Standish, who was working with Dr. Rossiter at the time, flew his airplane to Ennis to pick me up. I hate airplanes. Vern, with his scarf flying in my face as I sat in the open rear tandem-cockpit flew the contraption awfully low over the Virginia City pass. Right there the plane pooped out, quit. Dead. Vern pointed like in an Errol Flynn movie to the gas gauge, which read empty.

"At least he could have put gas in it."

"Listen to the struts whistle."

"Do I jump just before we land?"

"Or do I try to spring, pushing my feet to the floorboard just before we hit?"

Vern got it going again. I never forgave him.

We operated on the old boy. The Gavin Miller way! I castrated him—bilaterally.

And the hernias never recurred. Probably twenty years passed. In his nineties the old man liked nothing better than to ride with his neighbor Dutch Grauman in Norris on fuel-oil home-delivery trips about the county. On occasion the two men would stop in the Fish Bowl, Ennis' bowling alley—a busy establishment serving coffee, hamburgers, sandwiches, and pies. The lunch counter is always crowded at mealtime. One day I was seated at the lunch bar leaning over a "ketchupped" hamburger. On my right was our ninety-year-old friend nursing his cup of coffee. We visited about mundane things. Then and there, and much to the point, he said to me, "Doo, I wish you hadn't cut my balls off."

The Stretcher-Basket Rescue

THE TOBACCO ROOT Mountains lie northwest of Ennis. They form a snowcapped background behind a few low hills sprinkled with juniper clusters and underpinned by a long terrace formed in the last glacier age. The local Ennis seniors speak of electric lights that were visible at night, lights originating from the Missouri Mine that operated in these mountains during the Depression. Our family loved to drive the Jeep up to the mine from Ennis. What we thought of as the Missouri Mine was the ruin of a gold concentration mill on the north side of South Meadow Creek. The road followed up the creek westward into the Tobacco Root Range that surrounded the mill. On the way, the road crossed a flat glacial terrace until it reached the forest where it climbed the side hills precariously. The mill was a large, rough-timbered, and multiple-pitched-roof structure that complied with the steep side hill above the road. The ruins of the tramway that served the receiving hopper on the uphill end of the mill extended a quarter of a mile up the side of the mountain from the mill to the actual mine. The cable was festooned over the still-upright bents. The buckets, with their tram wheels still astraddle the cable, were on the ground at regular intervals. It was a "gravity tram." The buckets were loaded at the mine above. The weight of them, when descending, counterpulled the empty buckets from the mill back up the mine again. There was a large wheel that trochleated the cable at the top. It was controlled by a brake that must have generated an abundant quantity of heat along with the smell of hot and smoky grease when all buckets were loaded and swinging away! Miners must have bummed rides up the tram. Why climb that steep trail? There was no OSHA in those free days of low wages, bagged "Bull Durham" tobacco scrapings, and ultimate silicosis.

Oh, how I remember lugging big oxygen tanks in the middle of the night to the home of those hard-rock miners as they spent years choking and choking until blessed death, wondering what was so great about the practice of medicine, feeling as useless as tits on a bull.

The McKee Mine was established a few hundred feet higher up the mountain from the Missouri Mine. There was also a ruined tram system between these two abandoned works. The attraction of the McKee Mine was its backhouse, which faced the panorama of the southern half of the

Madison Valley. Every tourist exploring the acreage of the McKee Mine should test this privy for fun (or in earnest), by sitting on the splintery old hole with elbows on knees and chin on thumbs, door wide open, inhaling the beauty of the spacious landscape, seeing all, without being seen by anyone.

Following South Meadow Creek beyond the Missouri Mill the Jeep's road became even more rough. There were several large, bare rock humps that tipped the vehicle toward the left-hand steep bank lining the creek. These rocky projections in the road were known to knock a hole in the oil pan and immediately disable a vehicle. The road ended at the bottom of a lightly forested glacial terminal moraine. From here the traveler had to climb it a few hundred feet up a steep footpath and when the top was reached, the climber stepped out of the forest to the shore of a ten- or twenty-acre mountain lake. A cliff arose from the water on the lake's western edge, eliminating its shoreline for a hundred yards or more. This steep, rocky, treeless and mountainous slope sets the scene for the following anecdote of Wednesday, August 29, 1956.

Back at our log home in Ennis at one o'clock in the morning (the children asleep upstairs, with Buttons, their cocker-bull-dachshund-hound dog companion guarding them, half awake on a bed), the phone rang. Aerie Greydanus reported a man down on the side of the mountain, across South Meadow Creek Lake, beyond the Missouri Mine. "The other side of the Missouri Mine! We can't do that alone." We called our county attorney friend, with whom we had been playing bridge in the evening, to help, but he declined, saying he had to work in the morning. "Todd! He'll come!" Todd, our game warden, always would help.

The U.S. forest ranger also answered our call for help and brought a first-aid basket-type stretcher that I had not seen used before. We also got our neighbor Jack Scully to help us. (Superstitiously, Jack and his wife, Madeline, would never pay the last dollar of their doctor's bill. If they did, some damned health problem would return to their family and they would owe me again!) Jack recruited his schoolteacher comrade Maurice Hickey, and with a rubber boat we all set out for South Meadow Creek Lake in the middle of the night. Olive had made the sandwiches and the expedition was off.

We reached the base of the moraine by dawn and trundled the equipment up the terrace and laid it out on the lake bank. Mr. Scully shuttled us in his boat two at a time around the base of the cliff to the opposite shore. We all climbed one steep, schist-laden, treeless slope to a small hollow shelf in the slope on which the patient had spent the night. His son had made a small fire to keep him warm. He had dislocated his elbow, broken some ribs, and had become confused and unable to ambulate. We splinted him and strapped him to the basket and Todd, the ranger, Scully, Hickey, and I lowered him to the shore. Olive scrambled with us at the rear holding the intravenous bottle. It was an inch-by-inch slide down the very steep and rocky slope. There were skinned knees and ripped britches and sideways partial rollings of the patient-filled basket.

To get him by the base of the cliff we put him on plywood laid crosswise on the fat rubber boat. The board under his extended head and feet slapped the water like a teetertotter. One-foot waves added discomfort. Hickey did rapid and desperate paddling at the bow with Scully steering and paddling from the poop deck. In a situation like this, my old friend Dr. John Armour at the Royal Vic would say, "Pray to the Lord, boys, and pull for the shore. Pray to the Lord, boys, and pull for the shore."

It was downhill over the moraine to the parked travel-all bus that Todd used for his game-warden work. We decided the travel-all would be safer for the patient than putting him crosswise on the back of our Jeep. He was wrapped up in blankets and tied with a diamond hitch securely fastened in the basket stretcher.

It was midmorning, and everybody'd been up most of

the night, with only the last leg of the journey to go. And he had to urinate. Olive begged him to piss his pants, but he wouldn't. We stood the basket up. Two guys held the basket erect, undid the diamond hitch, unwrapped the blankets, turned the basket away from the crowd, unbuttoned and searched for the shriveled organ and hoped for as little spillage as possible. His valve was slow to release and he fainted as the urine trickled. Two more men helped support him. Blankets were rewrapped. His fly remained open. Diamond hitch was reapplied, and, finally, the man-in-the-basket was slipped into the back of Todd's van.

Back at the hospital, the elbow was set. I had to pour ether myself and quickly run around to reduce it. By then the waiting room was filled with disgruntled patients.

My old daybook records the total service charges:

Reduction, disloc. elbow	$55.00
X-ray elbow 14x17	$10.00
Suture Scalp	$20.00
Rx Shock	$10.00
Materials, 2 Ace band.	
2 Demerol amps	$5.00

Life goes on! On July 19, 1993, I was picking out a pair of sterile gloves to use for a minor tennis-elbow operation. A small man in his sixties with gray hair, a thin, tanned face, and deep-set hollow eyes, turned into the room where I was, and asked, "Are you Losee?"

"Yes," I answered.

"You hauled my father down from the mountain thirty-eight years ago. I was there when you done it. This is my sister." He indicated to me a black-haired younger lady, standing next to him. "They've got my mother in the hospital here and she wants to see you before we take her home today."

"Is your father retired?"

"Hell, no! He'd be a hundred. He died in his eighties."

The memory juices squirted and, with ebullience, I

recited the above anecdote. He made one addendum: "Yes, and after we got Dad in the van, Todd was driving down the mountain like crazy and you said, 'Todd, you son-of-a-bitch, take it easy. Don't kill him now after working all night to save him!' "

The little old mother with two beautiful, mischievous black eyes gave me a kiss from where she sat in her wheel-chair. I'm glad I was a doctor in this life!

By the Clock

MR. GRANGER OWNED a dukedom on the west side of the Madison Valley that stretched from the mountains to the Madison River and even across it at spots. He resided in New York City but spent the glorious summers in the valley. Besides having me doctor his dog (I was appallingly ignorant about veterinary medicine), he occasionally used my service as a physician who would treat humans as well. On this summer evening, perhaps in August of 1954, I attended the gentleman at his home. After the examination and consultation in a back room of the house, we both entered the living room again and I was served a highball in the presence of his wife and two illustrious guests, Nelson Rockefeller's sister and her husband. The husband asked if I would mind answering a personal question and I had no objection: I carried very few embarrassing secrets in my soul at the time. The question was very reasonable and not personal at all. He wanted to know if I prorated my fees. I replied that I didn't. Among my patients in the Madison Valley, a porkchop was a porkchop and a potato was a potato. The area was provincial and patients compared fees, mileage, time spent, shots given, babies delivered, name it, and they would be unhappy with varied charges. He then gave me a sermon on the value of time. He explained to me that if he came to my office, he would expect me to wait on him immediately. In fairness he would expect to be charged a higher fee. He made it quite clear that his time spent waiting in my office was valuable, implying, if not stating, his time to be worth more than the time of the local patients.

I asked the man, "How do you measure time?"

He answered in a commanding voice, "By the clock! By the dollar!"

"That's our difference," I said. "I measure time by the clock! By the life!"

It was time for me to say good night to all and go home.

And I walked out into the evening. The Montana sky was so boundless, and the stars so close. But I actually did prorate once at a later time. The patient was a retired, wealthy, blind old diabetic rancher who was alleged to have been stingy to his help. Nevertheless, feeling somewhat sorry for him, I asked him what he did all day.

He said, "I candle eggs."

I wondered about that and asked him, "If you're blind, how do you do that?"

He turned his head up to me and slyly grinned, "By not seein'."

Fetal Fatality

MAURICE STAGGERS WAS a free soul in his early sixties. Mrs. Alice Orr, who also ranched in neighboring Cliff Lake area, bordering Idaho, recognized bits and pieces of *her property* lying about in *his yard*. But, she silently recognized this as acceptable tribute. (Allegedly, Maurice was involved in cattle-rustling activities in the area, but Mrs. Orr had no problem with cattle rustling. It was also alleged that he'd beaten his father-in-law to death with the butt of his revolver many years ago.)

On another occasion he sat next to Olive in the Virginia City courtroom and requested, "Mrs. Losee, if I go to jail, would you give my wife, Mrs. Johnson, a ride home?" Todd, our game warden, had him before the judge for distributing a half a dozen elk to an Idaho market. The judge dismissed the case for lack of witnesses then rebuked the young county attorney (his first case) for wasting the taxpayers' money. It was purported that Maurice had affronted them on the previous evening by demonstrating his marksmanship within Duffy's Bar in Harrison. Maurice then stood and faced the assembly to advertise loudly the available supply of more elk for sale. The judge turned and swished to his chambers, thus stamping adjournment.

Later, Maurice appeared in my empty waiting room with a small black silk kerchief around his neck, holding the brim of his Western hat in both hands placed before him. Leaning heavily on his left foot, he introduced me to his younger friend.

"My friend, here, is in the family way and wants you to fix him up."

"Sure, Maurice, tell me his name."

His friend was a tall, younger man neatly dressed in black Western clothes, retaining his black broad-brimmed hat on his head and nursing an awkward smile. I sensed a touch of embarrassment here. Maurice continued to be the spokesman.

"George, this here is Doc Losee. He'll fix you up!"

To George, I asked, "Where's your wife? When's the baby due?"

"No. No, Doc," Maurice interjected, "that's not what we want."

George's smile broadened as he turned toward the window. Maurice waited for my response. I hadn't had much practice in answering requests for an abortion and initial experiences tend to generate awkward responses.

"I don't do that kind of fixing, Maurice."

"I gave money to your hospital," Maurice countered.

"I heard you did, Maurice, and we thank you."

"I gave money twice."

"I didn't know that."

"I gave a hundred dollars."

"I told you, Maurice, I don't do that kind of fixing. Why don't you ask for your money back. Tell the hospital board why you want it back."

"Come on, George, he won't help; I'll take you over to Dillon."

This topic repeatedly battered me in general practice.

I was armed with next to no instruction from Yale.

Frank Tanko described a Denver criminal abortionist's technique whereby she placed the end of a foot-long section of one-inch pipe on the abdomen, centered it over the head, and slammed the top end of it with a hammer.

"Less chance of infection, that way," said the cop, as we raced across Denver in the white Cadillac ambulance.

"Yeah, but, Frank, how many mothers did she kill that way?"

"I don't know but they finally caught her."

My last instruction was from Dr. Holtz, in Lander.

"You've got to curette them, Ron," he advised. "If you don't they'll bleed to death."

He attended a young mother who was bleeding to death from a failed self-attempt at abortion. This was happening in her home on the Wyoming plain far away from the hospital. He had no equipment. There was insufficient time to take her to the hospital. He curetted the young lady—probably on the kitchen table—with a piece of fence wire that he found, shaped, and sterilized. (Did he have time to boil it or did he just flame it with a cigarette lighter? There was certainly no anesthesia available.)

As an initiate and naïve practitioner, I thought *all* abortions were spontaneous. I was probably correct in most instances. My present geneticist friend, Dr. John Opitz, informs me that possibly two-thirds of all pregnancies are selectively and spontaneously aborted by nature and half of these occur before the lady even knows she is pregnant.

It took me time to distinguish between the patient's desire for a convenient abortion and the occasional patient's genuine need for a therapeutic abortion.

Mrs. T. entered my office having missed her period. I thought she wanted me to assist her through her pregnancy. Within three minutes of the consultation she asks, 'Have you got a shot, Doc, to make my period come around?"

I wasn't a Catholic, armed to the teeth with the tenets of the Church, nor was I armed with the Hippocratic Oath (thanks to Yale University Medical School, which did not subscribe to it). But I was armed with common sense and decency. I was glad no one had aborted me! I would have gladly settled with the sticker of "bastard" for the privilege of living.

I sensed the usual traps being laid by my prospective mother. I knew she would "pull out the therapeutic abortion stops."

"I'm too old for this. I'm nearly forty!" And she continued, "People are going to laugh at me!"

I couldn't let that one go.

"You mean to say, Mary," I suggested, "*you* have laughed at other old girls that have been in the same mess you are in now."

I had to dominate the conversation to try to save the fetus and convince Mary. I kept at it with, "You talk about people laughing at you, Mary; whose business is this anyway, *other people's or yours*? You talk about people laughing at you; I think you're really thinking how *you* laughed at Marjorie last year with her menopause baby. You're going to be the world's worst when your baby comes. I'll have to run over to your place every time an ant crawls on it. What are you going to do when all your kids leave the house in three or four years? You're a healthy old girl. You have your kids with one pain. You're too good a mother to abort this little one. You'll be a wreck with the guilt and empties. You're lucky, Mary. Let's weigh you right now and start the program."

Mary would not concede. There was no humor on that occasion and I felt foolish to have wheedled. My homily wasn't enough for Mary. She and her husband couldn't hack it. They had their private reasons and went to the abortionist in Dillon. That night she nearly bled to death in Ennis from a botched job.

Then let's remember the day in the southeast room of our hospital when we had two ladies under my obstetrical care in the same room at the same time. One lady was married. The other was not married. The married lady had her baby. Both ladies were ecstatic when the new baby was brought in to nurse. Within two days the unmarried lady delivered her baby, her baby who was *fathered by her married hospital roommate's husband.* Neither knew of the other's identity nor of the other's identical preference of a sexual partner. No problem! There was happiness everywhere! Two new step-siblings had joined our society! Both ladies inhaled their own and each other's baby, as ladies do, at every opportunity. There was an abundance of "prophylactic people manipulation" by the nursing crew in the rear, to be sure. The nurses prevented an emotional catastrophe from disclosure and neither of the happy two ladies was hurt that week.

One Wednesday afternoon years later I was in a side room in the state hospital for the retarded (more about that institution in the next section). There was a small sink in the corner, my chair and table (patients' charts scattered on it), and a single crib against the opposite stark wall. Bored with doing charts, I sat there, chewing on the ballpoint, turned my head, and studied the contents of the crib. Within was a "swastika child," suffering from a congenital disorder that was capable of being accurately diagnosed in utero. "Swastika" was the name I coined for decerebrate and rigidly spastic children whose arms and legs formed the symbol as they lay plastered to their beds by gravity. They would have to be turned over en masse. Occasionally a stiff extremity protruding through the crib slat would be accidentally injured by a passing attendant. This little living thing was on her back, looking at what and seeing what? I worried. I made a triangular paper cup like the ones we used to make in the Upper Red Hook Schoolhouse. I filled it with room-temperature tap water, carried it to the crib, and made a drip-hole at the bottom point of the cup. I held it above the child's mouth. The eyes widened. The feeble neck stiffened. The mouth opened wide. The dry tongue protruded. I could hear her pant. Her cheeks sucked in. She drank cup after cup then stared at the ceiling again.

"Jesus, what are we doing?"

Frequently confronted with threatened miscarriage, I worried about the possibility of a maternal fatality from hemorrhage or infection. In time I mastered the principles and lost no young mother from such catastrophe.

I diagnosed a chronic renal disorder on the multiparous patient in her forties. I gathered the data and with this I consulted with my obstetrician–medical-school classmate in New Haven and he supported me and confirmed the need for a therapeutic abortion because of the threat of a possible maternal fatal kidney failure. This was before the day of renal transplants. All along, I sensed that the pregnancy was not wanted by the mother or by the father. The two prospective siblings were now in high school and ready to leave home. There was the expected expense of further educational costs. The mother, who possessed a fragile temperament, dreaded the prospect of having to complete the pregnancy and rear a little one. The day came when we satisfied our consciences and reason dictated our duty. The mother's health was confirmed to have been in jeopardy.

This abortion I was about to effect was my first and I

had been instructed to merely break the amniotic membranes. Break the membranes I did under the proper aseptic gynecological technique. The amniotic fluid escaped. But no cramps ensued and after waiting with gracious patience while nothing happened, the mother changed her intent and decided with a bit of elation to risk kidney failure.

The kidneys didn't fail. The delivery was gentle. The babe was a healthy boy—whom the parents worshipped with exceeding joy, pride, and contentment. Together, we had many mischievous smiles of relief over the near-miss as the years progressed.

Thirteen years later I corrected a complex growth-line deformity (epiphyseal) this young man acquired from an injury. I was a better orthopaedist than gynecologist!

"Once a Boil on the Bone, Always a Boil on the Bone"

Orthopaedics in General Practice

IN 1945 WE were at the army's Winter General Hospital in Topeka, Kansas. It was so hot and miserable there that summer that Olive and I called the place "Toe-puke-ah." I was assigned to the officers' orthopaedic ward. There were only two recuperating officers of the two or three hundred I doctored who, at the time of their hospital discharge, wanted to return to service. Of these, one was a young aircraft pilot who dearly loved to fly. The other was a colonel about to be promoted. The happiest soldier I remember there was a kid with both legs and his left arm tied up in traction. He had a pinup picture of Betty Grable, a tiny radio, and a cigar in his mouth, as well as a box of them stashed. He had been rescued after surviving three days in a foxhole in New Ireland. He described lying in excrement and vomit in company with varmints and snakes with gun-fire above.

The news of Hiroshima was received by these broken men with silence. One soldier expressed *his* opinion to me. It was, "Jesus Christ, they'll have to put up a whole hospital every time they shoot one of those suckers off."

Here I picked up the finest textbook I had ever known. It was Sir Reginald Watson-Jones' *Fractures and Joint Injuries,* the orthopaedist's bible.

I read his book with the enthusiasm of a youngster reading *Dick Tracy* in the comics, and I couldn't put it down. I say to this day that it was Sir Reginald Watson-Jones who launched me into the orthopaedic world.

In October of 1953, Hank Rowe, a sheep rancher from Norris, Montana, came into my office. Seven years previously Hank had incurred a fracture of his tibia and fibula. It was a severely comminuted fracture (broken in many fragments), but not compounded. He told me his doctors talked of amputation at the time but they didn't cut it off. Dr. Roger Anderson in Seattle stabilized Hank's leg in an external fixation device, his "Roger Anderson Splint." To do this, they pierced the fractured bone fragments with thin stainless-steel rods. After they aligned the broken fragments, clamps alongside the leg held the pins solidly and thus stabilized the fracture. Infection can develop about the pin site, more often with the use of large pins than with the use of small ones.

In the four years since I had begun practicing in Ennis, Hank had been treated at least twice with penicillin for phlebitis by his surgeon. When Hank arrived at my office, I naturally had looked at the leg but could not see a sign of any superficial inflamed vein, nor could I palpate any deeper thrombotic areas.

In the back of my mind, I was certain Hank didn't have phlebitis of his old injured leg. But the course of penicillin ordered did seem to fix his painful leg until he had spent a few weeks in the mountains with his bands of sheep.

When he came back to see me that October, he had awful pain in the lower tibia and about his ankle. He had seen his surgeon in Seattle again. They had taken X-rays of the bad leg, diagnosed phlebitis for the second time, and referred him back to me for another course of penicillin.

But this time Hank's pain was excruciating. We both pondered over the problem in my office with his pant leg rolled up. I still couldn't find evidence of phlebitis. I wanted to take an X-ray, but he had just had this done in Seattle, so I sent him home after giving him his shot.

The next day Hank returned. The pain was intense. It was boring in character. Yet the leg wasn't hot, nor was it inflamed. Could this be a causalgia type of pain similar to the pain that caused the soldiers in Winter General Hospital to scream? (Today, causalgia is called "reflex sympathetic dystrophy," a painful complication of either trauma or a surgical operation.) Hank did have trigger points of pain about the ankle that implied causalgia. I thought, "Ethics be damned." Hank was in pain. His diagnosis did not seem correct to me, so I took an X-ray.

The film showed a thickened cortex throughout the lower half of his tibia. There were also small fenestrations, or areas with less bone, in the lower tibia. This could be chronic osteomyelitis, bone infection, I thought. Bad! Dr. Armour, in the Royal Vic, used to preach, "Once a boil on the bone, always a boil on the bone!" Hank's white-blood count was way up—it was 18,000—but his temperature was normal. So we decided the right thing to do was to send Hank to the Mayo Clinic in Rochester, Minnesota, eleven hundred miles away.

The Clinic reported that Hank had a large bone abscess of his lower tibia. They opened and curetted his leg. The cavity was loosely packed with furacin-infiltrated dressing (an antibacterial drug) and loosely sutured. After three weeks, when healthy granulation tissue covered the base of the cavity, they filled it with bone chips obtained from the bone bank. The wound closed and Hank recovered and bore weight on his leg in ten weeks.

Where had I missed? I had seen no large bone abscess in

my films. I corresponded with Dr. Young, Hank's surgeon in Rochester, about this. He had seen the abscess, which I had missed, on the original films they made of Hank's leg, and on additional X-rays using greater voltage penetration. Dr. Young thereby taught me a useful diagnostic technique: "Use different voltage penetration when a bone abscess is suspected."

As the years progressed, Hank developed a chronic drainage above his ankle. "Once a boil on the bone, always a boil on the bone!" He returned to Rochester several times, but the draining continued. A quarter of a century ago he told me he had spent thirty thousand dollars on his leg, a huge amount in those days. His favorite remedy through the years was to put bacon over the drainage and to soak the leg in the Norris Hot Springs that the Rowe family then owned. Perhaps fifteen years ago, about two years prior to his demise, Hank asked me to operate on his old osteomyelitic leg because it was so painful. I widely opened the lower area. The stench was acrid. His tibia contained an ounce or two of rot that had been there for a quarter of a century. The old bone-bank graft had turned to a stinking gray-brown paste, wet with surrounding pus. I was able to scrape out the dead tissue down to the living bone and Hank's draining leg dried up after weeks and weeks of drainage. It formed an absolutely dry and painless hollow with a shiny, thin skin covering. Dr. Amour's maxim failed, at least for the last two years of Hank's life.

Olive and I like to remember Hank in his middle age in the 1950s taking long running and limping strides at the head of his band of sheep, alongside the bellwether, as the thousand followers *baa*ed their way through Ennis, filling Main Street and its bordering sidewalks with waves of fleece.

The 1957 Doldrums

THE ENNIS FOLKS know that Ralph Paugh (pronounced *Paw*) suffers from momentary episodes of narcolepsy. Ralph is perhaps ten or a dozen years my senior. In 1957 he was actively working his ranch in the Jack Creek area. He and his wife Cloe lived in a one-storied house a couple of blocks south of Main Street in Ennis and Ralph drove his pickup truck back and forth to work. He was born in the valley and has become a fluent raconteur of its history. Because of his affliction, his story-telling is occasionally interrupted with a pause while he contemplates, and is momentarily suspended with a sigh and lowered eyelids. The hesitations enhanced the pleasure of his audience as they wondered, Will he be able to continue? Will he lose his place? But he always continued. Ralph had incurred a bout of encephalitis in the service of his country that resulted in his narcoleptic wound. He never insisted on compensation as is the expected practice of the veteran. One day at work he fractured his wrist. It was a simple Colles' (common wrist) fracture. I set it; even though Ralph reminds me today that, while pulling on his wrist while Dale Hirsch, Ralph's friend, counter-pulled the flexed elbow, we "ran out of power!" I took X-rays of his wrist. I studied the X-rays. I didn't know whether or not the set was correct. I took the X-rays to Butte, ninety miles away. I showed them to the orthopaedist. While slouching on a stool, he flashed them up, one by one, in two-second intervals, holding each film by its corner, and allowing the light from a dusty, half-open hospital window to shabbily illuminate them. His response

113

to my inquiry, that was about to consume a one-hundred-and-eighty-mile trip twice across the Continental Divide, was, "It's okay." And he proceeded to tell a dirty joke that I don't remember. I returned to Ennis thinking, "How could he know if Ralph's wrist was really set correctly with such a rapid inspection of the X-ray? He's an orthopaedist. He's supposed to know. I hope Ralph will be all right."

Then the sad, true, and consuming thought arose, "I don't even know when a wrist has been set correctly. That's dumb."

It was the end of the day in the office. I longed to run down the hill, around the corner, up the crumbly concrete sidewalk to the log house, and to just be home with Olive, Becky, Jon, and Buttons, who would be baying at the town's nine PM test-siren wail. Still, in the tiny five-by-eight-foot lab, I had pricked a patient's finger, spread the blood thinly on a glass slide, stained the smear, and was now looking at the blood cells under the microscope. The scope was on the east shelf beneath the window. The Madison Range was visible there, above the scope and through the window, with its old-rose alpine glow distracting me. I looked at the cells through the microscope. Red cells were everywhere. No problem. I thought, "Here is a mature polymorphonuclear leukocyte and there is a lymphocyte. I must make a count after I look at this slide. What the hell is this cell? Is it an immature white cell? How immature? It must have a name. I don't know its name. Here's another. It's not the same, though. I don't know what it is, either. I don't know anything. I can't even read a simple blood smear. That's dumb."

Margaret Best, the dentist's wife, was our next-door neighbor who lived above Gil Hansen's bakery. The second-story front window gave her the advantage of full disclosure of up-to-date Main Street events, including rare Saturday-night fisticuffs. And she was wordy in her descriptions, wordy to the point that Dr. Best could never get a word in edgewise. One night Dr. Best called me. Mrs. Best was critically ill. Her abdomen was tender and rigid. I suspected an acute pancreatitis. I thought she should be operated on. I wanted to send her to Butte. She refused to go. Both she and her husband *insisted* that I operate. I did. There were soapsuds all over her pancreas and on the omentum, too. I explored and found no other cause for her illness, labeled it an acute pancreatitis, and closed the abdominal wound. She remained very ill in our hospital. With gastric suction, intravenous fluids, and finally a bit of insulin to get her to eat again after a week, she recovered. Yes, she recovered, and after thinking about her case for a few days, I recovered, too. I then knew that it was wrong for me to have agreed to their wish and to have operated. I was too inexperienced, and I thought, "That's dumb."

I watched Dave Rossiter examining X-ray films of the chest. He had spent *two years* learning how to read X-rays. How many patients had I X-rayed, reading their films and proclaiming there to be no pathology? How many errors had I made in reading those films? Certainly, "That's dumb."

Portrayed here are but four examples of my appalling ignorance of commonly occurring medical problems. This included medical, surgical, obstetrical, pediatric, and psychiatric deficiencies. Insufficient knowledge had become my major anxiety in general practice.

My feelings of inadequacy were in no small part due to my mistaken belief that a doctor was supposed to *cure* people. I was a slow learner. This false idea ushered a sense of guilt at billing time. It was this guilt that produced my distaste for the economic part of the general practice. Gradually I came to understand that there are no *cures*, that healing is the in-built mechanism of the body, and without its genetic, immune, inflammatory, and adaptation processes, we are goners early in the game. Slowly I concluded that "doctoring" was the understanding and teaching of the natural and pathological processes.

I learned about the *understanding and teaching* function of doctoring when Marcie Scully had mumps and subsequently developed juvenile diabetes. I understood that the mumps virus had inflamed her pancreas and destroyed the islets of Langerhans that secreted insulin, and without her natural source of insulin she developed all the symptoms of diabetes. I couldn't "cure" this, but I could teach Marcie and her mother and father how to live with the diabetes and employ insulin.

When Wilbur Powell, the ranch hand, fractured his tibia while working for Jim Martin, his leg was bent between his knee and ankle. I could put a steel pin through his heel bone and hang an old paint can full of stones tied to a sash cord fastened to the pin in his heel. I could support, with the extremely important help of the nurses, Wilbur's broken leg on a pillow at the foot of the bed; I could order aspirin for his pain. I could put too much weight in the pail and keep the fractured ends of the bone too far apart to heal. I could put insufficient weight in the pail and let the tibia bend. But *I couldn't make the tibia unite*! This was to be the work of the incredible in-built healing process.

Also wearing on me was the economics of the practice. I hated the charging, the billing, the collecting. Medical bills differed from store bills; folks never *wanted* to *buy* medical service. Except for the mothers, they never received a thing for their medical payments. How could a waitress who contracted pneumonia or a cowboy who broke his leg while bull-dogging in a rodeo afford to pay a reasonable medical bill? They couldn't. Did that mean they deserved no care? Of course not. What happened when I lost a patient? The family had enough expense, the hospital, the undertaker, the extras, and now perhaps the wage-earner was gone. How could a man of conscience add to all this? How the hell could a doctor charge a widow? The youngsters with their obstetrical interruptions had a terrible time paying the seventy-five-dollar doctor bill, let alone a slightly larger hospital charge! The ranchers complained about paying high wages to their help, their laborers, who sometimes became my patients. The wages were not enough to pay doctor bills. Therefore I had to pitch in and help subsidize the rancher. I *hated* the business part.

Doctoring should not be a business, and I think that the surgeon who operates needlessly, as it were, possesses the morality of a rapist.

Doctoring must remain a profession.

The true professional should remain dedicated to uphold a sacred charge and should not be constantly de-professionalized, degraded, and dishonored by governments, the media, the courts, or corporations. Let these four properly attack, de-professionalize, regulate, and punish derelicts among us who deserve this, without crushing the autonomy of the professional American doctor by turning him or her into a cold-hearted business person, a technician and tool of the administrator.

One of the other nagging difficulties of my general practice was the unrelenting demands of the people for my time. Obstetrics required continuous availability. This moral mandate had persisted since the first delivery in the basement house early in 1950. In 1955 the Ford Foundation gave ten thousand dollars to the hospital to build a furnished two-bed maternity room, a nursery, and a delivery room. Wayne and Ed Miller built the new hospital addition to the east. Olive designed the floor plan that was and remains very functional. Now, at night, with the eastern extension we had a new light issuing forth from the back of the Madison Valley Hospital when a mother arrived for "deliverance."

During the 1957 doldrums, one night while I was rushing back to Ennis from assisting at an operation in Butte, knowing that a mother was due, I nearly drove off the road looking to see whether the light in the back of the hospital was lit. It was lit. I drove hell-bent to the front of the hospital, making tire marks in the sand. By this time I knew that the baby had come and the mother was bleeding to death from post-partum hemorrhage. I rushed in the front door and ran to the obstetrics wing. The ladies were just cleaning the joint!

The next Sunday we went as a family up to the Jack Creek ski hill. We had a wonderful time wearing out that homemade rope tow. We were home by five. It gets dark early in the winter in Montana. I had just taken my ski boots off and was ready to settle down with a beer or a cup of cocoa when the phone rang. No beer, no cocoa! How bad will this next problem be? I'd just warmed up, I was feeling groggy, and against all my instincts I'd have to say, "I'll be there as soon as I can!" Such is the problem of the Solo Practice of Medicine.

The decision to fix my medical inadequacy loomed like a tsunami wave one February night in 1957 after I had finished with the day's office calls. My feet were on the ten-dollar, cigarette-burned desk and my back was to the window. With no other consultation I picked up the phone and called Dr. Stewart Baxter in Montreal, my first mentor on the surgical service of the Royal Victoria Hospital.

"Have you got an internship for me in surgery? I'll take anything."

"How old are you now, Ron?"

"Thirty-seven."

"You want a residency?"

"I'll take anything you've got."

"I don't think there'd be a problem if you returned as a senior intern."

"I'll take it!"

"Okay, I'll talk to the powers."

It was a disturbing, disruptive request to have dumped on Olive, Becky, and Jonathan without extensive consultation. There was so much love for the papa, I never heard an objection, just anxieties—what-ifs, how-can-we's, and I-don't-know-buts. Their sacrifice made a father's dream come true.

Thirty-seven years old, I still owed Uncle Darb two thou-

DOC

Then and Now with a Montana Physician

Ronald E. Losee, senior year at Yale Medical School, 1943, in Private 1st Class uniform

Ronald E. and Olive T. Losee, Elizabethtown, Kentucky, 1947

Denver General Hospital interns and wives' picnic, June 1948 (Losee's Jeep)

R. E. Losee's office in Ennis, Montana, 1950

Losee's Jeep, at Olive's mother's house in Westfield, Connecticut, loaded up for trip west, August 1949

Lab in R. E. Losee's office in Ennis, 1950

Madison Valley Hospital, Ennis, 1950

Main Street, Ennis, 1950

Madison Valley Hospital, Ennis, 1965

Dr. Roland P. Jakob of Bern, Switzerland, demonstrating the knee ligament deficiency teaching apparatus to R. E. Losee at the 4th Congress of the European Society of Knee Surgery and Arthroscopy held in Stockholm, Sweden, June 1990

R. E. Losee (left), Werner Müller (right), and H. U. Staubli (center) testing EKT 1000 at Stockholm, Sweden, June 1990

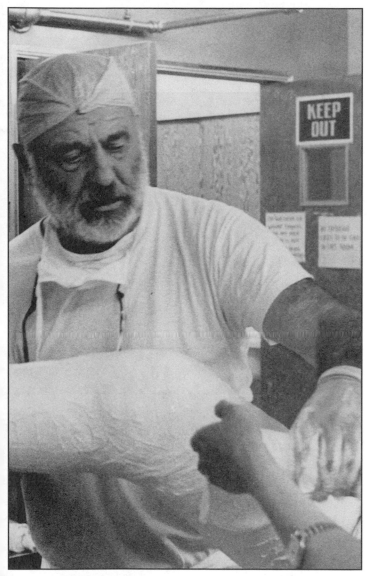

R. E. Losee, Madison Valley Hospital, Ennis, June 29, 1982
(Patient: K. Stevens)

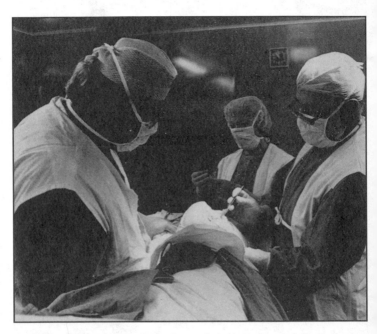

R. K. Handlos (left), Jody Sprout (center), and R. E. Losee (right), Madison Valley Hospital, Ennis, June 29, 1982 (Patient: K. Stevens)

R. E. Losee (left) with Guy Liorzou, 1990

John Feagin (left) presents Olive and R. E. Losee with the first copy of his book *The Crucial Ligaments*, March 18, 1988, in Billings, Montana

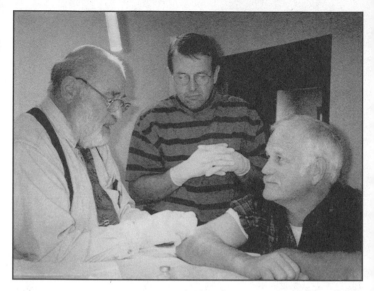

Drs. Gerry Key, Danielson, and R. E. Losee (cutting), Ennis, September 1992

Olive waves from restored GPW 28810 in the Fourth of July parade in Ennis, 1992

sand dollars. We had a Chevy station wagon and we might have had five hundred bucks in the bank. There were thousands owed to me on the books. When we left, those who owed us figured, "They're gone now, what-the-hell!"—except Bill and Ginny Judd and a couple of others. Glady Chamberlain, Hank Rowe, and Tommy Williams wrote to us when we were away. Our friend Buddy Little said we were crazy to leave Ennis.

Surgeon Allan Iddles from Pennsylvania agreed to take over the practice and to live in the log house. We packed our household goods in the deceased Miss Tits' barn. We boarded Buttons at Chuck and Fanny Aaberg's home at the Sun Ranch and left Ennis the day after school was out. Jonathan was strangling with the whooping cough. We stopped on our way south and said good-bye to Blue Evans who was working for the Park Service along the lonely (in those days) highway, the other side of the Fishing Bridge along Lake Yellowstone. He pointed out a grizzly cub down the road. And we were on our way.

Connecticut and Montreal, here we come!

PART 3

Bones, Joints, and Knees

Dr. John C. Armour

Senior Surgeon of the
Royal Victoria Hospital, Montreal

JULY 1, 1957, was a sad day as I watched Olive, Becky, and Jonathan drive away from the back of the intern quarters in the Chevy station wagon to return to Connecticut. Now, thirty-seven years old, I was to undertake a surgical training in Montreal. Olive returned with the kids to Middletown, Connecticut, to finally finish her nurse's training at the Middlesex Memorial Hospital. In her first days as a nursing student in 1944 she had contracted a Flexner's intestinal illness while on duty in the Norwich psychiatric hospital. Because of her forty-five days' absence, she was denied her RN diploma in 1944. Olive was told in 1957 that if she offered a *full year* of service as a student nurse to the hospital, the diploma would be granted—the usual academic extortion!

The waving family drove out of sight. The instant heavy sinking tug at my heart began. It was accompanied by a fearsome self-examination about the wisdom of our decision, a discomfort that lasted all too long. It was immediately intensified when I took a drink of warm chlorinated water from the fountain by the front door of the hospital. As I wiped my mouth, I looked out of the door and realized Montana was far beyond the citified horizon—Montana with its pure, crystal-clear, cold, Rocky Mountain water to drink! Why had I left? I poked at myself. The shoes I had on were my only possession. The white clothes and the pen in my pocket were hospital issue. Why in hell had I left?

Duty each day began at six AM and ended each alternate night when the work was finished.

The first operation at which I assisted was performed by Dr. Gordon Petrie, the chief orthopaedist. It was an attempt to unite a young man's hip with a bone-grafting operation. Before he made the incision I was delegated to paint the skin with iodine, which was simple enough until Petrie hollered at me, "You don't do it that way! You're doing it like a general surgeon! You can't work with me if you fritter like that! Paint it like a barn. Do it right!"

I don't think even my father hollered at me like that. We operated all morning. Petrie also fused the arthritic wrist of another man while his new orthopaedic resident from Ireland, Bill Woods, scooped slabs of bone from the patient's iliac crest for the boss to apply to the wrist. A week later, I, having been assigned to care for him after the operation, noted that the wound from which the iliac bone had been gathered was gaping. I had never seen such a problem and I knew it wasn't right.

That day's surgery was over, and I accompanied Dr. Petrie on his rounds. When we came to the patient whose wrist had been operated on, I said to the professor, "Dr. Petrie, I think you ought to take a look at this man's graft-site wound. It doesn't look good."

I removed the dressing. The wound seemed as if it was not just gaping; it seemed cavernous! Petrie looked, then in a very loud refrain shouted, "How long has this gaped? Are you waiting for *God* to heal it? Call Miss Warnock. We'll take him to the operating room right now. Do you treat your patients like this in Montana, Dr. Losee? This wound has to be closed now!"

And he closed it.

It took but a few days on the orthopaedic service to make me an orthopaedic enthusiast. I liked the anatomy, the surgical craft, the extremity of doctoring, and the mechanics of orthopaedics better than the complexities of general or thoracic surgery. The senior-internship program was divided into two-month intervals. I swapped with the other interns to stay on Petrie's and Fred Moseley's services to capture all the orthopaedics I could that year. (Dr. Moseley was an authority on the shoulder.) But it so happened that I had one month's work with the great general surgeon John C. Armour. Like Dominie French during my adolescence, John Armour became a hero and a permanent fixture in my soul thereafter. Dr. Armour's life's lesson was his insistence on the practice of *impeccable professional honesty* by his students, and he taught in an undisguised manner. My first encounter with Dr. Armour had been during my first internship in Montreal in 1948.

Each of the ward areas in the hospital had an entrance hall from which service closets and isolation rooms were accessed. In one of these large closets was a lab bench under a window facing the courtyard of the building as well as a large sink on the right of the door as one entered. One night I was working at the Ward F lab at the table against the window, doing a blood count, when Dr. Armour came in and turned to the large, black, square slate sink with the corroded brass faucets.

"Jesus," I thought, "he's going to pee in it!"

He did. He finished and turned to me and said, "The sink test. The sink test!"

The "sink test" we all knew was performed delinquently by overworked interns when they poured the urine they were obliged to test down the sink—and then forged a laboratory report on the patient's chart indicating a healthy urine.

Dr. Armour was a happy, overweight, white-coated man (we all used coats) in his fifties. After relieving himself, he gave me a devilish smile of wisdom, knowing damned well that even if we had never done the sink test, and we hadn't, both he and I had been frequently tempted to do this. I also remember that he neglected to button his fly until he walked out the door and then noticed his oversight. He buttoned, then brushed the front saying, "Dead bird never fell out of the nest. Dead bird never fell out of the nest."

I was not his resident then but I started to worship the

old boy immediately. He peed like I did, and had fun doing it. And he was tirelessly overloaded, trying his best, during the night, to help his patients on the wards. These people on the wards were poor folks. I never saw the great chief surgeon on the wards at night. Dr. Armour was there many, many a night. I am told that he grew up in an agricultural area of Perth, Ontario, and perhaps it was this earth source that made him so rich in human understanding and compassion. It's true he was sometimes uncouth, but this great man was passionately dedicated to the care of his patients.

It was when I returned to the hospital in 1957 that I came to know him well. The professor would scrub twice as long as was customary before his operations. He would scrub, using the stiff brush and his own can of "Mechanic's Delight," a sassafras scented, *sanded*, and naphtha-infiltrated soap paste. His large hands were soft and white, though one would think they would have become raw from such use. This lengthy scrub had two purposes. One was to give the resident a welcome chance to open the wound without supervision. The other must have been to provide, for himself, an opportunity to think about the operation he was about to start.

As I would scrub with him he would quiz me. There were lots of answers that I knew not. I would apologize to him and he would say, "That's all right. You're not supposed to know it all yet. I'm a generation older than you."

Later, operating, elbow-deep in surrounding abdominal wall as he palpated the patient's sigmoid bowel, he withdrew his moistened arm and motioned to me to examine the gut.

"Dr. Losee," he quizzed, "tell me what you feel in this man's sigmoid."

I buried my arm and rolled warm guts between my rubber-gloved fingers, trying my best to distinguish ileum from sigmoid. When I *thought* I had sigmoid bowel in my hand, was I feeling a tumor, or more likely an encased turd?

"Take your time," he'd say. "What do you feel?"

I'd have to tell him, "I don't know. I can't tell a turd from a lump."

"That's all right, that's all right," he'd answer. "We'll bring it out where we can look at it and settle the matter."

Scrubbing (for a long time) in preparation for performing an abdominal-perineal resection on a man with carcinoma of the rectum, referring to another patient on the ward and leaning over the scrub sink, he said, "Cystosarcoma phylloides, cystosarcoma phylloides—I didn't have the guts to call it yesterday. I didn't have the guts to call it. The breast looked like a turned-on electric lightbulb. Dr. Losee, did you see the lady yet?" (He was referring to a lady patient on the ward.)

"Yes, but I didn't know what it was. I'd never seen anything like that before." (Nor have I ever since.)

"Cystosarcoma phylloides, cystosarcoma phylloides" was the slogan he repeated twenty times a day for a week.

We commenced the abdominal-perineal resection on the man who was suffering from a cancer of his rectum. Dr. Armour let the chief surgical resident do the abdominal work (which was more dramatic) while he did the dirty job of carving out the rectum. He did this by sitting on a low stool at the foot of the operating table between the patient's flexed hips and knees supported by the stirrups. In this way his face faced the patient's anus as he worked. I was on the liver or right side of the patient assisting the resident above, who was mobilizing the large bowel in preparation for bringing it through the abdominal wall as a permanent colostomy. The time had come to transect the large bowel above the diseased lower tissue. Dr. Armour's large right rubber-gloved hand arose like Lazarus from the dead—arose from the depths of the pelvic basin of the supine patient! The hand from below was reaching, reaching to greet another person's right hand from above (the operating resident's). There was a sincere handshake.

The voice from below boomed forth:

"Dr. Livingstone, I presume. Dr. Livingstone, I presume."

(I still think of this every time I reach through a small door in the Madison Valley Hospital in Ennis where X-ray films are stored. The tiny closet containing the cassettes is between two rooms and has an access door at each end. There are times when Jody, our technician, is reaching from the other side and our hands shake. "Dr. Livingstone, I presume. Dr. Livingstone, I presume," I recall.)

I learned about the Girdlestone's orthopaedic operation from Dr. Armour one day, as again I was passing his operating room, No. 8. I always passed No. 8 on the way to Gordon Petrie's operating theater, just to get a glimpse of the old boy. This day while I was passing, Dr, Armour called me in.

"This is a Girdlestone operation. This is a Girdlestone operation. Here, have a head, have a head."

He tossed me the femoral head, the ball of the hip from the woman, which he at that very moment had removed. I caught it.

The lady had fractured her hip, the neck of her femur. It had never healed and she couldn't bear weight on that side.

He fretted, mumbling,

"It seems wrong. It seems wrong to cut out the head of the femur. But they get better. They can't do the Highland fling. But they get better."

(In Canada at the time the general surgeons would take care of fractures and even do meniscectomies on the knees and plate-fractured femurs.)

There was a time after I had left Dr. Armour's service when I was working on Ward E with an orthopaedic patient. Dr. MacBride was then Dr. Armour's resident and he asked me to examine the breast of a lady on the other side of the aisle. I remember the examination to this day. It was a left breast. I palpated and palpated the breast and the axilla and couldn't find a lump. A week later on the same ward, Dr. Armour approached me and asked, "Dr. Losee, did you examine Mrs. Nadine?"

"I did."

The doctor then took me across the aisle to the bedside of Mrs. Nadine so that I faced her while he told me that I had missed the cancer that he had found.

Then, away from the lady and out of her hearing, he asked me, "Is that the way you would want your wife examined? I'm not going to let you forget this. I'm going to remind you. I'm going to remind you."

And remind me, he did, many a time, always concluding his teaching reminder with, "It makes you humble. It makes you humble, doesn't it, Dr. Losee!"

One day, perhaps a week later, when he knew it was time to stop, he chuckled, "Gavin Miller—the surgeon-in-chief—missed the cancer in her breast too, Dr. Losee."

Dr. Armour liked to eat. If ever a patient had candy or nuts by the bed or if candy was offered, rounds were stopped and there was an instant sharing with everybody. One day there was a lady patient on the west side of Ward E, in the seventh or eighth bed away from the entrance. A dish of cashews was on her bedside stand. The professor gathered a handful in his right hand, and with the nuts still in his hand he put on the rubber glove. Standing at the left side of her bed, he reached over the supine patient and did a thorough rectal exam.

Yes, after the exam he did lift the gloved hand to his face in such a way that by stretching the cuff with his other hand he was able to permit the remaining nuts to pour into his open mouth. This was Dr. Armour.

Dr. Armour had operated for breast cancer throughout his career and he was always consulted at grand rounds whenever this subject arose. He always squeezed the utmost from the pathologist at biopsy time, studying the slides over and over again, and wondering about the outcome and the treatment methods. One day he passed me as he came out of the pathologist's laboratory mumbling, with a downcast look, "Carcinoma of the breast! Carcinoma of the breast! I've spent my whole life looking at it and I don't know a damned thing about it!"

The new surgeon-in-chief, Dr. Webster, asked his old master, Dr. Armour, to consult at the bedside in the private pavilion. We'll call Dr. Webster's private patient "Lady Snodgrass." She *was* a member of the queen's court and was indeed addressed as "Lady." The consultation was about a potential breast lesion. I stood by the side of the bed while the master, Dr. Armour, leaned over to examine. As usual, it was a most thorough exam. I observed him make an "antique-radio-dial maneuver." (He twisted the flattened breast very much like that of the radio dial.) I thought it was an unusual maneuver. Actually, Dr. Armour vigorously twisted both breasts at the same time, or so it appeared to me! But Lady or not, royalty or not, the professor vociferated, "Sex, sex. It makes the world go round!"

Webster was used to the antics of his old boss. He didn't say a word. He smiled to me with a twinkle. The Lady was being studied by the great master. Nor was she perturbed. I think I was the only victim of embarrassment. There was no malignancy on that occasion.

There was always a possibility of a sleep-induced erection on a supine male during an operation. To a sensitive soul, such a disclosure of male sanctity in the presence of our nurse sisters in those days was a disastrous embarrassment. By this time I had reached thirty-seven years without having experienced such an incident, but the occasion finally arose at the conclusion of Dr. Armour's last operation of the day. The flag went up beneath the thin green sheet covering the patient. There was the momentary scurry of the circulating nurse in charge. Not a word was said for many moments. Finally, standing and watching from a distance that was halfway between the operating table and the doorway, John Armour turned directly toward the patient.

He leaned back a bit and raised his right arm, pointing directly to the spectacle, and like the New England town crier of old, he said, "Look at that, look at that. It must be gas. It makes me jealous. It makes me jealous."

As he walked out of the operating-room door, he reminded us all, as he so frequently did, that "The sum of the assumption equals zero!"

I never did know just what that meant!

Petrie

Chief of Orthopaedics at the
Royal Victoria Hospital, Montreal

IMAGINE STANDING TWO feet beneath a circular, four-foot-wide operating-room light that pours forth not only its shadowless, intense illumination but heat as well. Imagine being clothed in a pair of solid-green pajamas, then wrapped in a pea-green gown that has been gathered and firmly fastened down its back. Complete the attire with a green cloth hat that half-covers the ears and a square of thick green mesh covering the mouth and nose, tied there with a pair of strings, one knot unnoticed tied behind the neck and the other pressing its small, firm mass against the scalp over the occiput. The scrubbed hands, of course, are "condomed" into a pair of rubber gloves, gloves which squeeze a bit at first and which partially smother the God-given sense of touch.

This is not all. Imagine the fatigue of the one contained within the costume, still awake after twenty-six hours. The view, with the head bent forward, is that of a supine person lying on a narrow and mechanized table. The person is also covered with green sheets, only the right shoulder is bared and painted with tincture of iodine. The person's right arm and hand are now enclosed in a long, tight-fitting, dull-white stocking. The stocking is made of cheap material and resembles the stockings that we who were children in the 1920s were forced to wear above our knees and beneath our short pants or knickers. Sitting at the head of the table is another begowned and bemasked person who is rhythmically squeezing a rubber bag attached to an intricately mechanized stainless-steel washstand. He is squeezing with his right hand and maintaining a form-fitting rubber mask firmly against the face of the supine patient. The mask connects to the anesthesia apparatus through a snaking, inch-wide accordion-pleated rubber tube.

Across the table, standing opposite, is the chief orthopaedist in the same green apparel, with his steel-gray eyebrows roofing the orbits that pierce over the green face mask.

With a five-inch-long, one-half-inch-wide, flat stainless-steel Bard-Parker knife handle tipped with a razor-sharp No. 23 blade gripped in the right hand, imagine having completed a proper four-inch-long cut on top of the sleeping person's right shoulder. The cut was made with one smooth slash, deep enough to have exposed the slightly convex top of the attachment of the collarbone to the acromion, the top of the shoulder. This is the Fraser Gurd operation, a remedy for a damaged and painful acromio-clavicular joint. Now an inch of the outer end of the collarbone must be removed. Removed now! By whom? No one else!

Get at it, is the inner thought.

But I've never even seen one of these done is the counter thought.

The third man at the table is a similarly garbed junior intern who is spreading the cut with small stainless-steel rakes. He also cuts the sutures down to the knot after they've been tied by the operator.

Imagine having to plunge the tip of the knife accurately into the joint.

Do it! And it's done, very easily.

Easy also, is a vertical cut that opens the acromio-clavicular joint.

Now what? Oh, cut down the front of the joint. I'm making a few jagged tears of joint capsule here. Not bad though. I'm getting deep here. Watch out! Let's go where it's safer. Let's go to the back. Cut here!

"Can you see the meniscus yet? Is it torn?" comes from the boss.

Jesus, I forgot to look; I'm so damned busy doing it, I don't know what I'm doing! I can't pry apart the joint enough yet to see anything. There's too much joint capsule deep on the underside to let it open.

"Here, Ron, let me slip a bone hook in the end of the clavicle," the chief says and he slips it in sideways, gives it a twist, and yanks it toward the front.

Oh, that helps. I can see the joint now, I realize with relief.

The joint is all scoured. The meniscus is buggered. We all three agree.

I've got to cut the under-part of the joint now or we'll never be able to take out the outer inch of the clavicle. What's under there? Is a subclavicular vessel likely to be cut? Jesus, that would be horrible!

It has been fifteen years since I have seen a cadaver specimen of the shoulder. There has been no time to study the anatomy in preparation for this unexpected invitation to excise the acromio-clavicular joint. I'm uneasy.

At this moment I hesitated and pondered how to protect the tissues beneath the deep part of the operation. I gently placed the scalpel on the sheet at the side of the wound in order to contemplate.

"DON'T PUT THAT KNIFE DOWN! PICK IT UP! QUIT YOUR HEN-SCRATCHING, DAMMIT! DON'T OPERATE LIKE A GENERAL SURGEON! KEEP CUTTING! KEEP CUTTING, DAMMIT! IF YOU *EVER* PUT THAT KNIFE DOWN AGAIN I'LL TAKE IT AWAY FROM YOU AND YOU'LL *NEVER* GET IT AGAIN!"

Petrie is shouting.

Whew! He's mean. He damn well means it, too. Okay, I'll cut. But I'll be damned if I'll slash. I'll hang on to the knife all right. I'll hen-scratch if I have to, but I'll hen-scratch as fast as I can. I'll keep cutting right against the bone, right around the end of the joint. I'll cut upward from the bottom so I don't cut a subclavian vein or a nerve or something. I've got to look this area up again tonight in the anatomy book.

Then as I've nearly recovered from the embarrassment of the rebuke, a seed of confidence sprouts. "Will somebody pull harder on the bone hook so I can get underneath the clavicle better?" I say.

The collarbone is lifted. The last of the posterior capsular ligament is cut. The end of the collarbone now protrudes.

"I'll have a periosteal elevator," I blurt out, and the scrub nurse at the instrument stand passes the tool.

It's easy to scrape the periostium off the clavicle in front, but the damned elevator won't cut underneath.

"Use your knife again, Ron, to cut underneath but DON'T CUT THE SUSPENSORY LIGAMENTS!" says Petrie.

I think, *I know that much*, then request, "Can I have a dull elevator, please?"

A dull elevator is handed to me. It is just a nice name for a flat, round-ended lever. I put it under the end of the collarbone and cut the outer inch of the bone off.

"Can I have an osteotome and a hammer?"

"An osteotome and hammer! Don't use an osteotome, Ron. Give the doctor a Gigli saw. Somebody adjust the light for him," commands the boss.

A Gigli saw! Oh, it's the serrated wire Petrie uses in his Keller's operation for bunions. Sure! Here come a couple of Kelly clamps to attach at each end of the saw. It's going under the collarbone easy enough. Oh, oh, I'm sliding the wire saw back and forth against the bone. It is too tight and forming a U against the underside and won't saw. It sticks. Now it's going a little. It's sliding too far toward the end and won't saw. It sticks. Now it's going a little. It's sliding too far toward the end. I'm not taking enough off!

"Watch the skin for him so he can cut vertically," addresses the chief to the junior intern. Then to me, he speaks, "Now SAW, DAMMIT, SAW! WE'LL *NEVER* GET OUT OF HERE! NO RON, DAMMIT, NO! NOT LIKE THAT! HOLD YOUR ARMS APART. DON'T LET GO! PLAY IT LIKE A VIOLIN!"

That was PETRIE speaking.

We removed the outer end of the man's clavicle and he fared well. I never forgot how to do a Fraser Gurd operation either. It was Gordon Petrie's way of teaching the orthopaedic craft. "Petrie is rough!" John Armour said one day. "If he gets too rough, tell me." I never did that, but it was nice to know I had a friend. Petrie's way was not boring. It turned into a game. The game was to be able to get by a day at a time while working for him without getting hell. I never could go more than two weeks, but his way of teaching worked. For instance: He used the Gigli saw that day instead of the osteotome (chisel) to make a smooth end of bone that would round off. He never said these things at the time but afterward it became apparent.

And so went 1957 at the Royal Vic. In June 1958, Dr. Petrie asked me to share a residency on the orthopaedic service for a year and then work another year at the Shrine Hospital. I accepted.

July came. It was customary to give the residents a month off, but Petrie directed me, "Take ten days off, Ron. That's all you need." I didn't even get to see Olive graduate from the Middlesex hospital, having achieved the highest grades ever given. We took the time to find a place to live close to the hospital. Olive got a job at the Vic. The kids were accepted in King's School, a public primary school; and the second year away from Ennis began.

One Long Blast—Evacuate

I SHARED THE orthopaedic residency with Dr. Matt Erdowan who was the boss resident the first half of the year. When my turn came to be the boss, Olive and the kids were forced to return to Connecticut. Olive had been working as a float nurse in the Royal Victoria Hospital. She scratched her hand on the bed of a patient just deceased from hepatitis. You can bet that she didn't escape that infectious contact. She turned pumpkin color and became very ill and was hospitalized. The children were inoculated with gamma globulin and sent off, by themselves, to Olive's family by rail. Three weeks later, out of the hospital, Olive followed and convalesced in Connecticut for the remainder of my residency.

We weren't quite as broke as we had been in Hood River, a decade previously, but money became worrisome. It took every cent Olive had earned as a nurse to pay for that small scratch. Thank God it was before AIDS.

It became impossible to spend another year away at the Shrine Hospital in Montreal as planned and I was gracefully excused by the chief.

My father had preceded us and welcomed us back to Ennis from Montreal. He loved to come to Ennis and we had been away for over two years. Buttons, our dwarfish, seal-skinned, snub-nosed dog was retrieved from Chuck and Fanny's. It was a comfort to be back with friends and patients, back to Winifred's log house, and back to where even the water was free from chlorine. The practice immediately resumed its night-and-day continuous charge of phone-ringing, daily-crisis recurrences, requests, demands, and wheedling. Yes, in addition to all this, Phil Pallister, the chief clinician serving the residents of the Boulder River State School and Hospital, needed help. On August 17, 1959, Olive and I were invited to come to Boulder, the seat of Jefferson County, Montana.

Pallister wanted orthopaedic help with the multitude of problems endured by the retarded population of more than a thousand inmates. ("Residents" was the kinder euphemism that Phil Pallister and I subscribe to.) Olive and I drove to Boulder in our blue 1956 Chevy station wagon. We had never seen so many rattlesnakes, squashed and wiggling across the road as we drove to the State School that evening. Upon arrival at the institutional hospital we went right to the operating room, where Dr. Buddy Little and Dr. Pallister were working. They had finished a general surgical operation. The patient was tardy in breathing spontaneously during his recovery from anesthesia and there was fussing about in the surgery. The confusion was now increased by a gathering of not only the two operating surgeons, but also Buddy's brother Spif, who was my Dartmouth college roommate, and now Olive and myself. The conversation was not only about anesthesia variances but about many other subjects that interrupted the prime concern of the moment.

Suddenly a bizarre nausea momentarily encased me. An eerie, rhythmic swishing sound seemed everywhere. The operating room started rocking. The operating lamp swung. The more prudent members of the party found themselves standing in the doorway entering the surgery from the long hallway. I looked out into the hall. The hundred-foot-long hallway floor undulated. It seemed that the wavelength was not quite the length of the hall and the height of the oscillation appeared to be a foot high. The quake lasted long enough for me to remember being in two places, both in the middle of the operating room and in the doorway looking down the hall. Olive and Spif were having a whale of a time laughing at the more concerned members' reactions. I marveled at the groundswells, the plasticity of the hallway and the earth beneath it. It was hard to be convinced that the ground was making visible waves and I pondered the infinite energy potential seething within the earth. The patient began to breathe unassisted and conversation immediately turned from medical to very practical topics. Phil's house was constructed of concrete blocks, and he called his wife Willie to learn that the chimney still stood. We forgot about the purpose of the trip. All we could discuss was *earthquake*! We left Boulder for Ennis when Phil left the hospital to check his house, and Buddy and Spif left for Buddy's home in Helena.

What had happened back at Ennis, ninety miles away? On the way home we had to dodge rocks on the highway as we passed through the Jefferson Canyon and trailed past the Louis and Clark Caverns. Olive would periodically sneak a grasp of the steering wheel and give it a jerk while saying she felt another earthquake shock. I reacted by stopping the car and getting out so that I could stand on the ground to feel a tremor. KXLF radio announced that chimneys had toppled in Virginia City and Butte. He assured us *that the authorities had the earthquake under full control*! We arrived home safely and my father and the kids were up to tell their story. A few minutes after our arrival home, the Ennis town siren started. Buttons bayed at the front door and neither he nor the siren stopped after a reasonable interval. This dramatic persistence of the siren had never before happened in Ennis. We all hurried out of the house to watch the firetruck drive east on Main Street. But it didn't leave town. Instead it turned south at the corner of Hal Pasley's garage, blowing its siren as it careered down the four "city" blocks to the end of town, turned west going the one block available in that direction, then north back to Main Street again. It kept circling and screaming. The volunteer firemen didn't seem to know where to go! Pickup trucks followed. Some leader, standing in the middle of the street, in front of the telephone office, and frantically trying to stop the periodically passing fire engine with its living occupants, shouted to the mob some very important information. George Hungerford, the dam keeper at the Hebgen Lake, had called to warn Ennis that Hebgen Dam, damaged by the earthquake, might give way. With this message realized, the pickup trucks rapidly were filled with valuables, refrigerators and washing machines (with further monthly payments to be made), chickens in their cages, and ladies' wardrobes with scarves and blouses, caught in the tailgate chains, fluttering behind. With the thought of another Johnstown flood about to happen right here in Ennis we had to move the patients out of the hospital. We took them to the Sheridan Hospital where we had to use the outside ramp to get some of them in the upstairs room.

Our town's inhabitants gathered on the high ground, two miles west of town, along the Virginia City Road. Lots of beer and cases of whiskey were provided by the bar proprietors. Officials drove one hundred miles an hour, back and forth, between Ennis and Virginia City on purposeless missions they thought so important. It was a social event. We kept watching to the south, up the valley toward Yellowstone Park, and wondering whether it would be a wall of water or a slow seepage. (It took two more days before rational thinkers reasoned that only a two-foot water level could possibly cover the main street of Ennis because the valley was so wide and the distance so far.) Daylight came and some official drafted me to go on a mercy mission in the Fish and Game warden's airplane. I hated flying. The pilot asked, "Are you ready? Now is as good a time as any." And he took off without my answer.

We flew on the east side of the river and I was amazed to see a fisherman casting along the banks of the Madison River. But where was the water in the river? It was only a quarter full and muddy at that. This was inexplicable. What? Why? How? I felt totally mentally blank, blah, bad. What in hell is *drying-up* the Madison River?

The fisherman knew there was an increased concentration of the fish in the trickling river. He certainly didn't give a damn about earthquakes or floods. As I peered down on him, I thought, *piscatory fool*.

"This is as good a place as any to land," the pilot said as we descended along a country telephone line whose distance from the wing tip I kept mentally measuring. We landed on the two-lane highway at the mouth of the Madison River Canyon north of the Missouri Flats. Dust and smoke and small landslides were seen on the steep hillside in back of Garnet Oliffe's place. We joined a group involved in the rescue mission, but they seemed unconcerned as they stood about with their backs to the mouth of the canyon, the possible site of a gigantic belch of the entire Hebgen Lake. If nonchalance was their game, I could play it too. Gene Todd, the legendary game warden, was in the group along with the highway patrolman and Maurice Staggers. Maurice asked me for "a cc or two" to calm his nerves. He had suffered one hell of a night, because his cabin was situated against the unstable mountainside, and he thought a little morphia would do him well. But the real problem at hand was a young man of sixteen or seventeen lying in the back of a pickup truck with a compound fracture of his tibia. Accompanying him was his mother who had also been battered and traumatized. They were survivors of a great landslide that damned the river in the canyon. The slide was not visible from where we were gathered nor was it mentioned by the party at hand. Still, considering the likelihood of a ruptured and weakened Hebgen Lake Dam a few miles up the canyon, I resolved that it was time to drive the injured back to the hospital. I drove quite smartly, alone in the cab, with the patients bouncing in the truck bed. There was much looking backward at every opportunity. There was much assessment of possible off-highway escapes to higher land when the flood came roaring down from behind. There was no flood, but the highway was split in places by the quake and huge boulders obstructed the road where the quake had loosened them from above.

Back to the hospital and two days of pretty intense doctoring. We operated on the young man's tibia and held clinic the rest of the day and spent the following night patching up victims. The young man and his mother had been camping in a tent with the father and two sisters when the slide occurred. They were at the west boundary of the slide. There was a tremendous gush of displaced air that tore off their clothes and even their shoes. They thought the wind must have somehow blown them across to the south side of the river where they were rescued. The rest of the family was lost and buried forever in the slide.

A tourist who was staying at the Riverside Motel in Ennis that night was said to have fled in his car at the time of the quake. He rushed back once to pick up his dog, left town, and then returned to pick up his wife. The Red Cross came to town and set up headquarters at the Ennis School. They provided the injured mother with a luxurious dressing gown which she didn't need and then immediately billed her for it. The Red Cross flag flew proudly on the school flagpole. Later that day I discovered that the landslide had dammed the Madison River, accounting for its draught. But flood was still on everyone's mind. Jack Scully put up a sign in the middle of Main Street that warned the people to leave town immediately if the siren sounded. The sign read: ONE LONG BLAST—EVACUATE!

Speedy

IN JUNE 1992, I received a letter from Dr. Sim of the Mayo Clinic that concerned a common patient from Ennis. He had operated on her on two occasions, and because of his success the lady now is able to work full shifts sorting talc at the Cypress Mines, twenty miles south of Ennis. His note brought back vivid memories of the Hubner family. Perhaps it was in the fall of 1951, during the bird-hunting season, that I had an urgent call from Josephine Jeffers to get to her neighbors, the Hubners.

She said that Steve, the fourteen-year-old Hubner boy, had been shot. He had been shot all right, shot in the cheek of his ass by a slightly older hunting partner who let fly from only twelve feet in back of Steve. The other boy just wanted to see what would happen when he fired. The wound of exit was in the adductor region of Steve's right thigh. You could put your fist in it, but all the parts were left hanging in proper order, including the femoral artery, vein, and nerve. Adduction of the thigh was a bit weak, however. I surmised that this was one of the first proper transfusions performed in the history of the Madison Valley. The whole town of Ennis turned out to offer blood and check on Steve's progress. I must have cross-matched Steve okay. He didn't die of shock, nor of a transfusion reaction. We moved him into the southeast room of the hospital. When the wound was debrided the best I knew how—without anesthesia—and when he stabilized a couple of days later, I sent him to Mayo's at Rochester, Minnesota, where Dr. Young finished the job. Some of the shotgun BBs must have immediately been sucked into his venous system and become lodged in Steven's lung. Every once in a while for a long time afterward Steve would cough up a BB. He said they would fly across the kitchen. Steven had three sisters; the middle sister became the patient of the above Dr. Sims.

Audrey, Steven's oldest sister, was a patient of mine ten or more years later. She was pregnant and very near her due date. Dr. Rossiter called me to attend a lady who had been struck below her knees by the bumper of an automobile while crossing one of the streets of Sheridan. She had been taken to the town's Ruby Valley Hospital with bilateral compound fractures of her tibiae. I gathered up tools in the original doctor's bag that Olive and I purchased in Portland on our way from Uncle Darby and Aunt Ag's so many years earlier. By then I had accumulated hammers and osteotomes, curettes and rongeurs, sharp and dull elevators, and a selection of Lottes nails. These were long, thin, flanged, and pointed nails with a slight curve at the pointed end that were used to stabilize a wobbly, broken tibia. They were inserted by driving the nail down the tibia through a drilled hole in front and just below the knee. The nail was hammered down the marrow across the fracture site and into the fragment below, thus securing the wobbly leg.

There was talk by my Sheridan colleagues of doing the job under local anesthesia. I remembered hearing Dr. Salter of Toronto at an orthopaedic meeting speak from the podium: "You call it local anesthesia. I call it vocal anesthesia."

So my friend Dave poured ether. Shirley boiled the instruments. It seemed as though it took many different boilings during the night. The bilateral-open-reduction-with-internal-fixation operation was a new event for the Ruby Valley Hospital. First one leg was operated on and casted, and after many drapings and redrapings the other leg was nailed. At one moment at the height of this activity, Olive looked up and standing well into the operating area was Audrey, facing Olive. She mouthed, without speaking, "Look," as she pointed to her abdomen, very heavy with child. I didn't see her, but knew she was there. She obliged and didn't have it then. The fracture job was done by daylight.

Attention was directed to Audrey. But Audrey stopped having contractions. We all wanted to go home. Olive had assisted all night. The kids were home alone, as was the case so many times in those days. If possible, Audrey preferred to have her child in Ennis, closer to her folks. A war plan was made. We would take off in our station wagon with Audrey in the backseat. If pains returned *before* Granite Creek, the halfway mark between Sheridan and Ennis, we would return to Sheridan to have the babe. If the pains started *after* Granite Creek, we would continue to the Madison Valley Hospital, a reasonable and elementary tactic.

Exactly at Granite Creek, Audrey announced that the baby was about to be born: "For Christ's sake, Doc, hurry."

We nearly centrifuged into the Bail of Hay Saloon as we rounded the corner at the west end of Virginia City. At the top of the Virginia City Hill we charged across the mile-long "Race Track." This is a flat area three miles east of Virginia City where the pioneers used to race their horses.

I considered stopping the car, opening the tailgate, and pulling down the backseat to deliver Audrey on the tailgate. We had nothing to work with but our shoelaces, and I pondered to myself, "Jesus, what a mess! I'll go for it, down the Virginia City Hill as fast as I can to our hospital."

We tore east, down the mountain and down Two-Cell Hill, swished down the Chowning Dip and back up, at one hundred or so miles an hour. The roller-coaster ride through the dip might have sucked the protruding child back to its original lodging long enough for us to screech to a halt in the front of the Madison Valley Hospital. We charged to the delivery room and Audrey got on the table just in time! The babe was born with a veil, a very lucky sign—a wonderful sign. The veil, this time, was not amniotic membrane but rather Audrey's underpants. The last time I saw Audrey this past fall, she said that "Speedy," the little heroine of this tale, was a mom herself with two or three children of her own.

Whisky Interference

THESE WERE THE days when an orthopaedic service started to erupt in the Madison Valley Hospital. General practice flourished but every time a patient with an orthopaedic problem presented, general practice came to an immediate grinding halt and all attention was diverted to *orthopaedics*. The old judge fractured his hip in Virginia City one night. The undertaker transported him to Ennis. Olive and I enlisted Joe Maitin, our schoolteacher friend, and Todd, the game warden, to help us. Todd scrubbed with us, and during the operation he broke a screwdriver while "helping" us. Joe was probably in the background diverting us with laughter at Todd's destructive strength. We put the old boy together.

Mrs. Munson needed a femoral-head prosthesis. She had suffered a hip fracture similar to that of Dr. Armour's patient, but now instead of removing the femoral head, orthopaedists were replacing the devascularized head with an Austin Moore prosthesis. Our Becky helped us do this operation. That morning the anesthetist drove all the way from Bozeman to help us. The operation was supposed to start at eight AM. At seven forty-five, Heidi Gorsage came in to have her baby. This interjection aggravated the anesthetist who had to meet a tight schedule in Bozeman, goofed up our preop medication on Mrs. Munson, completely diverted all nursing attention due Mrs. Munson, and threw a monkey wrench in my mental preparation for my first hip-replacement operation. Baby Candy was worth it!

* * *

A transverse fracture of the shaft of the humerus can be a bugger to unite. This is a crosswise break in the arm between the shoulder and elbow. Janis Clark, an older sister of Penny's who used to babysit our Becky and Jon, was married to a veterinarian, Bill, who had just such a break. They were taking care of him in Bozeman and his arm wouldn't unite. Bill was referred to my care. His right arm was flail. He had "two elbows."

Bill, with his painful, flail right arm, was now in our hospital and I was to operate on his arm in the morning. In preparation for this, after I consulted my bible, Watson-Jones' *Fractures and Joint Injuries*, I was impressed that the job on Bill had to be done correctly the first time or he would be doomed to repeated and failed operations. In the afternoon before the surgery, I prepared a shoulder spica, a cast that includes the chest and arm, for him to wear after his planned operation in the morning. I had prepared all my tools and was ready if we needed blood. We rehearsed. We checked to see that we had our side-plates, screws, screwdrivers, osteotomes, rongeurs, and curettes. However, there was a lot more to do.

It was late afternoon and I was working with "general practice" patients. One of the country's great cattle brokers—the one who had given us our eighty-dollar operating-room lamp that easily tipped—brought in Wayne, who ranched in the North Meadow Creek area, northwest of Ennis.

On my last encounter with Wayne, he had confided to Olive and me that Floral, his wife, was ready to deliver. He had said, "It's getting time. Floral is throwing all the clothes on the closet floor; she is making a nest."

At that time, he had four girls. One day, as Olive passed him on the sidewalk in Ennis, she spoke about the two bottles of whisky she noted bulging, one from each hip pocket. Wayne pointed to one bottle and responded, "Mrs. Doc, if Floral has a boy, I'm ready to celebrate with this one." He slapped the other bottle and finished, "But if it's a girl, I'll drown my sorrow with this one."

Floral had a gorgeous baby girl and, after consulting with her daughters, let me name her Becky.

He had a booze problem. Once, after Wayne had been on a binge and had slept on Otis' bar floor for ten nights, Floral told Wayne that she was "sick and tired of him and was going to pack up her stuff and leave home." Wayne is reported to have said, "I'm sick and tired of myself too. Pack up my stuff. I'm going with you!"

This time, in my office, Wayne was sopped and downright loathsome. The only medicine that would calm him for twenty minutes at a time was another glass of whisky. Floral came down and we decided to send him to Spokane to detoxify him. Floral would leave with him from Butte. I asked the cattle buyer, who had enjoyed getting Wayne drunk, to help me by taking the couple to the train in Butte. No, he had some cattle buying to do and couldn't manage it. I had words with him. I don't remember him speaking to me again. Floral and I put Wayne in the backseat of our car with a full bottle. The bottle was empty by the time we reached Pipestone Pass. The plane wasn't running that evening and we had to wait until a train came through at midnight, two bottles later.

By two in the morning I was able to continue with my preparation and by six I was ready to operate on Bill.

My first bone graft of a nonuniting humerus worked.

Bill later accidentally ran over our hound, Buttons. Our family had a burial under Winifred's lilac bush by the log house. The kids wept more over Buttons than over a grandparent. I must remember that. John Armour would say, "It makes you humble. It makes you humble!"

Not Even a Postcard

ONE OF THE ports of entry for transients destined for the state of Montana is the small city of Dillon, situated beside the Union Pacific Railroad, which pokes its way northward into Montana from Salt Lake City and Idaho. Parallel to the railroad tracks is Montana Street with its commercial buildings overlooking tracks to the west. Along this street, besides Skeet's Cafe (of strawberry pie fame), there are, interposed between pawn shops and other secondhand stores, a number of busy bars. The migrants gather in the bars for eventual dispatch to ranch employment in Southwest Montana.

One of our friends, seventy-year-old Alice Orr, ran the Bear Creek Ranch in Cameron, Montana, twenty miles south of Ennis. She was also a friend of the Madison Valley Hospital and an original hospital board member. She wore long woolly dresses, liked to play chess, and incessantly smoked strong, unfiltered cigarettes. They would hang down from the corner of her mouth in such a fashion that their smoke curled above, into one of the squinting eyes of her upturned head, while chunks of ash tumbled down her front. She ran her large ranch with authority and possessed the respect of every veteran rancher in the valley. They respected her for her wise managerial capability. She had been highly educated in the East and had been widowed by an American diplomat.

Mrs. Orr once told Olive of a Dillon recruitment story.

She drove her suburban to Dillon in search for a new hired hand. She had no luck finding a man in any of the several bars. She looked over the few prospects in the drunk tank of Dillons' Beaverhead County jail and picked out a likely candidate. She bailed him out, gave him a quart bottle of Old Crow whisky to nurse upon, put him in the back of her suburban, and shanghaied him back to her Bear Creek Ranch a hundred miles away. Her other hired man met her and put the new recruit to bed in the bunkhouse and all was well until the middle of the night when she heard a violent altercation beneath her bedroom window. Mrs. Orr looked out of her window upon the fracas below and saw a potential for a fatality brewing. She didn't want to shoot her newly hired man to save her established help, but alone, she had to take action. Mrs. Orr ran from her bedroom out the kitchen door; picked up a two-by-four plank and proceeded to stop the fight herself. She thought a good whack would do it. Not too much! Just enough. She thought a "mashie" golf shot would be just about right. She practiced by whacking the two-by-four against the large cottonwood tree until she thought she had mastered the proper Newtonian force needed for the project. Then, with one firm blow, the altercation was instantly stopped by the old girl. The new hired man proved to be the pick of that summer. He kept his job. Bail and the price of a bottle of Old Crow was subtracted from his first paycheck.

Twelve years later, in 1962, from this same port of entry to the state and from one of these same Dillon bars arrived a migrant named Sterling from West Virginia. He may have been recruited in a fashion similar to that of Mrs. Orr's hired man. That we do not know, but after a reported fall at work and after a reported fight and after a request for physician's service from the Beaverhead County jail, he became the patient of Dr. John Seidensticker, Big John, who had moved his practice to Dillon. The patient had a broken arm.

My old friend decided to test me, now that I claimed to be an orthopaedist. He sent his patient with a fractured humerus to Ennis. This was a worker's compensation case.

The patient claimed he fractured his right upper arm while at work. There was some confusion about a refracture in jail, much to the irritation of the sheriff. It was even possible he had fractured his arm in West Virginia! This sort of medical history is called "unreliable witness." Simple casting hadn't worked in Dillon.

I made my own X-ray and it showed the reason for the failure. This was not a simple fractured humerus but was a pathological fracture. I arranged for my pathologist friend Vol Steele to come over to Ennis from Bozeman at the time of the projected operation to help me diagnose the lesion. We obtained the biopsy and Vol diagnosed it as a hypernephroma. That being a malignancy, we were obliged to study the patient further. There was no other disclosure of a metastasis elsewhere. The "mother" tumor was known to be growing by either the right or the left kidney. If the mother tumor could be removed and the metastasizing lesion in the humerus could be eliminated, we could save the life of this forty-year-old man.

I called Dr. Alan Iddles, my general-surgeon friend, also from Bozeman, to remove the mother tumor from the top of whichever kidney was its site. We tossed a coin to determine which kidney to explore. The coin came up RIGHT. Alan operated on the right side and there it was! He successfully removed the other tumor.

Now it was up to me, the man who was supposed to know his orthopaedics, to finish the job. Professor Fred Moseley, general surgeon at the Royal Victoria Hospital in Montreal, was interested in the shoulder and had written a book, *The Forequarter Amputation*. He had generously given me a copy. I had never memorized an entire book before. However, I spent until two or three o'clock each morning after the removal of the mother tumor memorizing Moseley's directions for doing a forequarter amputation. The anatomy of the operation had been distinctly and beautifully illustrated by his assistant, Mrs. Helen McArthur.

The day arrived and Alan Iddles came back to Ennis to help me. The operation went without a hitch, thanks to

Moseley and Mrs. McArthur. The sutures were removed in ten days.

Sometime during the course of Sterling's treatment, Olive drove the West Virginian to the Bozeman Deaconess Hospital for radiation treatment. She escorted him into the elevator of the old Deaconess Hospital on the second floor, where he had undergone his treatment. The elevator in the old hospital did not always stop exactly level with the floor. On the main floor, with the patient now ready to exit the elevator, there was just such a discrepancy at the doorway. Olive observed the patient purposely poking his foot between the elevator platform and the sill in an effort to injure his foot on hospital property—apparently an attempt at gaining a possible remuneration in tort. Olive, now wise to Mr. Sterling from West Virginia, aborted his effort in time to save his lower extremities, by maneuvering a sharp lift within his only remaining armpit.

When it was time to eat, the patient mentioned to Olive that Madeline, our nurse supervisor, on the previous trip to Bozeman for his therapy, had taken him to the Baxter Hotel Restaurant and had provided wine with the meal. Olive's response? Hamburger for Sterling.

His arm? Kept in the cellar of the hospital and used repeatedly to refresh my memory of the anatomy of the upper extremity before operations. The arm eventually retired in grace to the cemetery, but with neither funeral nor tombstone, and Sterling got no wine from Olive!

The job was done. But a man without a shoulder appears unpleasantly distorted to the viewing public, so we fitted and provided him with a prosthetic shoulder-filler that he could wear under his shirt. The compensation people paid for his biopsy only, and not for Dr. Iddles' services, nor for the forequarter amputation, nor for Madison Valley Hospital's bounteous services. He was ready and able to return to West Virginia. At the time of his departure Olive provided him with a carton of cigarettes and a bunch of stamped postcards. We wanted to hear of his subsequent progress.

That's thirty years ago. We're waiting. We haven't heard a word, not even a postcard!

Horrendeoma

IN 1963 AN active orthopaedic operation was in effect in Ennis. One desperate Veterans' Day, I made my weekly service trip to Helena to accommodate physicians' requests for consultations, but not one physician's office was open. Troubled by a wasted trip, I sought comfort from my old pediatric friend, and I held him to his suggestion that I ask his doctor friend in Nebraska to come to Ennis to do the general practice. By now I *never* wanted to see another hemorrhoid or puke from the anxiety of delivering a babe. That day produced a life-long colleague, Dr. Wilkins. He was to arrive and to take over the general practice in Ennis the next February.

The Madison Valley Hospital had been expanded to eleven beds. There was a bit of sadness for me in the project because no longer did the magnificent Madison Range with its alpine glow in the late-winter afternoons, or a full moon just up from behind the "Beehive" (Willson's Peak) illuminate our activities through the five side-by-side east windows of our surgery. Instead, we had constructed a twenty- by twenty-five-foot operating room in the new north addition. It had green Formica walls that were washed down after operations. As time passed, I favored the white that I remembered in the Old Royal Victoria operating amphitheater. The contrast of that white with the patients' color gave a clearer indication of their proper physiology. Is he white from hemorrhage? Is he blue from an obstructed airway? But, one gets used to green. We accumulated a new operating-room lamp just like the ones used in the operating theaters at the Royal Victoria Hospital in Montreal. And, yes, the Madison Valley Women's Club purchased *a brand-new operating table*. It was like the tables I had worked with at Montreal. Only our new operating table seemed to slowly sink a few inches, slowly, ever so slowly, toward the floor. There was a bottom limit to the inferior drift so we never had to operate on our knees. There was always an accumulation of hydraulic fluid around its base. The service people, I used to think, would merely wipe up the fluid, say the seepage was fixed, then return to home base leaving a service fee that would take a great number of "operating-room charges" to fulfill. In those days operating-room service in the Madison Valley Hospital did not cost the patient a dollar a minute. Tuesdays became a busy operating day in the Madison Valley Hospital. I would always pick out the instruments the night before so that I would have what I wanted available. I didn't want to lack a tool in the middle of an operation. I remembered how frequently that would happen in the Royal Vic and what friction it caused. Besides, we didn't have a rapid method of sterilization. The most important reason for me to pre-pick instruments was to go over the operation in my mind the night before and to rehearse possible deviations that might occur. Most of the work was elective. Patients came from all over the state to see the bald-headed man in Ennis. There were but few practicing orthopods in the state in those early days. At that time, general surgeons flooded the country and their specialty was more popular than orthopaedics. They considered it more elite and less carpenterlike. This was also before the days of the "sports medicine specialist." Ennis was so small that the town provided but a small fraction of the work. We would operate. Olive scrubbed. Lois Olsen circulated. Denny Klemp from Butte would give anesthesia when the sisters at his St. James Hospital would let him come to Ennis. If Denny couldn't make it, Tafford Oldtz or his wife, Laurie, from

Bozeman would administer gas. After each operation the same ladies who helped us operate would clean up in preparation for the next operation. The hospital had hired a cook by now. Either Glady Chamberlain, Millie Miller, or Alma Oliver would prepare enormous soporific lunches for the crew. Operating then was not the way it is now for my present-day dear French friend who operates in Bordeaux and whose modern team can help him to do eight or ten orthopaedic operations in a day. In those times we were lucky if we could accomplish four or five operations on a Tuesday.

After finishing the operations on Tuesday, I had to pick out and pack my instruments to take to Boulder, ninety miles northward, in readiness for operations there on Wednesday, where I would help my friend Dr. Phil Pallister. Wednesdays had become orthopaedic day there.

A "horrendeoma" was the term that Tafford coined to describe our operating experiences in the new brick Ruby Valley Hospital in Sheridan. (Tafford never knew the real "horrendeomas" of the old Sheridan Hospital, nor did he know of the twenty-degree ramp to the "operating-room closet"!) "Horrendeomas" implied certain difficulties that seemed to occur during operations in the Ruby Valley Hospital. For instance, the operating room X-ray service was such that lateral X-rays of the hip were next to impossible. The only way I could pick a proper length for a hip nail was to pass a guide pin through the head of the femur from the side of the thigh, guiding the stout pin while feeling the fractured area. In addition, as I blindly advanced the pin, I wiggled the thigh until the wire protruded through the head of the femur and stuck in the socket. I then knew that withdrawing the wire enough to release the hip enabled me to subtract from the protruding portion of a nine-inch pin to give me a proper measurement. Driving the nail blindly might easily cause it to protrude through the neck of the femur and damage the ball. Blind nailing would not even secure the fracture. I could even gouge nature's beautiful hip socket. I would continuously palpate along the femoral neck as I was driving the nail home. In that way I could *feel* when the three-flanged nail had properly sought its home in the head of the hip. When the operation was over, we would take a "frog-leg" projection with the ancient X-ray machine and would get a barely readable picture to check our work.

Another example of a "horrendeoma" would be a power failure during operating time.

A fly landing on an already-inserted prosthetic stainless-steel hip replacement would be considered a "horrendeoma."

It was at the end of such a trying day. We had been operating in Ennis until eight PM. We were hungry, tired, and looked forward to quitting after picking the tools for the trip to Boulder the next day. But there would be no quitting until a hip was pinned in Sheridan, at the Ruby Valley Hospital. Tafford would render his services. No one but myself picked the instruments.

The hip-pinning in Sheridan was easy and straightforward that night. The patient was a very old woman and it seemed that her nieces were of the same generation. The lovely ladies were patiently waiting, sitting side-by-side on a bench against the wall of the hallway right outside of the operating door. The hip nail was placed. The post-operation X-ray that night was astoundingly satisfactory. Marilyn Doggett was taking the pictures. This particular hip fracture needed not only a nail to obtain a purchase up the femoral neck into the femoral head, but also a side-plate to attach the fixation device along the side of the shaft of the upper femoral bone. (The femur is like a hockey stick with the ball head at the end of the blade and the knee knuckle at the end of the stick handle.) This fracture was at the angle and it had to have an angular fixative device. There were either solid angular devices to use or adjustable angular devices of two parts. One part was the three-flanged nail that was driven through the neck into the head. The other part was the side-plate to be bolted to the protruding end of the nail. The side-plate could then be screwed tightly against the upper shaft of the femur.

The nail was perfectly placed. The proper side-plate was bolted to the end of the nail and rested perfectly alongside the femoral shaft. The first drill hole was made through the shaft.

"I'll have the screw guide, please." The screw guide is a crochet hook with depth markings used to measure the correct length of the screw to be employed.

"That'll take an inch and a quarter screw, please," I added.

There was silence.

No problem, I thought, the nurses in the Ruby Valley Hospital aren't used to measuring screw sizes. They'll figure it out.

Oh, oh, this is taking a little too long. . . .

"I can't find any screws, Doctor."

A classic horrendeoma had occurred!

I had forgotten to put the screw set in my bag when picking out the instruments in Ennis.

I thought, "Will wires work? No. What will? Nothing. Jesus! Ennis, where the screws are, is one hell of a long ways away from here! The nail alone in her hip is worthless. It's a catastrophe without a side-plate! There's nothing to do but call Ennis and have screws shipped over. Shipped over! Now? Midnight? As we did for Audrey and Speedy, a few years ago, we could meet at Granite Creek."

"How's she doing, Tafford?"

"No problem, Ron."

At times like this I would frequently go to the toilet and sit on the pot, hoping I might pass a mental stool.

I walked out of the operating room and instead of going to the toilet, being a tobacco addict at the time, I lit my pipe filled with Sir Walter Raleigh's tobacco. Immediate relief and clear thinking resulted. I turned to the right to face the dear old relatives.

"How is it going, Doctor?"

"The pin is in the hip okay, but I forgot to bring the screws over from Ennis to finish the job."

"What do you need, Doctor? Perhaps we could help."

Bless your hearts, I thought, *no way*.

The elder sister said, "We'll go to the hardware store, they'll open up. Tell us what kind of screws you need. We'll get them."

"No. Thank you very much, ladies, but we need special screws from Ennis. I'll call up Mr. Loucks and he'll bring them right over and then we can get along with it. Excuse me, I need to phone now."

I called Phil Loucks. He was our hospital administrator in Ennis. What's more, he was a retired State of Montana highway patrolman and speed was no problem. Henrietta Black was the nurse on duty in Ennis and I told her where to find the screws and the proper antiseptic juice to contain them.

The screws arrived thirty-five minutes later, from thirty-five miles away—the midnight ride of "Phil Revere."

This was not quite as long as it used to take to get an X-ray of the hip in the Ruby Valley Hospital!

Gatekeeping

TWENTY-FIVE YEARS ago a patient came to Ennis from Deer Lodge, Montana. He was in his late thirties and entered my office on crutches. His left thigh was draining pus a year after he fractured the shaft of his femur. His thigh pained him especially at night, or during the day when he tried to bear weight upon his left foot. He told me he had fractured both thighbones a year previously while working for the phosphate mine at Garrison, Montana. The doctor in Deer Lodge had saved his life in treating his shock and had successfully operated on his right thigh so that he was able to walk with crutches. However the operation on the left thighbone didn't go so well. It never healed and was still draining. He wondered if I might be able to help him.

He let me operate. His infected left femur had not yet united. I removed the stainless-steel side plate that had been screwed across the fracture site. It was easy to unscrew the plate because the screws were bathed in pus and had dissolved bone around them. I freshened up the fracture site, which was packed with nature's scar tissue and got bleeding bone of one fracture end to press against bleeding bone of the other. I shaved long, kitchen-match-sized staves of cancellous bone from the crest of his left ileum (one of the bones above the hip that keeps the belt from sliding down). I put these matchsticks of bone all around the fracture site and left the large wound open to "fill in." I kept the bones aligned long enough by using a traction apparatus to let the fracture ends stick together. I then encased the victim in a plaster cast that enclosed his entire left leg and thigh and reached around his belly and chest to armpit height. He still could wave his right leg freely in the air. Urine and stool spillage was a problem then and now. God bless the nurses. At that time I had employed my Montreal friend Louis Papineau's method of treating infected nonunions without knowing it. The femur united. The drainage ceased. The man walked without crutches.

A year passed. It was time to make an impairment rating for the Montana Industrial Accident Board. Deciding when an injured workman can return to work is a "gatekeeping" function that some physicians enjoy. It is a minor power play that appeals to some men who seem to need the feeling of self-importance that gatekeeping may impart to them. I never thought of impairment ratings as a pleasure. I thought of them more as being a necessary and tedious duty. There was a book available to guide the gatekeeper. The guide concentrated on the range of motion of the injured extremity and not much else. No mention was made of the possible difficulty that a stiff knee might force upon the injured workman's sex life! Our patient had a stiff knee. This was because the pus around the fracture site had involved the muscles in front of his thigh and had caused them to adhere to the bone. He could only bend his knee a few degrees. I had tried to break the adhesions loose by putting him to sleep and attempting to force the knee to bend, but it was too tight. I had no experience at the time in cutting the front muscles loose from the femur, and he was not enthusiastic about undergoing another operation by a third doctor. I made the impairment rating. I gave him the maximum amount the book allowed. It awarded him nine thousand dollars.

He returned a year later for a checkup and he gave me a big smile.

"Doc, I saw a lawyer and got six thousand dollars more on my settlement!"

"Great!" I answered. "How much did the lawyer keep of the six thousand?"

"Only two! I got four to keep. That's pretty good, isn't it?"

"What did the lawyer have to do to get you the money?" I asked.

"He wrote a letter. It must have been a good one, eh, Doc? It worked."

I didn't answer him. I picked up my telephone and called the chief of the Industrial Accident Board at the time. When he was put on the line I asked him, "It is true that lawyer so-and-so was paid two thousand dollars for writing a letter in behalf of my patient?"

There was a confusing fussing on the other end of the line with the eventual request, "Let me call you back. I'll get his record out."

"I'm sitting here waiting," I responded.

The voice returned, "The lawyer wrote *two* letters!"

The phone conversation was now over. I said no more to my stiff-kneed patient, but the offense nauseated me.

It wasn't until the next day that I thought about the settlement as I was drawing a glass of water to drink at our kitchen sink. I started to think at a pretty discouraged level.

I thought, "I can't believe it. I undertook the risk of performing a surgical operation on the patient. I worried. I spent hours on the problem. I eliminated his infection, grafted his femur so that nature could do the job, and his femur became whole. For the total year's care I got between two and three hundred dollars. I was also paid twenty-five dollars to make a rating. The lawyer wrote two letters and was paid *two thousand dollars*! There's something morally wrong here!"

It stuck in my craw.

Perhaps six months later the chief of the Montana Industrial Accident Board asked me to speak at a gathering of insurance men, lawyers, and accident-board people. The meeting was to be held in Helena. That pepped up my ego! I said, "Sure, I'll give a speech! What do you want me to talk about?"

"Anything you want. Your orthopaedic cases would interest us."

I gathered up slides that I had made of particularly bloody operations and other slides that I thought would open the eyes of the bureaucrats.

The day arrived. The meeting was held in the same room in the capitol where I had taken my examination in 1950. Yes, the spittoons were still there, as I remember. To address the audience, I suppose I stood at the lectern used during legislative sessions by a very powerful political Montana statesman. I showed the bureaucrats and lawyers a few slides, the ones exhibiting masses of cut flesh. I remember looking around at the screen to see if the slide was showing all its gory majesty. A wave of disgust infiltrated my soul. I shut off the projector. Addressing the audience in a loud voice, I proclaimed, "I'm not going to talk about this stuff any more. I'm going to talk about something far more important, which you all should think about."

I related the story of my patient just as I have related it

above. Concluding in a louder voice, which came rolling out of the Montana State Capitol chamber to be heard by listeners outdoors, I railed, "Yes, the patient got his four thousand dollars! The lawyer got two for writing two letters. What's immoral is: That's two thousand dollars the injured workman *didn't* get for his impairment and suffering. What's practical is: That's two thousand dollars the taxpaying employer had to pay out of his pocket for that exorbitant letter-writing service."

I expressed my disgust to my entire satisfaction and declared that I would not make an impairment rating again.

"Let the lawyers do it!" I sassed.

I regained my calm, suggesting that the act of impairment-rating required more thought and consideration than just the measurement of joint motion. I proposed an "impartial commission" versed in the project and consisting of qualified doctors and other judges. But never again for me!

After the scene, while I was getting into my car, some politician, a Democrat, approached and invited me to be on some political committee or other. I declined. I was too busy doctoring. I never heard whether my message stimulated any thought. At least for me, my role was reconfirmed. I had judged that the man's stiff knee was worth only nine thousand dollars! The lawyer did four thousand better than I. I wouldn't take a million dollars to live with a stiff knee. From that time on when I was asked to make a rating I would repeat this story on my patient to explain my stand on the matter and would conclude, "*You* know how much your impairment is worth. *I* certainly don't. You'd laugh at me for putting a price on your injury. Think of it. If you have to set a price, *all* impairments are worth a million dollars! At least that's what it would be if I were injured! No, I won't make a rating. There are doctors who love to make ratings. Watch out you don't get a company man!"

And the session would end with an unhappy, "I know, Doc; thanks anyway."

The Ivory Tower

IT WAS 1963. I was forty-three years old and we were still living in the rented log house in Ennis. One day Olive and her cub scouts were sewing together a teepee, outdoors, in our front yard. A crew of little boys passed up reams of canvas duck to Olive, stationed at her sewing machine. At last the teepee had been completed. Visiting dignitaries from the bars had crossed the street to gather against Winifred's fence to watch the erection of the seventeen poles and the ceremonial wrapping of the canvas about them—when the whole monstrosity collapsed, blanketing several screaming cub scouts within. Eventually the teepee was resurrected that day. Night occupancy, with a small fire illuminating the interior, was followed by a whooping encirclement of juvenile neighbors armed with boy-made bows. There was a wild galloping around the teepee as they shot their arrows of flaming newspaper at the new, inviting structure. The skirmish ended with bodies doused with water. The teepeee survived. It was the only home we owned. We thought it time to build a house.

While I was searching for a home site one fall day, Albert Thexton, a rancher on the Varney Road, joined me. He knew my thoughts. He took me to a corner of his ranch and agreed to sell us a few acres overlooking the Blaine Spring Creek channel of the Madison River. I sketched my idea of a French-Canadian-style house on paper and made an inch-to-the-foot model. Olive designed the interior. Our friend Ed Miller, who had built the hospital addition, started the project just before Christmas.

Having acquired the land in Montana, it is the duty of the owner to protect his lawn or garden from cattle by fencing in the area. So occupied, one Saturday morning in November, I was struggling to extract a boulder from the earth with a crowbar at each fence-post site. Our friend Pete Womack drove up. Without getting out, he announced from the side window of his pickup truck that the president had been assassinated. A black day!

The following month, on a cold, black, winter night, Olive and I met Dr. Gene Wilkins at the station in Bozeman and hustled him back to Ennis. The doctor had come to check the place before he moved his family from Nebraska. In spite of its being a tiny, frozen cow-town in the boonies, he decided to move to Ennis.

Two months later in late February 1964, Olive and I were in Chicago at a hockey match. We were sitting with Dr. Gordon Petrie, who, like us, had come to Chicago to attend the meeting of the American Academy of Orthopaedic Surgeons. It was a warm reunion with my old boss from Montreal. We had enjoyed a dinner together and talked orthopaedics and patient problems at the table. As we left the hockey game, after he gave me hell for not having attended an orthopaedic meeting since I had started my practice, he said, "Ron, I want you to come to Montreal. Red Yablon, our resident at the Shrine, broke his hip skiing. He'll be out of action for two months. Come for two months to take his place. Be ready to start Monday."

My answer was quite negative. "I've got patients scheduled. I can't leave my practice that fast. We're building our house."

"You know you can come if you want to. I'll give you until breakfast time to let me know. I'll be eating with Dr. McCarroll from St. Louis in the hotel, downstairs. Be there. Eat breakfast with us and let me know then."

It seemed as if somebody had set the thermostat to 100° in our hotel room that night. I might have drifted off to sleep at five minutes to six when the wake-up call came.

At breakfast, I agreed to spend two months at the Montreal Shrine Hospital.

The following March and April 1964 at the Montreal Shrine Hospital superseded in excellence any training experience I had previously had. This tiny bite of orthopaedic instruction was so delicious, so properly concentrated, and an extremely pleasant adventure. This hospital was a haven for youngsters, not a house of sadness and distress. I remember a whole ward of boys and girls shouting and screaming from their beds at the television screen as the Beatles descended on the tarmac; the pride that radiated with the first steps taken on a casted but now straightened leg; the smiles shared upon first looking at a surgically untwisted club foot; and the pride of an accomplishment of the first few unaided steps with a new brace.

We examined, we studied, we operated. Yet there was time to read the great *Journal of Bone and Joint Surgery*, time to spend learning with the therapists, time to copy and collect case studies, time to make a collection of transparency slides and to make X-ray copies of classical orthopaedic syndromes. And the good people at the Shrine fed me, for sixty breakfasts, the largest hens' eggs I had ever eaten.

I had spent two months in an ivory tower.

Wednesdays

ON THE NIGHT of the earthquake, August 17, 1959, after meeting Dr. Phillip Pallister in Boulder, Montana, I decided to help him with his horrendous orthopaedic problems. We finally got together on February 14, 1960, to operate on

Joann Krapmann. We transferred a tendon at her ankle to straighten the clubbing of her foot. This was the start of a weekly ninety-mile trip each Wednesday to Montana State School and Hospital in Boulder that lasted until 1975.

Pallister came to Boulder, Montana, with his wife Willie and their boy-children to survive and live. They eventually had twelve sons, one daughter, and three other adopted boys. They used to say, "It's a good thing we're not Catholics!" He started a general practice in this small Montana village that accommodated the state institution for the custodial care of the mentally retarded. He immediately became the physician for the institution, and involvement with the Boulder School started. He stopped the practice of transporting inmates from the dormitory to the small infirmary in a child's Radio Wagon express cart during blizzards. He threw away the mercurochrome that was used to paint all patients' throats "just to make them feel better." He forced the state administration to obtain Kotex for the women residents instead of the commissioned despicable and primitive facilities.

After ten years, Phil finally inveigled an orthopaedist to come to Boulder to help him care for a variety of diornal problems. Two operations were rendered, but Phil couldn't get the specialist to return for necessary follow-through care. (This was the same specialist who flashed the X-ray of Ralph Paugh's wrist up the hospital window.) On August 17th, 1959, the night of the earthquake, I agreed to help him.

The orthopaedic problems facing our friend were awesome. Here were patients with the most severely disabling genetic defects which at the time no one had attempted even to diagnose. Phil and I, both from American medical institutions of repute, had not been trained in genetic disorders. We were even taught the wrong human chromosome count in our day (Down's syndrome). "Goofy kids" confronted us as green young doctors, and we were privately embarrassed at our profound ignorance. We professionals were supposed to know. We suffered as we managed our own appalling ignorance, and what is worse, we would sometimes try to hide it behind a hypocritical, juvenile, role-playing behavior.

A thousand or more dependent, mentally deficient souls were under his charge, and this alone mandated that he try to eliminate at least a portion of the horror that he was seeing every day. Phil taught himself and his assistants everything and anything in examination and laboratory techniques that would help to diagnose these people. Bit by bit examinations were recorded, photographs were documented, laboratory tests accomplished, and chromosome studies commenced. Consultations were obtained through invitations offered to pertinent faculty members from Washington, Duke, Wisconsin, and Johns Hopkins Universities. Not the state, but Phil and Willie would board them and entertain them, in return for intensive clinics and seminars. The orthopaedic program was a fair fragment of the whole project.

With no contract and with only a proper Montana man-to-man agreement between Phil, Dr. Westwell (the school's superintendent), and myself, we began our orthopaedic project. When the state saw fit, I was to be paid eighty-five percent of the Blue Shield allowance for each operation performed, but not for any other service (such as consultations, clinics, examinations, follow-ups, etc.). That didn't matter. There was a lot of work to do. After three years, the state paid my eight-thousand-dollar bill. Of the eight thousand, I think three of it was transferred from the state to the feds, through me. A good year!

Wednesday after Wednesday, our day started, seven o'clock AM, at Willie's breakfast table—always competing for *the* anecdote of the week relative to some moral issue.

The conversation one morning might have gone like this:

"Phil, do you remember that little room in the back of the elevator in St. James Hospital? [in Butte]" He laughed, hilariously. I thought it couldn't be. He answered, "Yes, I know that little room. Why?" And he laughed again.

I told him a story of the early 1950s when Drs. James and MacPherson had me in that little room and offered,

"Losee, we know what it's like working in a place like Ennis, where you do. It's tough. I tell you what. You bring 'em in here to operate and we'll split, one-third for you and two-thirds for us. How about it?"

Now we both choked with laughter. Phil had the same offer. In the same little room. By the same two guys.

"What didja tell 'em, Phil?"

"What'd joo?"

We told each other. Willie interjected. "Shshsh, boys, shshsh, the children are up!"

Actually, as with every new shocking experience, neither one of us knew quite *what to say*, but we both knew *what to do*. Neither one of us ever had anything further to do with them.

Phil, the atheist, used to say that as a kid he wanted to be president of the United States. I countered that "I had some cosmic aspirations, myself."

The patient was on the table. Margaret Keating was the boss nurse and Jo Phelan circulated in the surgery. Dr. Dave Bossler, the anesthetist from Helena, was at the head of the table. Indicating the overhead surgical lamp, Phil loudly said, "Margaret! Throw on the lights!" Margaret laughed. We all laughed. What's so funny about that?

They all knew my Madison Valley Hospital story of the 1950s.

A mother had delivered her child precipitously, having never before consulted. She had been obliged to spend the last of her confinement period with a fond relative, one of my favorite patients. The reason for the mother's Montana sojourn was that her husband was wanted for bigamy in Wyoming. The accouchement passed without an untoward event. The next day the fond relative related an incident to our chief nurse that had occurred in her home on the eve of the delivery. She told her, "I heard a commotion in the next room. I went in and 'twas just as I suspected. *So I throwed on the lights* 'n' I says to him, I says, 'Get off'en her you, son-of-a-bitch, 'n' go out the shithouse 'n' jack-off!' "

Thereafter, any operation that enjoined Phil Pallister and myself would always start with that quintessential sacred litany. It "purified" any operation procedure that we might render. We "threw on the lights" 417 times together from 1960 until 1975, trying our best to rectify some of nature's horrors. Highlighting this project were Dr. Frank Bassett's two pro bono visits from Duke University to audit and to teach us in our orthopaedic adventure. He helped us tackle some difficult cerebral palsy problems and enabled us to get some more youngsters ambulatory. He operated with us. (We "threw on the lights" when he was there too.)

It was a typical Wednesday. Ramona Sedgewick, a resident, had the day off from her duties in the kitchen where it was warm. The outside temperature was 20° below, and there were snowdrifts along the paths. Ramona forgot it was her day off and walked to go to work in the kitchen. She walked outside from her dormitory to the kitchen in her cotton dress and without her coat. She never made it. Someone found her frozen, yet still alive, in a snowbank. They guessed she'd been there forty minutes, but actually, no one could know how long. She was taken to the ward and Phil and I saw something we had never seen before. *Ramona's extremities were frozen solid! I could knock on her shoulders with my knuckles and make them ring like a block of ice. This icy solidification extended to her fingers.* Frost had stiffened her lower extremities from the hips to the toes. I couldn't believe it. I had to lightly tap the iced arm, the calf, and knock on it again to make it ring: Am I really doing this? Her torso was soft and she was conscious and breathing. Phil and I knew the tissues were to be handled very gently. What to do? Now, I have forgotten her "core" temperature, but we had to raise it. We put her in the bathtub very carefully. We didn't know how fast to warm her, so we guessed at room temperature. We knew she would shock. We knew she might shut down her urine. She shocked. We pulled her through that. I remember how nauseated she became. We gave her heparin, worrying about thrombosis. We had to consult with somebody who had seen this before. I suggested the University Medical school in Edmonton and called. I told them I wanted the trauma physicians to guide us. They directed me to the plastic service. The plastic surgeons could give advice only on reconstruction treatment of frozen extremities, very good advice, but *we could find no authority to advise us how to treat acutely and solidly frozen arms and legs that cold Montana day*! We injected a local anesthetic into the sympathetic-nerve trunk in her neck (a sympathetic-nerve block which dilates the blood vessels) to try to assist the circulation. We worked and worked, knowing very, very little about thawing out a solidly frozen young lady. Why she never lost a toe, I'll never know, but she did permanently damage some of her fingers.

Phil and Willie made awfully good sauerkraut. One Wednesday supper at their table, the day's work over, a manhattan followed by lots and lots of sauerkraut was a good send-off for the ninety-mile ride home that October night. The next morning Pallister announced his arrival at the Madison Valley Hospital by ringing the bolts off our emergency room door. Our nurse, Madeline O'Neill, rushed to open it, only to be confronted by our laughing, bearded friend. Madeline barked at him and the day in Ennis started. Phil came to assist me with a Bankart operation on a young fellow's recurrently dislocating shoulder. In making the surgical exposure needed to do the deep repair, I had an urgent message from below.

"Phil? Will you take out the cephalic vein, please?"

A few moments later I rescrubbed, regowned, and returned to the table.

"Jesus, Phil! You and Willie make powerful sauerkraut!"

"I know."

The Montana legislative Budget Subcommittee on Institutions, chaired that year by State Representative Francis

Bardanouve, came to Boulder one February a few years after Phil and I had established our orthopaedic program. By that time we had treated dozens of the residents. The chairman gave strict orders to Dr. Pallister and chief nurse Margaret Keating, with whom they had gathered, *to stick to the budget discussion only*. The chairman admonished Phil, "There will be no powerful presentation nor impassioned demonstrations this time. We are going to cut the budget by twenty-five percent."

That was a positive indication for immediate responsive action. While Margaret and Phil were with the legislators, Jo Phalan and I rounded up the kids. With the legislators' heads deep in the scattering of budget documents at the table, entering into the same room came a young retarded resident pushing another in a wheelchair. Silently and smartly the kid pushed his charge past the politicians. Directly following, two youngsters pushed a gurney carrying a nonambulatory resident. Then in marched youngsters in walkers and braces, smiling and curiously touching the committee members. By now a continuous stream was passing by, in one door, out the other. These were residents, whom we had operated on and successfully made ambulatory, pushing the nonambulatory ones needing help. The committee wanted to know what was going on. Phil and Margaret explained and challenged, "Do you want us to cancel this program?"

The chairman seemingly tried to distract the committee by announcing, "You know, of course, that Pallister is the highest-paid employee of the state?"

To which Pallister instantly responded, "Yes, and by God, I'm worth it!"

They said we were tough customers to argue with. They voted for a proper Boulder school budget that year.

Thirty years ago a nineteen-year-old boy suffered with a low-grade septic arthritis of his knee joint. We had planned to do a synovectomy on him (that is, remove the diseased inner lining of the joint). Because there was no anesthetist available that day, Dr. Pallister gave the spinal anesthetic. The patient was conscious during the operation. The knee joint was surgically opened and was so badly deteriorated that it had to be solidified (arthrodesed) to enable the young man to become pain-free and to ambulate again. This required chiseling off the joint surfaces down to the spongy bone beneath the articular surface of the knee. The two raw ends would be solidly held and pressed together until the femur and tibia became one long bone from the hip to the ankle. This requires a lot of hammering. Phil and I were consumed with grinding up the kneecap to use as filler graft material in the procedure. A sterile screen had been placed over the patient's chest across the operating table so that he could not see below it or sneeze over the wound. The patellar chips were prepared. The hammering continued.

From above the screen, there wafted the voice of the young man upon whom we were operating. With the tempo of a woodpecker, it said, "Tap, tap, tap, tap, tap, tap, tap, tap, My mommy won't like this. Tap, tap, tap, tap, tap, tap, tap, tap. My mommy won't like this!"

As the years passed, it would seem that every time our family was in Great Falls, Montana, I would see this same gentle young man, perhaps a block away, walking with his fused stiff knee. He had long since left the institution.

"It makes you humble. It makes you humble."

"I Wish the Farmer's Wheat Would Grow"

GAVIN MILLER, THE chief of surgery at the Royal Victoria Hospital in Montreal, ridiculed a colleague surgeon who

prayed. The chief asserted that a surgeon who had to pray
during an operation was not fit to operate. I think I'd be
pretty nervous, too, if I heard my surgeon praying at his
task. When techniques have been perfected and are no
longer controversial, they go to the back burner, are nar-
rated, and are talked about more in a cool, scientific manner
than hotly debated. When a difficult operation is still in the
debating stage and the surgeon is committed, a silent prayer
(heavy thinking) is not to be shunned. I *like* the young and
inexperienced surgeon to use prayer (fiercely heavy thinking). It will help him to reach the so-called "master" stage.
In medicine I think prayer (heavy and urgent thinking)
waits in the foyers to be summoned when ignorance rules.
There is a lot of praying in the AIDS clinics, I am sure. For
instance, a good surgeon doesn't have to pray. "Lord,
should I wear surgical gloves when I operate today?" However, there was a lot of prayer years and years ago, by all
involved, when the obstetrician delivered the baby with his
bare hands after walking in from the autopsy room and un-
knowingly infected the mother who was to die from subsequent sepsis.

The patient was a young man in his hospital bed waiting
for me to operate at eight AM. He had wrecked his ankle
and an orthopaedic surgeon had operated to fuse it, to so-
lidify it. But the operation failed, and the ankle never did
fuse. It became even more painful than it had been before
the surgery. I decided to redo the operation to attempt to
succeed in solidifying it. By this time I had experience in
fusing (or arthrodesing) ankles employing different techniques. Also, at the time, I was most comfortable using a
compression technique that squeezed the operated and
roughened joint surfaces very tightly together. I liked to approach the ankle joint with a long incision that crossed the
joint over the inside knob of the ankle. However, the skin
over the inner knob of this man's ankle was scarred badly
and it was not wise to operate through this scarred side.

It was seven-thirty that June morning of the scheduled
operation. I was sitting on an old schoolhouse desk-seat Ol-

ive had acquired and had placed against the outside kitchen wall. There was nothing between me and the Madison range but the broad pastureland on the other side of the noisy, shallow, stony-bottomed river below. My thoughts were, "How am I going to get at that ankle with that awful skin in the exact area where I want to cut?" After another ten minutes passed with no idea forthcoming, the mental turbulence screamed within. At that moment I remembered every patient I had seen with osteomyelitis (a boil on the bone) saying, "Jesus, if I cut through that scar, the wound *can't* heal. The wound won't close. It will first drain blood, then serum, then pus. The edges will retract. Bone will be exposed. The ankle will never ease. The pain will be bad. He'll drain and drain. Drain pus and stink! It will mean an amputation. An amputation, if I cut through that side! Why can't I figure this one out? It's getting late! I've got to go!"

My mind had a little pressure kink. Negative thoughts had won for the moment. Time was passing and I hadn't come up with a plan. A big shot of healthy anxiety hit. True to my good old Sunday School days in Upper Red Hook, New York, I asked. I made a prayer. I thought urgently and hard. I humbled myself.

Some of us were taught, "Ask, and it shall be given you."

The gift?

The state bird of Montana is the meadowlark.

A meadowlark was singing what every Montanan knows so well: "I wish the farmer's wheat would grow. I wish the farmer's wheat would grow." (Rita Gress, our scrub nurse taught me that one.)

The bird changed its tune to an even more beautiful melody.

I got up from my seat and knew—"Sure, that's it! I don't have to operate in exactly the same way I've been doing ankle fusions these last few years. I'll change my tune, just as the meadowlark did. I'll go in the other side. I'll use another technique and it'll work, too. Let's get at it!"

I got his ankle to arthrodese.
I like meadowlarks.

The Bucket-Handle Tear

BY THE MID- and latter 1960s the Student Health Service of
Montana State University at Bozeman kept us on our toes.
After a full Wednesday at Boulder I would return home to
pick out the surgical instruments needed for the next day
when Olive and I would drive to Bozeman. There were
rounds to be made that night in the Deaconess Hospital to
check the patients that were going to be operated on the
next morning. We'd sleep in a motel and I would operate
in the morning, then consult with the general practitioners
and surgeons at their offices in the afternoon. Olive would
help with nursing and secretarial efforts. At the end of the
day we would spend all evening examining injured students
and athletes at the student-health-service building, then
make another round at the hospital to check the patients I
had operated on that morning. We usually were home in
bed in Ennis by two or three in the morning. The next day
at the office in Ennis, Friday, could be a terror because of
our Wednesday and Thursday absences. But, we could look
forward to the weekend. Perhaps there was time enough to
take care of our garbage on Saturday morning. By three
o'clock Saturday afternoon I was on the way to Bozeman
again to check the knee (or the wrist or shoulder) of a university football player. Marshall Cook, at the time, was the
trainer for the university. He had been educated in the sci-
ences in Louisiana and was versed in his knowledge of
anatomy and in the physiopathology of extremity injuries.

Marshall, who liked to be called "The Cajun," would have his injured players lined up. We would examine them together and operate together, either in Bozeman or back in Ennis, where we sometimes took the patients. Knees, knees, and knees!

At that time, Drs. O'Donoghue, Hughston, and Slocum were leading American teachers of the surgical management of knee injuries. To their orthopaedic audiences, they emphasized the stabilizing importance of the medial ligament of the knee and the importance of its immediate repair when ruptured. Importance was placed on a "golden period" of five days in which to repair a freshly ruptured knee ligament. I subscribed to this idea and believed I should operate on the knee with the ruptured ligament as soon as possible. Hence, we were up late Saturday night after Saturday night, and weekday nights too.

Logistics became a terrible problem. One late night in Bozeman, looking at the big football tackle's smashed wrist, I advised that it had to be operated on in the morning.

We scheduled his operation for seven-thirty AM in the Bozeman Deaconess Hospital, which had no orthopaedic instruments of its own at the time. However, my surgical instruments, needed for the morning's operation, were in Ennis, fifty-four miles away. Moreover, my books were in my home as well. I had never fixed a fractured carpal injury just like this one before. I had to read all I could about it, even if it took all night. Back to Ennis by midnight! Then I confidently went to the surgery of the Madison Valley Hospital to pick out my tools from the glass-enclosed case in which they were stored.

I thought I could pick out the instruments I'd need for the morning's procedure and I'd still have plenty of time— the rest of the night—to "study up."

But as I stood in front of the instrument case, in a flash, it was obvious that there were gaps on the shelves. "Jesus! Boulder is a long ways away."

Ninety miles north of Ennis—ten or fifteen of those

miles were on dirt road in those days—I drove to the State Hospital in Boulder. The night nurses there laughed in sympathy as I picked up my tools and slurped a cup of watery coffee. I completed the extra hundred and eighty miles in time to read about the operation in *Campbell's Operative Orthopaedics* and arrived in Bozeman by seven-thirty the next morning. The wrist turned out fine. The same tackle had me operate on his shoulder the next year. Did I *ever* leave one single, solitary, lonely surgical instrument or screw in Boulder or anywhere else thereafter? Yes, I've already recalled the "Horrendeoma Operation" in Sheridan. "It makes you humble. It makes you humble!"

Continued obligation to the needy university athletes and students advanced my orthopaedic interest in injuries of the knee. By the end of the decade, patients with bad knees were coming to Ennis to see the bald-headed man who was supposed to know something about the knee. The most frequent operation performed on the knee was the meniscectomy.

The meniscus is a new-moon-shaped piece of rubbery cartilage that nature has positioned above the periphery of the knee joint. Chickens have menisci in their knees. So do rabbits and so do dogs. In cross section the meniscus appears wedge-shaped, with the outside of the wedge being thick and the inside becoming paper-thin. The outside and thick portion curves like the outer edge of an imaginary two- or three-inch new moon. The little new moon lies flat between the knuckle of the "knee end" of the thigh bone and the platform (or the *tibial plateau*, as it is called) of the upper end of the leg bone. Each knee has an inside or *medial* meniscus and an outside or *lateral* meniscus. The combined effect of both the inside and the outside meniscus is to contain and to help stabilize the inside and the outside knuckle of the lower end of the femur as it presses against the tibial plateau. The meniscus becomes a cushion and shock-absorber to the joint.

An injury to the knee may tear the meniscus. A common tear is called a "bucket-handle" tear. Imagine this kind of a tear splitting the little "new moon," or the meniscus, length-wise down its middle. The thick outer edge of the meniscus is naturally fastened to the outside ligaments that join the knee together. With the meniscus now split by an injury, the middle portion slips into the center of the joint while each end remains attached, one at the front and the other end still attached to the rear portion. One can imagine the displaced torn part appearing like a bucket handle. The displacement obstructs the joint and the injured patient cannot straighten his knee. The patient now is forced to walk on a bent knee.

Gordon Petrie, my old boss in Montreal, said, "Ron, get those menisci out. Get them out! They're like tonsils, better out than in." At that time I watched the orthopaedists remove the *entire* meniscus at each operation. They would cut any remnant cartilaginous material from the rim until there was no "cushion" left. When the time comes to operate "on your own," it is reasonable to do as taught. Therefore, I removed the entire meniscus of the first few patients with torn menisci on whom I operated. They took a long time to recover! Then one day in 1961 or 1962, with my anesthetized patient on the operating table and with his leg bent over the end of the table and the knee joint "opened" (incised), I saw the displaced portion of a bucket-handle torn meniscus between the two knuckles of the knee. I slowly extended the bent knee and could see the displaced portion of cartilage (meniscus) obstruct the two closing joint surfaces.

I thought, "Why, why in hell, take the rest of the rim of meniscus out of this man's joint?"

But tradition held me back as I continued to think, "They say that the remnant rim will tear and you'll have to remove it later. That will be two operations and anesthetics for this man. He will never forgive me for that."

I concluded my thought with, "The hell with what 'They say.' It's destructive to the joint to carve all the cartilage out. I'll operate again if I have to! Let's see what happens."

It was very simple just to cut loose the two attached ends of the displaced portion of the meniscus and then quickly sew up the wound. *And the patient did wonderfully well. He was back to work in two weeks. And neither he nor subsequent patients needed second operations to remove remnant menisci.* That was the end of that nonsense. And soon it was the end of the nonsense of treating the meniscectomized knees with long plaster leg casts. And soon they were out of the cottonwool knee dressings by the next day and out of the hospital in three days.

But I still didn't know what happened in the knee joint when it *went out*, as the young men and women would so frequently complain.

Tribute to Butte

BUTTE! OLIVE AND I entered with our miner's lunchpail. This was Carl Rowan's place on West Park. Carl announced our arrival and shouted to all. His compliments rolled. And *rolled*. Jesus, it was embarrassing and wonderful! Carl grabbed the lunchpail, sat us in a booth, and rushed away as he said, "Give me a minute." He returned with the pail filled. Hot coffee filled the bottom half. The heat below warmed the two Cornish pasties he had placed in the inset container above the coffee-filled bottom. He completed the lunch with a blueberry pie set in the bucket's top tray. Carl reminded us that Italian miners filled the bottom of their buckets with wine and the Irish with whiskey or sometimes tea. Olive and I passed the pail back and forth while driving away from Butte—coffee and pasties, coffee and pie. Later our Ennis friend Milt Crooker, a longtime Butte miner, fixed our old prize with a coiled spring that secured the lid. Milt confessed those same lunch buckets regularly returned small, well-earned, company bonuses home each night.

Butte on the Fourth of July: I marched in the left file. Son Jon marched to my right. Friends Tom MacKee from Kansas City, and Dr. Warren Swager from Sheridan marched to Jon's right. Another eight or ten of us were all squeezing a bagpipe under our left armpits. We droned, we doubled, we threw our Ds. We purred. We cut loose with "Highland Laddie," "The Green Hills," and "Bonnie Dundee." We were hot! The sun was hot. "Scotland the Brave" was hot. Then comes, "Hi, Doc!" from the folks in the crowd and a big tug at my argyle sock, with a cold, cold can of beer stuck against my hot calf. "Oats in the sporran? Hell, no, another can of beer!"

It was in Butte, with Olive, Laura Wilson, and Dick Avedon where we devoured Walla Walla sweet-onion sandwiches at the Met Bar. We watched a dozen Butte miners line up in front of Avedon's white-paper background. We saw these men bare their souls in their proud momentary presentations of themselves to the big camera. His photographs in *The American West* portray people as I have known them and as I wish them to be remembered.

Butte is Dan Harrington's town. Dan, with his Butte American-Irish dialect, sold me two or three tools at a time from his surgical supply house, then waited, and waited, and waited, for months and months. Finally, in Ennis, comes Dan's voice: "Doc, it's income tax time and I need something on account, in a kind of a hurry. Can you help me out, a bit?"

Butte ladies always honored me when they came to see me, the doctor in Ennis. They dressed for me in their Sunday attire. Thank you, you lovely ladies from Butte.

Butte, where else? The wonderful Serb-American family presented Olive and myself with a huge povitica for our holiday coffee times, over and over!

Butte! I've been honored to try to help the injured miner the best I knew how. I've listened to his way of life—the heat of the underground, the drifts and slopes, the stretch of the cable as the seven miners in their cage spring to a stop a mile deep in the earth.

Butte—my favorite city. That's because of them. These good people have trusted me and honored me with their confidence for decades. This Butte scene has been one of the precious rewards of "doctorhood."

"That's It!"

IT IS JUNE 16, 1969. I am now a forty-nine-year-old, middle-aged, self-proclaimed orthopaedic surgeon about to examine my supine patient on the examining table before me. We're beneath the big east picture-window in my office. I gaze out and relish the sharply outlined entire Madison Range, totally distracted, as if my patient were but a scarf on an ironing board.

I look at him and think, *He comes down to Ennis, all the way from Helena with the chief complaint of "My knee gives way." What the hell does that mean? I hear it all the time. Dozens of injured athletes at Montana State complain of it. A lot of them have had anterior-cruciate-ligament ruptures.* I keep thinking, *Doctors take out menisci in the hopes that it will help, but it doesn't. After they lose their menisci their knees still give way. I saw doctors take out normal menisci for this in Montreal. They also recommend meniscectomy for "loose" menisci at the recent Academy meetings. What the hell are loose menisci?*

Gary, here, didn't say his kneecap dislocated. That would cause a knee to "give way." I ask him, "Gary, did your kneecap ever slide off to the outside? Did it ever do that and then you had to push it back again?"

"No."

My thoughts continue, *His patella is stable. It's not that. His kneecap is tighter than a bull's ass in fly time.*

I keep poking his knee. *I don't feel a loose body. Loose bodies get caught between the joint surfaces and that hurts like the devil. That makes a knee "give way."*

I ask him, "Gary, did you ever feel a bean move about in the front of your knee?"

Before he answers, I know he'll say, "No."

"No," he says.

I look above and through the window again, notice the recent clear-cut in the Jack Creek area, and cannot believe that I've lived here twenty years and have still never wandered in among the mountains.

I shake my head a little and muse, *His quadriceps aren't paralyzed or especially weak. Weak quads cause giving way, but the knee just bends forward when that happens.*

I ask him, "Gary, when your knee gives out, does it feel like the times when we were kids and used to come up behind the girls and bend our knees in the back of theirs to make them fall?"

He quickly responds, "No, Doc, it's not like that. It feels as if it comes apart when it does it. It hurts enough to make me puke."

I poke his knee again and rethink. *The only thing left that I know will do it is a locking cartilage. I've got to check for a torn meniscus. I'm going to check for it hard. If his meniscus is okay, I don't know what the hell makes his knee give way. It's that old thing. I don't know why the hell anybody's knee gives way without dislocating kneecaps; torn cartilages; floating, loose bodies; or bad quads. The big boys are always talking about the quads. I don't think it's always weak quads. I don't think the quads have a damned thing to do with it.*

And I do every meniscus test in the book and I even do one I swear I made up, thinking, *It's probably known. Gordon Petrie says, "Nothing is new."* (I would pull the 90° flexed knee forward by clasping both hands behind, and a sharp yank would displace, with a dramatic thud, the center of the meniscus if it were torn at its rim. I later ascertained that "my" test was actually Finochietto's Test and was written up by Ricardo F. himself, who wrote from Buenos Aires and published in the *Journal of Bone and Joint Surgery* in 1935. I wish I could tell him that he gave us an extraordinary test.)

Well, I think, *He sure as hell doesn't have a sign of a torn meniscus! He denies locking too.* (It is a symptom that occurs when the displaced bucket-handle portion of the torn meniscus becomes pinched between the front joint surfaces, preventing full extension of the knee.)

I look out the window again and see a bunch of Canada geese about to land in a large, irrigated field just beyond and below the alluvial terrace in back of the hospital.

The silent, enduring patient is still there. And, *I don't know why his knee gives way. He has that same old giving-way complaint they all have, the complaint that nobody knows a damn about. And he comes here all the way from Helena. I'll ask him more questions.*

I learn nothing more from the patient about his trick knee than that he'd give a year of his life to get rid of it.

I check his ligaments. *Yes, he has a little increased lateral wobble with his leg bent fifteen degrees. The joint spreads on the medial* (or inside) *side. It's tight when he's completely extended. This means his medial ligament is a bit slack, but that won't make the knee give way. I'll do a draw test. He has a very positive anterior draw test, therefore I know that his anterior cruciate ligament is ruptured.* Dr. Petrie used to say that you don't need your anterior cruciate ligaments, and he used to snip torn ones out when he operated.

Then I remembered what the great Harrison McLaughlin, professor of clinical orthopaedic surgery at the College of Physicians and Surgeons in New York, which my granddad attended, wrote in his book *Trauma*, published in 1959. He wrote, "Complete absence of the anterior cruciate ligament produces no demonstrable adverse effect upon the stability of the knee if the collateral ligaments and the quadriceps muscle are intact."

Disregarding those teachings, I concluded that Gary had an old tear of his anterior cruciate ligament and that had to be the reason for his knee giving way. I recalled athletes I had cared for at the College (Montana State University of Bozeman) with ruptured anterior cruciate ligaments, who complained of giving way.

I continued to ponder, with the window distracting me again. *Now the horses are running in Tillinger's field. There must be a storm coming up.*

I still don't know what I'm going to tell the patient.

Perhaps out of sheer boredom, sheer frustration at my ignorance, or the pathetic hope that I might learn more, I elevated his partially flexed knee a foot off the table by holding the back of his left knee in my right hand. I took his left foot in my left hand and drew it toward me while pushing the knee away with my right hand. Why? I don't know. Perhaps I was reviewing a perceived slackness from a slightly stretched medial ligament, the king of knee ligaments, as preached by the authorities at that time. I further flexed the knee while holding it this way. I must have been squeezing the lateral (outside) compartment of the joint while bending it this way. Nothing happened. But, when I extended the knee in this same manner: The knee GAVE WAY.

Jesus, I thought. *It's coming apart! I'm dislocating it! This is what all the patients are trying to tell us! This is the trick knee! This is the giving way! I MADE THE SON-OF-A-BITCH GO OUT!*

The patient sprang to a sitting position with both knees sharply flexed. As he still sat that way on the examining table, he clasped his infirm and flexed left knee in both hands and hollered, "THAT'S IT!"

I was forty-nine. I had been examining knees since I was thirty. I had never seen or felt the knee jump like this before. I had never read about it. I had never heard the big guys talk about it. It wasn't in the texts. I hadn't read about it in the *Journal*. I thought, I *knew*, I was on to something big. *What the hell is it?*

A mental curtain of intense concentration closed the magnificent window.

I could repeat the new test and get the knee to give way every time. It never failed. All I had to do was to push the knee away from me with one hand while I pulled the foot toward me with the other, then lift the leg enough so that I could bend and straighten the knee. I helped exaggerate the sign by twisting the leg below the knee inward (making the toes point toward the toes of the other foot).

At this stage I had no idea what was happening. I had to figure this out because I was convinced I had made a discovery. I was at a disadvantage because the authoritative teaching of that decade was that the tibia toed outward during knee-instability episodes. What's more, a knee operation designed to check this outward twist was being extensively employed by the orthopaedists at the time. I had done three of those operations and had not become enthusiastic. I was also strongly influenced by the stressed importance given by the authorities to the function of the medial ligament of the knee. (The medial ligament, like a hinge strap, joins the thigh and leg on the side where the knees can touch together.)

Because of this strong influence, I immediately thought that there was a *defect of the medial ligament* that allowed the leg to twist abnormally inward (toe in) instead of outward, as taught. But as I repeated the test I could see absolutely no pathological action on the medial side. But I did see, every time I tested, *an impressively unusual shift at the lateral (outside) joint line*. I then knew that the authorities had it ass backwards! But, I also thought for a few moments that such a finding was too simple and too fundamental to have been missed by the entire orthopaedic society. I thought that a discovery this big couldn't possibly be true. But I knew it was true because I could repeat the test ad lib and *the test reproduced Gary's dysfunction every time I did it.* The next thing I had to do was to see if I could prove and document my idea with an X-ray.

"Come with me, Gary." And we went to the X-ray room.

Gary let me twist his knee to keep it out of mesh while I took the picture.

Because of the strong traditional teaching—even though there was only one way to interpret the X-ray—it took me until a week later, when Gary returned for a repeat X-ray study, to accept the proof of my discovery with no further amendment. It was a big one, and I wanted to tell the world about it. At the time, I described the knee pathology as "anterior subluxation of the lateral tibial plateau." And I knew it was caused by a ruptured anterior cruciate ligament (the front ligament of two, deep within the knee joint, which, to the anatomists, appear to cross each other).

I had rediscoverd in Ennis what Ivar Palmer had described in Sweden in the 1930s. But his great discovery had not been well taught. He had been a Jesus, but he had no St. Paul to spread the news. I had independently rediscovered what Marcel Lemaire in Paris and David MacIntosh in Toronto had also just perceived. I had not yet read Palmer's article. Lemaire had just published in the French literature. I didn't have an inkling about his article. MacIntosh had not yet written his findings.

The next week I was able to obtain a positive test on another patient. Then another and another. Anyone with a suspected anterior cruciate ligament rupture was a candidate for a positive "giving way" test.

Sure, this was known, but not by me! I had the joy Palmer, Lemaire, and MacIntosh must have had. I was lucky. Although I consider myself a clinician and not a scientist, I rejoiced in my finding. Rosenstock-Huessy wrote in 1944 in a letter addressed to Cynthia Harris, M.D., and now published in a monograph entitled "Hitler and Israel or, On Prayer":

All scientists rejoice in their findings. If they didn't, their discoveries would not be worthy of much respect. You have to throw yourself into the unknown, in fear and trembling, and yet in the white heat of faith, if you hope to hear God's answers to your prayers.

There *was* the unknown to me. I didn't throw myself into it; I fell into it. I had an overwhelming sense that I had arrived at an understanding of a principle of great magnitude. After only a few months of repeated substantiation I had an intense passion to get the word out, to publish, to share what I thought was my discovery. There *was* a little fear and a little trembling with the first operation to come, an operation to remedy the troublesome dislocation of the knee—not a heart operation! There *was*, there *had to be* faith—not a white heat, but a hot conviction.

A Remedy

WHAT TO DO now with the patients who started to come to Ennis with the complaint of giving way of the knee? By the end of 1969 I realized that the anterior-cruciate-ligament-deficient knee with its giving way was a common dysfunction. The surgeons of the day recognized the anatomical but not the functional deficiency of the ruptured ligament. They knew the cruciate ligament was torn and in time dissolved, but had no idea of the mechanics of the dysfunction. When the athlete tore his anterior cruciate ligament, the surgeon diagnosed it by the traditional anterior-drawer test and had available a variety of popular operations for the acute tears or the neglected ones. One concept employed in the reconstruction of the neglected injuries was substitution of the destroyed ligament with a strip harvested from the ligament between the kneecap and the leg, the patellar ligament. Another turned out to be a misconception garnered from the misinterpretation of the dynamics of the joint observed during surgery.

Prior to my understanding of the mechanics of the trick knee, a young man tore his anterior cruciate ligament skiing. His big complaint was, "I was carrying my girl, my knee gave way, and I dropped her. I don't want that any more." I didn't know what giving way meant. I knew his cruciate was shot and it made sense to repair it. I replaced the torn cruciate with a portion of the patellar ligament. The replacement turned into an obstructive chunk of bone and the man still had giving way. This failure influenced me to seek another way.

I was glad I didn't get sucked in to doing many operations for chronic anterior cruciate ligament deficiency using a different method popular at the time. I did three too many and wasn't impressed with the results.

After my finding of June 16, 1969, and after repeating and refining my test for many months, I started to think of a remedy, realizing I was in uncharted territory. I knew of no authority to call upon. I knew the cruciate was destroyed in the trick knee but I hesitated to replace it with the patellar ligament because of my previous failure. My failures were mine alone, unsupported by any professional group or institution that could offer rational encouragement. A failure in a small town meant gossip, an immediate rejection. I had to meet my failures at all-too-often intervals!

What could be an alternative way to fix the trick knee? When the knee gives way, the patient is bearing weight on it while it is slightly flexed. The foot stays on the ground, and the body twists toward the affected-knee side (i.e. with a bad right knee, the body twists to the right). If the anterior cruciate ligament has ruptured, the knee partially twists out of its socket, causing the lateral femoral condyle (the outside knuckle of the knee) to twist too far backward and the patient to have a sensation of hyperextension. Understanding this, I started to think of ways to make a check rein beneath the skin on the outside of the knee joint that would keep it from twisting too far. Two available sources for such a structure are the biceps femoris tendon and the ilio-tibial tract. The first can easily be palpated in the back of the knee while sitting and twisting the foot outward.

But a year went by and I continued to do nothing for my patients with their trick knees. A sacred rule in medicine is, "Do no harm!" (In this age, the malpractice-specializing attorney will probably cry, "Doing nothing is doing harm!" Dammit: Let him be a doctor!)

In September 1970 a beautiful tan-faced, blonde, twenty-four-year-old English teacher came to see me about her unstable knee one Thursday when Olive and I were working in Bozeman. This young lady had been in a motorcycle wreck and she had "anterior subluxation of the lateral tibial plateau" of her left knee. But I could offer her no operation. I sent her to the therapist to teach her how to strengthen her biceps femoris muscle, hoping it would help stabilize the knee to keep it from tricking. These techniques were called "dynamic stabilization procedures," a captivating name, but I thought, *How in hell can a muscle stay tight all the time to keep the joint from coming apart?*

In May 1971 the English teacher, Linda Shadiow, my number-one star patient-to-be, returned to Ennis, this time to my office with the big window facing east. She was on crutches. She complained that she had faithfully exercised her biceps femoris night and day, "until the cows came home." "I've spent over two hundred dollars on physiotherapy and *my knee still goes out,*" she cried. "Can't you do anything to keep it from dislocating?"

I said, "I don't know what to do. I don't know where to send you." (I didn't know about Lemaire in Paris nor about MacIntosh in Toronto yet.)

But, I didn't send her home. I fretted and I stewed and I spun my wheels for two hours. I had considered transferring the ilio-tibial tract. *No,* I thought, *I better do nothing.*

Then an idea flashed. I had attended a San Francisco orthopaedic meeting the previous two months and listened to a fine speaker from London, Ontario, Jack Kennedy. I thought he was an excellent thinker and an investigator of the cruciate. I called him. I was a bit nervous. I had not spoken with many big shots in my life. I told him I believed everybody had it backward. I emphasized that the leg below the knee twisted excessively *inward* instead of outward when the anterior cruciate ligament ruptured. I told him I thought it to be rational to use the ilio-tibial tract to fix it. What did he think? He asked me to write him a letter. He promised to send me a letter after he attended a meeting in Toronto. Linda went home. I promised her I would keep thinking about her lousy knee. And I did.

I wrote the letter. Later I discovered how the orthopaedic grapevine works. Kennedy sent copies of my letter to interested professors; my old friend, Dr. Frank Bassett from Duke University, got one.

Dr. Kennedy answered my letter. We corresponded over the summer. He had learned that Professor MacIntosh in Toronto had performed ten or a dozen operations using the *ilio-tibial tract* to stabilize these tricking knees. I liked Dr. MacIntosh's idea in which he used the tract to make a sling on the outside of the knee to stabilize it. I didn't want to depend upon a sling alone because I thought it could stretch out in time and fail. Over the summer I formulated the hypothesis that it would be better to reinforce the sling by making a longer strip, still using it to make a sling, thereupon using the excess to reef the outside capsule of the joint. Using the tract to reef resembles what a seamstress does when gathering or pleating material. This is done in the posterolateral corner of the joint.

By November 1971, I had formed my plan, but I still needed a large needle to manipulate the strip of ilio-tibial tract. My mechanic friend Hugh Black made me a set of needles out of Olympia beer can openers. He did this in the back of the Texaco garage in Ennis, and each needle still retained the Olympia beer logo, "It's the water."

We operated on Linda's left knee in the green operating room Ed Miller built onto the Madison Valley Hospital in

Ennis. Poor girl, we kept her in the hospital for three
weeks. It worked! Linda "number one," sent me a picture
of her running in a California marathon twenty years later.

To Linda!

LINDA SHADIOW, DO you know that you are a brave lady to
have let me operate upon that wiggly left knee of yours
over twenty years ago? Do you know that I operated upon
your knee without first dissecting a knee in the anatomy
lab, without practicing upon a laboratory animal, and with
absolutely no prior descriptive text or orthopaedic journal
source to consult? You do know I talked with a Canadian
surgeon about a possible technique and you do know that I
described a plan I intended to pursue.

Neither one of us really was sure that an operation would
work. My brain kept repeating that the plan *had* to work
because I understood the anatomy and mechanism of the
dysfunction. In November 1971 there was no record available to tell us that an operation might be effective for
twenty years. Think of this: We did not even know of any
of the pitfalls that could be encountered from such an operation at that time—total failure, future cartilage tears, or
reinjury. We did not know then that if infection supervened
it would take a season to resolve; it would leave a deep
scar, but the knee would not stiffen. We had no idea of the
chance for arthritic degeneration. We didn't even know of
a better operation! Which there are now. We did not know
then that if we operated, the other knee was at an increased
risk of rupturing its anterior cruciate ligament. Linda, we
knew very little. Was our adventure blind faith? Faith, but

not blind. There was a lot of prayer, if prayer can be called hard thinking. There were both, Linda, we have to admit. Know you are THE PERSON of that first job, my friend.

The Doctor Now Farts

A MONTH AFTER Linda's operation, a Butte youth let me do the same operation on him. His knee had already been giving way for a year. The operation was forced because the knee had become locked from a meniscus displacement. It was too soon to know Linda's outcome and thus be assured there had been at least *one* success. However, we had "done one." Here was a brave boy with trusting parents who let me operate. His remedy, his repair, still works, more than twenty years later. A couple of months later followed another young man, this one from Livingston; then a miner from Butte. These first four patients have had lasting successes for twenty years but, definitely, not all the operations have succeeded. It was a slow, deliberate, and cautious start.

I had operated on only seven patients when I attended a knee meeting in Eugene, Oregon, in 1973. The same old stuff was presented about knees. Medial ligaments! Medial ligaments were preached as usual—until the last lecture, when Dr. Hughston presented a patient with an anterior cruciate ligament deficiency. His resident tried to demonstrate the patient's knee instability on the stage but couldn't make the knee go out. I nearly shit my britches trying to get up there on the stage to show the world how to do it! Things rolled by so fast, the meeting was over and everybody went home before I could get my dibs in. That day I saw the orthopaedic world edging toward new knowledge about knees, and I knew that I was ahead of them in the concept of knee instability but couldn't get the message out.

By the next year I had operated on twenty knees. The operation continued to work. I was getting antsy to tell my story. I kept corresponding regularly with Dr. Kennedy in London, Ontario. We had a nice exchange of letters and photographic transparency slides. I sent out a letter telling my story to seven of the great North American knee surgeons. Dr. Larson from Oregon and Dr. Jackson from Toronto responded. I realized I had a problem: How in hell, can a country doctor in Ennis, Montana, who is doing orthopaedics with no orthopaedic board qualification, ever get a hearing in the scientific world? I had no idea. I kept working, hoping, and fantasizing.

In 1974 I had a break and made a new friend. Dr. Sig T. Hansen invited me to talk about my knee project at the University of Washington in Seattle. What a thrill! I forever thank those good men for their kindness to me. I had a wonderful time telling about "anterior subluxation of the lateral tibial plateau" because it was all new to them. My crayon slides worked.

These were the "bagpipe years." Olive learned of a two-week course in bagpipe playing and urged attendance. Son Jonathan and I strapped our backpacks and bagpipes to our Honda trail bikes one late-July summer afternoon and took off from Cactus Rock Ranch, named for our home on the bank of Spring Creek. The second night out, we nearly froze on Hoodoo Pass in the Bitter Root Range, but we made it to Coeur d'Alene, Idaho. The third day, on the campus of Northern Idaho College, we were before the bagpipe master, demonstrating our skills. At our completion, Professor Seumas MacNeill from Glasgow exclaimed, "Ghastly!" However, in two weeks' time he had taught his pupils to proudly play the piobaireachd, "The Company's Lament." Olive and Becky joined us to complete the holiday. While there, Becky fell in love with Kit Ashenhurst, who had come from Canada to enjoy the piping activities. At their wedding, the following New Year's season, we celebrated with our kids' friends for nearly a week, our home pulsing with jigs, strathspeys, piobaireachd, and the snapping staccato of young Lee Wilson's snare drum. There was so much joy at home, the couple forgot the honeymoon escape. Becky and Kit raised their three in Alberta, Canada. Jonathan became a landscape architect, and he also was attracted to Canada where he had made friends with several young bagpipers.

In 1975, Olive and I had promised to take Jon and Becky with her family on a visit back East to show them our roots. We met at Shelby, Montana, close to the Canadian border, where they joined us from Alberta. We all piled in the train the middle of one September night and were away to the East.

Olive insisted I take my data and slides, as well as a crude X-ray movie of the patients' knees. The idea was to stop in and visit with Dr. Kennedy in London, Ontario, and to show him my slides in the pathetic hope that the famous doctor might be willing to publish, with me, a scientific paper about the anterior-cruciate-ligament-deficient knee. Wild, wild dreams, that one!

Our family descended on Olive's mother and sisters, May and Julie. I immediately flew back to London, Ontario, and was taken by the good professor in his wide-open little car from the Holiday Inn to his office.

Dr. Kennedy was exceedingly nice to me. He generously gave me a couple of days. He let me scrub with him in the operating room. I watched him do an Ellison operation for a knee with a pivot shift and was secretly disappointed he didn't do my "sling and reef" operation.

I offered to take him out to dinner that night.

He objected, "That would be a waste of time, Ron." He fed me chicken sandwiches late at night at his kitchen table and he asked me, "Ron, what do you do when you have a failure?"

My answer? "It wrecks me. I puke. I can't sleep. It's all I can think of. I wonder why I do orthopaedics. I have to hurry to admit it to the patient. That used to be hard, but it's easier now that I'm older. I have to know, 'Why did it fail?' It's hell when I can't figure it out, and we both know damned well we can't figure out a lot of them. But, at least, I won't do it *that way* again. I've even driven eight hundred miles to Seattle from Montana to consult and be present at a redo of my failure."

In the basement room of his home he practiced a lecture he was about to give in London, England. He asked me what I thought of the operation he had used to reconstruct the knee on that day. I used the phrase, "fiddle-string operation" to convey my skepticism.

I left him standing at the front door of his home shaded by huge eastern deciduous trees along the sidewalk as I parted for the railroad station. Leaving London, I concluded that *no one* would ever be interested in my ideas about the anterior-cruciate-deficient knee.

Grandpa was glad to be back with his loved ones in Connecticut! We celebrated by going to Rocky Neck Beach the next day, all day long. That night in the little bedroom at May's, Olive began coughing inordinately from lung congestion caused by mitral stenosis. She became a patient in her own alma mater, the Middlesex Memorial Hospital in Middletown for a week. Olive's cousin Lois and her man Lem Hoops lived at Old Lyme, Connecticut. A couple of days later, Lois asked if I would like to visit her neighbor, Dr. Wayne Southwick. I knew he was the chief of orthopaedics at Yale. "You bet, Lois! I'd like nothing better."

The next evening at eight Lem escorted me to the front porch, overlooking the mouth of the Connecticut River, of Dr. Southwick's home. I was loaded with my slides and movie. The doctor and his wife Ann had just returned from a community project organized to save the Saybrook railway station. The professor's eyes were heavy with sleepiness and I felt like an intruding ass. Nevertheless my fantasies were starting to boil over. We watched my entire presentation in his living room.

When it was over, he asked, "Would you show these slides at rounds at Yale this Friday, Ron?"

"I'll show these slides at Yale yesterday," I agreed.

And Friday I found myself standing before a group of thirty or more whom I thought *had* to be *serious surgical critics*. They turned out to be a great bunch, and human, like the rest of us. I did my thing. There was a place in my lecture where I referred to an occasion when I was stumped and didn't know what to do for my patient with a knee instability. As I stood before my Yale audience, perhaps having isolated myself in Ennis, Montana, a bit too long, I vernacularized, "I stood around for a long time with my thumbs up my ass before I figured out such and such."

The talk was over and I, a very lonely man, went up to the hospital café to have a cup of coffee. I sat at a table for two, alone and dejected. All I could think of was what I had said, using the Ennis vulgarity, when a handsome young surgeon sat himself down at my table and with his pen in his hand, he asked me, "Can I pick your brains?"

No one, absolutely no one, had ever honored me before with that question. In zero time, I agreed to have my brains picked. Dr. Tom Johnson, assistant to Dr. Wayne Southwick, picked them to the bone.

Olive improved. Our kids returned to their homes a few days before Olive and I to ours.

A month later Dr. Southwick wrote and insisted that I get busy and write a paper and prepare to present it at the American Orthopaedic Association meeting in Boca Raton, Florida, in June of 1977, a year and a half away. If the paper were accepted, he said there would be a good chance that the *Journal of Bone and Joint Surgery* would publish it. I started writing it on our kitchen table that night.

In mid-October, Dr. Southwick sent Dr. Johnson to Ennis to study my knee cases and to see how I did my knee reconstruction. This was not quite as amazing as it seemed because Dr. Johnson *grew up* in Harlowton, Montana, and it gave him an opportunity to get back home. Nevertheless, I was thrilled to have a staff man from Yale come to Ennis! When he arrived we did four "sling and reef" operations to remedy trick knees. We studied thirty more patients whom I had operated on for this problem.

I was asked to come to New Haven to demonstrate a "sling and reef" operation in March 1976. I was beside myself. Finally comes a chance to teach my tricks. March arrived. I reported. I was to do my operation at the West Haven Veterans' Hospital.

My first shock was to see policemen stationed in the hallways of the *hospitals!* I was told that it was necessary to protect against the frequent episodes of violence, drug-related and not, that were occurring in the hospitals. We never saw *that* when we were young American medical students roaming these same hospital corridors.

Dr. Johnson was ushering me. He told me that my talk at Yale had come at the perfect time. The week before my forty-minute show, the renowned knee surgeon Dr. J. A. Nicholas had spent three days at Yale teaching the Connecticut boys how it was done in New York City. The patient we were to operate on had previously undergone the New York surgeon's five-one reconstruction for anteromedial instability of the knee and it had failed. The knee was still unstable. With this background to the case, Tom led me toward the operating room. We were in hospital operating pants and still in our own undershirts. I was kind of proud of my pink Wallace Beery undershirt (of "Tug Boat Annie" fame) with a few undone buttons at the neck. Here comes Ms. Official United States Veteran's Administration Bureaucrat Nurse to inform me that my pink Wallace Beery undershirt was not appropriate in this United States Hospital.

"This is my undershirt. I like it. So what?"

Exercising a bureaucratic power play, she indicated that it was disturbing and that I would not be permitted to operate. Since we all were about to cover our personal underwear with sterilized garments, this had nothing to do with antiseptic protocol. I indicated that I would take my toys and go home rather than insult the memory of Wallace Beery.

It all calmed down. But my abdomen was getting tight as a balloon with emotional irritation, nervousness, New England beans, and brown bread. We entered the operating room. It was crowded with doctors waiting to see what was going to happen. There was movie-making paraphernalia crowding the area and the movie technician was busy making ready his outfit. Always one in a crowd, this young, smart, busy, snappy-eyed anesthesiologist carried his loaded syringe to the head of the table and squirted the excess out as if he had a water pistol. I was watching him. He sat down. He then flashed a white paper with heavy red-crayon printing (similar to the way movie people clap boards together and say, "Take two!").

In red type, the sign read, SCENE 4: THE DOCTOR NOW FARTS.

At that magic, once-in-a-lifetime, and opportune moment, what else could I possibly do with a bloated, tense abdomen but *oblige*, with unlimited force, duration, audibility, and total satisfaction.

The spell was broken. There was much scurrying and tittering and a temporary emptying of the operating room. My nerves were soothed and I started to operate just as if I'd been in the Madison Valley Hospital. The operation was a success. I never did see, or hear, the movie.

"The Senior Author Is Not One of the Acknowledged Doyens of Knee Surgery"

SINCE THE FALL of 1975, when Dr. Southwick asked me to prepare a paper for the American Orthopaedic Association meeting in Boca Raton, he had become my mentor. The evening I received his written invitation to this proposal I sat at our round kitchen table and started to write the article on an 8½" × 11" yellow legal pad. My *first* words on the *first* draft were, "Recurrent anterior subluxation of the lateral tibial plateau of the knee is a common type of instability. This subluxation can be reproduced clinically and when this is done, the patient immediately recognizes this very demonstration as being the mechanism of his impairment. The instability follows trauma."

The article was roughly completed. After a couple of years and ten revisions, Olive and I walked in the front door of the old Boca Raton Hotel in Florida. They didn't put us up in "The Tower" with the big boys; instead they put us in the old part where we had a big bathtub and a very noisy air conditioner.

At nine PM, Wednesday, June 29, 1977, three prestigious eastern orthopaedic surgeons hosted me around a small cocktail table in a quiet corner of "The Tower" club room. The men kindly offered me piña colada. They told me it was a pineapple-and-coconut mix, which made my tongue hang out with desire. However, because on the following morning I was to address the austere audience of orthopaedic professors, members, and guests of the American Orthopaedic Association, I declined. It was *not* the time to bridle the brain with alcohol. I politely refused the offer.

These three distinguished orthopaedic surgeons were all looking at me. I sniffed kind smiles coming from the men, but I tasted a tiny inquisition. This was and remains quite acceptable to me. After all, these men were leaders in the orthopaedic world. Perhaps they were guarded because they themselves along with the entire contemporary orthopaedic community had not yet gathered the collective concept of the ubiquity of the unstable knee as I had. A grave responsibility, to maintain the integrity of their society and to maintain the integrity of orthopaedic academia, rested upon them. It would be a serious error to give rein to some imposter from where? Oh yes, from Ennis, Montana!

They came directly to the point and one of them asked me, "Tomorrow, you are going to present forty cases of a knee instability that you are describing and have operated on, is that right?"

The answer to that was easy. "Yes."

The next question posed, with all six eyes fixed upon my countenance, was, "How is it that you have gathered *that many cases in Ennis, Montana*? How many people live there—fifteen thousand, perhaps?"

My slightly heated answer was, "Ennis doesn't even have a thousand people in it. Yes, I have operated upon *forty patients* for their trick knees."

Continuing the proper inquisition, one of the men "put it to me" with, "But, Ron, forty patients is a large series to have gathered in such a little place!"

I felt defensive. Were they challenging my honesty?

"Yes, Ennis is very small," I explained. "Patients drive long distances in Montana to show me their knees. I operated on forty patients. I'm trying to tell everybody that this is a *common* instability and that it follows a ruptured anterior cruciate ligament."

The final query was, "What are you going to tell them if *they*"—the accepted authorities of knee ligament surgery—"challenge whether the instability you're going to talk about is as common as you say?"

"My answer will be, 'It is *very* common.' What is wrong with that?"

And suddenly I realized what was happening. These professional leaders were protecting their colleagues from the pain and humility that the evolution of ideas is bound to inflict. But I knew then that they must have thought I had a significant message to spread. It shouldn't be pain. It shouldn't be humility. It should be, "It's time to step on my shoulder, young brother!" Dr. Southwick, one of the three, then kindly taught me: "Ron, Andy Young gets everybody upset when he tells us we're all a bunch of white Anglo-Saxon Protestants. He's right, but it doesn't sit well with us when he states it that way. Don't forget, Ron, some of these men have spent years, a big portion of their lives, on their pet ideas and beliefs about the way a knee works. These are fine men and have given us a lot of knowledge about the knee. The idea that the knee instability you are describing is 'common' may be disturbing to some of these good men because it lessens the importance of their contributions. We just shouldn't be raw, that's all."

I understood their recommendation. No problem with the rawness. Who the hell wants to offend, to be juvenile, or to be injurious? However, let's remind ourselves that the function of an inquisition is to kill the imposter, not the prophet. Let the good ideas not be the temple but happily become one of its bricks!

Sleep, the night before, was impossible. Dr. Southwick had coached me, both previously in New Haven and now in Florida. He was my partner. We left Olive at the side and sat together in the front row, waiting our turn, in the auditorium. Dr. Finder from Chicago presided. The Association had honored Dr. Mark Coventry, the great orthopaedist of the Mayo Clinic. In return, Dr. Coventry had shared his exquisite slides illustrating his recent visit to the Soviet Union. A famous South African orthopaedist was also being honored and preceded me on the docket. He spoke and he spoke. Up to that time, in the course of the meeting, no one had been cut off. I had expressed a worry about this to

Dr. Ward Cassells, a fellow attendant. We had previously become friends in New Haven, where he had given me a lesson in arthroscopy. Dr. Cassells assured me they rarely cut off the speaker. But the South African was taking an awful lot of time. I knew damn well the time of leniency had passed and that I had better keep a fast pace when my turn came.

My turn came. There was a little light issuing from the top of the slanted surface of the pulpit. My text was before me. My slides had been checked twenty times. The world "out there" was dim and consisted of hundreds of heads, thinking heads of orthopaedic critics, heads of the masters of the craft, scholarly heads from Harvard and Oxford. I must have mumbled as I searched for the slide controller. The quiet mumbling resonated in my head, sounding a little like Gary Cooper. I didn't know where *it* came from but I thought, "Cooper's got a good Montana voice."

And I cut loose with the words, "Dr. Finder. Dr. Coventry. Members and Guests."

It was a pinnacle experience to have told my story to all those assembled heads! *However*, as I showed my thirty-eighth slide, a slide of a young man, well slung in his hockey shorts, demonstrating his long leg-brace, which I wanted to discuss, Dr. Finder pressed the button. The red light started to flash. This indicated the gas tank was just about empty! Gary Cooper instantly converted to high-pitched shouting. As the red light kept flashing, Dr. Southwick, gesticulating to me from the first row below shouted, "Keep going, Ron. Keep going!" I raced. Use my notes? Hell with them! They slid off the pulpit as I twisted and turned, I flashed slide after slide. The absolute halt, stop, quit-or-we'll-have-a-train-wreck sign came on at the fifty-sixth slide. To this day, I don't know how anyone could have understood my closing blast. It doesn't matter. I had one hell of a lot of fun delivering during my turn at the party!

After I sat down, Dr. Leach, from Boston, presented the critique of my paper. He later kindly sent me a copy. He said, "This is an informative and provocative paper on a sophisticated subject. The senior author is not one of the acknowledged doyens of knee surgery, but a man who has had extensive clinical and surgical experience and who has given much thought to a problem, the trick knee, which bothers all practicing orthopaedic surgeons. And, most important, he has with his coauthors taken the time and effort to put all this together and present it to us." The rest of the critique was technical and defended the status of the thinking of the day.

I don't remember a thing until the recess. A man in a dark suit came from the back of the room and sought me out. He shook my hand and asked, "How did you get here? Fantastic!" He was Dr. William Harris, professor of orthopaedics at Harvard. Dr. Harris remembered a two-week experience we had together in 1950. As a young medical student visiting Montana in the summer of 1950, he coincidentally spent two weeks doctoring with us. He remembered sleeping in the back room of the log house in Ennis. He reminded me of the slides we prepared from a persisting lesion on Clinton Frisbie's wrist. We found concentric rings and diagnosed blastomycosis. As a couple of young doctors, we were pretty proud of the way we doctored Clinton.

On September 20, 1977, I sent my thirteenth revision of my article to the *Journal of Bone and Joint Surgery*. By then, Dr. Southwick, Dr. Kennedy, my geneticist friend Dr. John Opitz, and my editor friend Mr. Nat Adams had all helped me with the job. The paper was accepted by the editors of the *Journal*, and Dr. Thornton Brown of Boston became a new professional hero of mine.

My paper was returned in an unrecognizable state. Dr. Brown had rewritten paragraphs, condensed sentences, eliminated clauses, inserted "becauses," scratched out cumbersome duplications, and clarified phrases; and after all this, which must have occupied days, he would inquire, how many? more than what? why? I don't understand. Each return of my manuscript put me to work again for at least a couple of fortnights. I revised my manuscript. He followed. Dr. Brown revised the third more gently than the first two drafts. That was the final buffing. About this great man? I gave him the ingredients. He made the cake! He extracted my observations, my experiments, my experiences, my data collections, my thoughts, and my ideas. He then, *with absolutely no distortion or amendment,* labored, guided, and assisted me to write a worthy document of which I am very proud. Thank you, Dr. Brown.

In the December 1978 issue of the *Journal of Bone and Joint Surgery* our article was published. My coauthors, Dr. Tom Johnson, who greatly assisted in the project and was the first man to have "picked my brains," and Professor Wayne Southwick, who listened to and believed and promoted my story, both helped to make my monograph possible. It was the lead article of that month. Thank you, Dr. Johnson. Thank you, Dr. Southwick.

The abstract in the *Journal* started, "Recurrent anterior subluxation of the lateral tibial plateau is a common type of chronic knee instability resulting from trauma."

I picked up that issue of the *Journal* in the Ennis post office next to Heinie Rakeman's drugstore and in front of our old log house. What a day!

PART 4

Now

Are Highs Really High?

A COUPLE OF times a decade ago, at our place, while sitting overlooking Spring Creek and the mountains beyond, and while waiting for Olive to spoil us with supper, my friend Richard Avedon and I talked about our eventual metamorphosis from men into geezers. We were curious and had a dread. Like death, the idea envisions limits and demands an economy of our allotted time. Are we geezers now that we have told our stories? Perhaps. Perhaps our storytelling is geezerhood's scream to the children to revere life with passion.

My rediscovery of the cause of the trick knee and its remediation, and my promulgation of the subject were unquestionably a pinnacle for me. Following this comes geezerhood, but because I deny it, I recall some highs, lows, and hassles that have come with the present demise of the American doctor's autonomy.

After the publication in the big *Journal of Bone and Joint Surgery*, exciting invitations for me to expound on the knee were offered in different parts of the country. Olive reminds me to explain that all of these trips were self-financed at the cost of a garage or a sunroom we never enjoyed. I can't deny that it was a pleasure.

Olive, Tom Johnson, and I, with the help of a graphic designer Dana Aaberg, built a fine display of our knee work that we intended to exhibit at the San Francisco meeting of the American Academy of Orthopaedic Surgeons in February 1979. In preparation for this, we had produced a movie hologram to illustrate the pathological motion of the knee slipping out of its joint, slippage caused by a ruptured anterior cruciate knee ligament. We worked on the hologram at night after climbing many flights of stairs in an ancient building at Montana State University. The television department helped us in our project. This hologram was to be produced in San Francisco and we were to retrieve it just prior to the meeting. To transport the clumsy exhibit, we rented a large recreational vehicle from a Bozeman source and drove the monster home. Our quarter-mile-long driveway from the country road to our house had been plugged with a quarter-mile-long east-to-west snowdrift since November. All we could do was drive the monster across the snow-blown fields of our neighbor and park it on the other side of the fence, sixty yards from the house. At loading time, ten o'clock at night, two things happened. The water system of the vehicle froze, and a driving blizzard from the north was upon us. With extension cords, hot water, cardboard "toboggans," ripped snow pants, and Olive's leg skinned from repeated fence-climbing, we did the job.

We left our snowbank and, with only one breakdown in Sparks, Nevada, we reached San Francisco. We found the "hologram factory" in some back alley. As we approached the entrance to the production studio, in an adjacent doorway stood a juvenile couple, belly to belly with their drawers at the ankles, keeping right at it. Apparently our presence had not interrupted their pornographic productions.

We acquired our hologram, then proceeded to unload at the San Francisco civic center. We paid one crew to empty the vehicle, and another to truck it to its assigned station. We assembled the display which we had produced. As we were finishing, a very tall, Celtic-countenanced, middle-aged man stood in the background for a few minutes. Olive was using screws to assemble the skirt to the exhibit when the man advanced. He was a tough union boss. He threatened to call the entire labor force of the civic center to a halt if Olive didn't put down her screwdriver and stop work. He didn't know Olive! We finished our assembly ourselves, heated but unscathed. Our exhibiting neighbor's projector was stolen, wrecking his display right away and making us apprehensive.

It was an ego trip to stand by our exhibit and answer questions from renowned North American and European visitors. It was a memorable experience to demonstrate our test on the knee of a famous American knee authority, an old hero of mine whom I had never met before. I overheard one of our old fathers of knee-ligament surgery, sitting across from our exhibit, telling his friends with gruff grunts, "There's no such thing as a 'pivot shift'!" ("Pivot shift" had become the accepted name of the trick-knee dysfunction we've been relating.) I was curious. Why? Because his untroubled defiance of a newly entrenched concept suggested either he hadn't read about it, hadn't been taught about it, or hadn't thought about it. He was either a wise old skeptic or, possibly, and sadly, he suffered from the ultimate liability of longevity, geezerhood.

After the hiring and paying of three labor groups to take apart and load our exhibit, we left San Francisco and drove the recreational monster up the California and Oregon coastal highways. We arrived home with our quarter-mile drive still buried beneath its quarter-mile-long snowdrift. We unloaded our stuff, back and forth, over the barbed-wire fence now sunk in even more snow. I'll never know why we bothered to take the exhibit home! Then, my fantasy told me I better keep it: "I might need to show it in Boston! Perhaps they may even call me to display it in London!"

I first heard Dr. John Feagin speak in San Francisco in 1975. His chosen opus has been an in-depth, extraordinary, international search for, and distribution of, complete knowledge about the cruciate ligaments of the knee. He has organized a study group dedicated to this. He has sought, befriended, and urged authorities to compose and deliver the knowledge each has accumulated on the subject. This has resulted in his textbook *The Crucial Ligaments*. His work is critical because, through his book, he has distributed knowledge, enabling orthopaedists to better care for their patients. Whenever I receive a letter from John, I know I'm in for a month's work. I like to oblige him when I can. He has enriched my life by having enlisted me to talk at symposia, to write in an orthopaedic periodical, and to enter "The Pivot Shift" chapter in his text. Dr. Feagin has honored me many times and in many generous ways.

Soon after giving the paper in Boca Raton, Dr. Tom Johnson returned from Yale to join in an orthopaedic practice with Dr. Perry Berg in Billings, Montana. I am proud to call these two men and their group my colleagues, and they have been extremely generous to me, time and again, in many ways. For years they have invited me to lecture at the Perry Berg Symposia, then always wining and dining Olive and myself. I pretty nearly burst, a few years ago, when they named one session a "Ron Losee" meeting. They never object to my obscene titles, "The Pus Factor" and "The Rot Factor," not even to the title of my talk at last November's session "Anterior Crewshit Stories."

I didn't know one could be called "professor" when awarded an honorary Doctor of Science degree. At seventy years old, I attended a knee meeting in Stockholm with Olive. Dr. Roly Jakob, from Switzerland and one of my orthopaedic heroes, approached and called me, with a big smile, "Professor." He went on to say, "Ron, congratulations. You're a professor now. I sent enough material to your University in Montana to give you the Nobel prize! They told me they gave you your doctorate." Thank you, Dr. Jakob.

In March of 1986 a Bordeaux surgeon politely asked to visit us in Ennis. An orthopaedist from *France* coming to Ennis? You bet! Up goes *le drapeau de France* to top the flagpole of Cactus Rock Ranch! *"Bonjour,"* to our new, smiling, black-haired friend at Bozeman airport. He had been royally treated in Toronto and Philadelphia. He then came to Montana, directly from, he said, "God," a very famous American knee surgeon from no-matter-where, who, preoccupied, had slighted our friend from his "kingdom of kneedom." M. le Docteur Guy Liorzou was our guest from Wednesday until Sunday. At the time, he spoke some English. I spoke less French. No communication problem, just a few detours. Dr. Johnson came from Billings to help. On Thursday, we did our "sling and reef" operations. On Friday we showed patients we had operated on more than a decade previously and patients we had *not operated on*, who lived comfortably with the pivot-shift dysfunction. X-rays of their knees suggested deterioration had not occurred as might have been expected. Dr. Liorzou had not heretofore seen a surgeon showing those of his patients who had been selectively *not* operated upon. We showed our new French friend our failures. It is essential to show failures. It is dishonest *not* to show failures, and *studied failure* becomes our great teacher! From Saturday noon until that midnight, Dr. Liorzou quizzed me in my study, which he now calls the "orthopaedic jail." The session ended in time to send him off to Oregon for his next search. I had never had the honor of such a prolonged brain-picking session. We hated to see him leave on Sunday.

Dr. Liorzou completed his study by visiting renowned knee surgeons in Europe and North America. From these surgeons, he gathered the tests each had devised to diagnose the different and intricate ligament deficiencies that spoil the function of the knee. Liorzou was convinced that the overuse of modern instrumental techniques was harmfully supplanting the traditional, lucid ways used to diagnose knee dysfunctions. He thought orthopaedists were losing valuable and basic clinical diagnostic skills.

By 1990, Dr. Liorzou had published his book in French, *Le Genou ligamentaire*, which was later translated to English as *Knee Ligaments*. Professor Werner Müller of Switzerland and I share the dedication page. I am simultaneously proud and humble, proud of my French friend's accomplishment and humbled by his sincere honor.

On Olive's birthday, June 13, 1990, our Becky and her

family saw us off from Calgary. We flew east. The narrow, pink line of a northern horizon over the Atlantic was perhaps the most lonely natural sight of my life. While looking, I remembered listening to Lindbergh's arrival in Paris, listening over a one-tube, homemade radio set, listening by sharing one of the round Bakelite ear-pieces of the headset with grandma's neighbor, Mrs. Rall. That was in the spring of 1927. Soon the green fields of France filled our window with their clustered, red-tile-roofed villages. The view told us: "Olive, Ron, you two old kids are in France!" Dr. Liorzou and his loved ones gave us hugs as we stepped off the train in Bordeaux. Our friendship has become cherished. Orthopaedics did that!

We attended the knee meeting in Sweden and finished our trip with a three-week stay at the home of our distant cousin in London, Justin Howse, who is also an orthopaedist. Justin has had a more extensive orthopaedic training and is honored to care for the extremity problems of the Royal Ballet. He has become a subspecialist in extremity pathology of the dancer. Justin crowned my orthopaedic career by arranging an invitation for me to speak to a group of London orthopaedic surgeons.

We gathered in a stone-cold, dark hospital amphitheater. Olive was a guest also and sat in front as I talked to a group of the Royal National Orthopaedists in London about the pivot-shift dysfunction of the knee. Twenty or more surgeons that day were kind enough to listen to my story in that austere gallery in London.

As I lectured, I thought, "Jesus, Ron, you are talking to these British surgeons, in this London hospital in the pit of this cold, semicircular steep slope of men looking down. These men are British doctors! They are serious. They *are* my kind. They have the same interest. They have trained vastly more than I. Think of the orthopaedic knowledge these men have gathered! Why compare? My career is most over now! Where's Justin? There he is in the front row. There's Olive with Shirley over there. How am I going to show my tests? I'll step right up on the pulpit and lift my pant leg. I'll use my own knee.

They let me talk an hour. No red light flashed this time!"

Nannie Writes to Becky

FOR A CHRISTMAS present of all presents to her parents in 1982, our daughter Becky prepared a notebook full of yarns about our general practice days in Ennis that had been related to Becky in letter form.

The following tales are written by Nan Taylor, the granddaughter of a pioneer physician of Virginia City, Montana. She worked for us for years as a practical nurse in the Madison Valley Hospital and now no longer lives. Her words come from her heart and accurately convey insight, and she was able to relate what I could not.

Above and Beyond the Call of Duty

It was after midnight and Doc was just getting ready to go home—He looked so tired and worried I ask him what was wrong. He said the tube in the X-ray had burned out. Said it cost $750 to replace it, he didn't think he could do it. Just then the front door bell rang, when I answered it there stood a young couple—The father was holding a little girl in his arms. He said, "our baby is sick." A beautiful frail little girl that was convulsing. The father said they had been on the road ten days with very little money—had been sleeping in the car and eating in the car; they were trying to get to Seattle to his family. After the little girl rallied Doc had me give her a bath and put one of the gowns from the nursery on her and a clean blanket—He sent her to a neurologist in Great Falls with a letter to get the diagnosis and the name of a Dr. in Seattle. Just before they left I saw Doc give the father a roll of bills. After they left Doc said "Pray I don't get a call out of town tonight—I had him put my tires on his car and I'd never make it out of town with those tires. He said he'll pick up some tires in Great Falls that will get them on to Seattle." When I walked back to the desk, I had a feeling that from somewhere above he looked down on the little scene tonight and smiled and said "This is how I meant my world to be, that ye love one another." When I went to work the next night the people were gone to Seattle and Doc's tires were back on his car. A few days later a good Samaritan had had the X-ray tube put in and all was well with the M.V.H.

The Fish Weighed 8 lbs. on the Baby Scales

It was always a happy day when I could gather my little fishermen together. Jon and Becky Losee, Jim and Penny Phillips (our chief nurse at the time, Mrs. Bea Phillip's children), and Eddy Taylor (Nan's son) and take them to the fish hatchery to fish in the ponds. This day Jon had really caught a big one. After I had cleaned him we came home. At the top of the hill Jon asked me to take him to the hospital so he could show his Dad the fish. But when we got in the waiting room the office girl told Jon his Dad was with a patient and to take his fish and go home. At that Jon opened his mouth and started yelling—Papa, Papa. Doc came charging out of the office to see what had happened to the No. one son. He took Jon through the hospital and let him show his fish to all the patients, then he took him to the nursery and weighed his fish. I wondered if this wasn't the first fish that was ever weighed on the baby scales in a hospital. Years have passed by since that day, and my little fishermen are all grown and out in the world on their own.

A Dark Night in November

It was midnight—the dark hour, and we were just finishing up a busy shift at M.V.H. Doc Losee had four surgical pts (patients) booked in starting at 8 AM. I was sitting at the desk signing off the charts for the night shift. Doc came to the office door and said Nannie watch the little hill tonight. Its icy and slick and we don't want a car wreck in tonight. Little did either of us know that our trails would cross again that night as the results of a car wreck. It was 2 AM there was a knock on my door—it was Ellis Thompson. He said Aunt Nan, Eddie (Nan's son) has had a little wreck hurt his foot and Doc Losee wants you to come to the hospital. When we got to the hospital the ambulance was pulled into the emergency door. I went down through the hospital. I stopped at the door. Doc was with my son. It was a bad scene. Doc looked at me and said Nannie I know you've had a lot of trouble but your facing the worst trouble here tonight you've ever faced. I think Doc thought I would go to pieces—but he forgot that he himself had taught me to conceal your emotions around the sick—that a time of crisis was no time for hysteria or tears. I walked over and kissed my boy and said a prayer. Harlow (the combined undertaker and ambulance driver) took my arm and helped me to the waiting room. As soon as they had Eddie in his room Doc told me to stay with him and keep checking the vital life signs, that he and Dr. Wilkins were going to have a piece of toast and a cup of coffee. Rev. Nick McKinny was with Ed (Nannie's husband in the waiting room). In just a flash the blood pressure and pulse changed—I thought no this can't be happening to my son. I called the head nurse in—she immediately called the Drs., they came in and looked at Eddie—went out and into the office. I looked at Nick who had his hand on Eddie's chest—his head bowed in prayer. I went and knocked on the office door and went in. Madeline was smoking. Doc Losee was standing at the window looking out. I turned to Dr. Wilkins and said "My boy isn't going to make it is he?" He said "It looks awful bad." Doc Losee whirled around and said "Hell tell her the truth he's dying and Madeline won't give the anesthesia." She (Madeline O'Neil, our chief nurse and anesthetist) said, Doc, I can't give anesthesia to a dying boy. Doc said "I only wanted to try." I said if you want to try—I want you too. Doc asked Dr. Wilkins "Gene, will you give a spinal?" He said yes.

I saw Olive come and go into where Doc was, and I felt comforted because I knew these two working together were a wonderful team, and with Dr. Wilkins to assist I felt Eddie had the best. Olive came out in a few minutes and said they were taking Eddie into surgery, she said "Nan if we have to come out in a little while and tell you he is gone—will you blame Doc?" I said "No never—if it had to happen tonight in Alder Gulch or on the steps of Rochester (Mayo Clinic in Rochester, Minnesota) I would want him here with Doc Losee." It was a little after noon when Rev. Nick McKinny came out and said they had taken Eddie to his room, and I could see him for a minute. Doc was sitting on the floor leaning against the wall. His surgical suit was soaking wet from perspiration and he looked almost as white as his patient. He looked up and said "Nannie don't build up any hopes he has his hand on deaths doorknob and all he has to do is turn it." It was nine days later he called me to his office and said "Nannie, Eddy is going to make it." What do you say to a man who has just given you back your son? I could find no words except, "Thank you my friend."

(We must remember: this is a mother's story. The eating of the toast at 2 AM is probably quite accurate. I don't remember the "doorknob" part of this story, but on that "Dark Night" Nan's Eddy *was* seriously injured. He had incurred a chest injury, along with a tension pneumothorax, that seemed threatening to us. After we had "stabilized" his respiratory function, he also needed an anesthetic to enable us to operate on a serious lower tibia-fibula fracture.)

In the Heart of a Hollyhock

In working with Dr. Losee I had noticed when he was real tired he seemed to walk with a slight limp. This had been a long tiring day for him. With four surgeries and a boy in with a broken arm. He came to the office to write his final orders for the day, and when he walked out I noticed the limp and I thought how tired he must be. In just a few minutes he came back and said, "Nannie, come here I want to show you something." Just out in front of the hospital were hollyhocks blooming. He said take my camera and look down into the hollyhock through the lens. I did. It was like looking into a chasm of beautiful crystals of every color. This so impressed me that as tired as he was he would take time to share this beauty with a friend. That night I wrote this poem.

Doc

Deep in the heart of a hollyhock,
I looked into the heart of you—
Saw all the things you had done
and those things still left to do.
I saw you rushing
from one hectic day into another—
Always telling yourself that tomorrow you
would rest. I saw you putting aside the
things for which your own heart might yearn.
I saw you giving to your people so much
and asking so little in return. I saw

the speed of the passing years—The
rapidity in which all things must end.
I saw all this in the head of a hollyhock
at days end.

A Little Cloud,
a Little Threat

THE FINALE BEGINS. The fatigue, the tender day-and-night
years of family practice have passed. The challenges of surgical drama are over. The luck of discoveries and
rediscoveries, the innovations, the searching that comes
with daily work now subside. The thrill of presentation is
a memory. This is all the natural and aging program. There
is new urge to play a little, to tell and teach, and yes, dammit, to shout to the young, to urge them to look within, to
find a star, to serve each other, and for God's sake, to pre-
serve their idealism throughout their lives. Olive and I have
tried to do that with neither apology nor embarrassment,
nor are we sorry. To tell and teach! Doctor, translated from
the Latin, means "teacher." They call me "Doc"! Otis
Crooker used to call Olive "Mrs. Doc."

I watch modern changes rapidly de-professionalize and
steal the old autonomies, freedoms, and joys of the medical
practice. Instead of, "Is it right?" I hear over and over
again, a pitiable, "Is it legal?" In medicine, law cannot be
enough, because law trails the Golden Rule.

Forty miles south of Ennis, the Hutchins' Bridge across
the Madison River repeatedly and mercilessly rattled in the
late spring and then again in October when the cattle
pushed their way over the manure-strewn planks and

through the rusted truss-works. Governing the movement were the ranch families and their hired men, all mounted, weaving their quarter horses slowly and deliberately among the cattle mass. These movements were the transfers of the owners' herds from the individual ranches to and from the government forest grazing areas surrounding the West Fork of the Madison River. The Hutchins' log homestead adjoined the approach to the bridge. One of the daughters of this pioneer family, Edith Kirby, lived in this log home in 1950. One of her sisters, Bessie, was Mrs. Jimmy Shewmaker. Jimmy Shewmaker was my friend. He was teased by the community as being a bit slow to pay his arrears. Jimmy must have held a bill from me for a while. In my office one afternoon during that period his classic remark to me was, "Gee, Doc, if I *paid* you I wouldn't *owe* you!" Mrs. Kirby's other sister, Mrs. Cloe Hutchins Paugh, suffered with congenital hip dislocations and was forced to rock from side to side with each footfall. This did not slow Cloe down one bit. She seated herself low in the driver's seat of her big car. With a little effort you could see her head through the steering wheel. Cloe generously donated her expertise and service to the benefit of the Madison Valley Hospital from its inception until the end of her life.

In 1950, Cloe had me in her little office and advised, "Doctor, I think it would be wise if you took out malpractice insurance."

I agreed and I "took it out." I search my 1950 logbook and see that Cloe charged me $4.46 a month. For that year, I deducted a total of $53.52 as my medical-malpractice-insurance expense.

In 1957 and 1958, while we were working at the Royal Victoria Hospital, I paid no malpractice premium. Dr. A. A. Butler, one of my orthopaedic instructors, confided to me one morning, as we were scrubbing together in preparation for an operation, that his total Canadian medical-malpractice bill for the year was fifteen dollars.

Upon my return to Ennis in 1959, I did not purchase

medical-malpractice insurance. I had no intention of committing malpractice!

Perhaps two years later, one morning while sitting with my friend Phil Pallister at his breakfast table in Boulder, prior to a day's work at the institution, the subject of malpractice came up.

"Phil"—I took my stand—"I'm not going to pay malpractice insurance. I'm not going to practice *mal*! 'Mal' means evil, means bad, means abandonment, means drunkenness, means operating when you don't know how, means neglect, means battery, means wantonness. We don't do that crap, Phil! Why should we need malpractice insurance?"

Phil Pallister had given these matters more thought than I had. His immediate and towering closure of the debate was, "Ron, you're not thinking of the *compensation* component of medical-malpractice insurance. You don't *mean* to leave a sponge in the abdomen! But if you *do* accidentally leave a sponge in your patient's abdomen, at least your patient could be remunerated for the expense and misery resulting from the accident. The compensation part of malpractice insurance is morally right."

Phil won. I purchased medical-malpractice insurance again from our friend Mrs. Cloe Paugh.

Cloe passed on. Juanita Stalcup set up a lively insurance business in Hal Pasley's refurbished garage across the street from Cloe's place. After Cloe's death, Juanita sold me my malpractice premiums.

The price of the premiums went up and up. I paid Juanita $7,019.20 for the malpractice policy covering 1975.

On September 23, 1975, Juanita sent me a letter informing me that my premium would go up to $30,000.00 for the following year. A few weeks after I received this note, Juanita was kind enough to come to our house to hear our decision one Sunday morning. She sat in our kitchen in our home, now on Spring Creek. She was speaking from the two-seater in front of the kitchen fireplace. Olive and I were at the kitchen table. There was no problem. It was decided. We couldn't afford medical malpractice any more.

Would we quit? No. We *had* to keep on working. We *wanted* to keep on working. We were *going* to keep on working! It was a man-and-wife decision. We had nothing when we came to Ennis. We had made no fortune after we came! We all have to leave the earth with nothing. We were not going to let fear ruin our lives. We had more work to do. We'd continue doctoring.

I looked at 1975's logbook. Olive and I did not cheat. We paid all our taxes. In 1975 our net income was $46,250.37. From this we paid $13,712.51 to the I.R.S. and $3,111.42 to the State of Montana. This left us a fat $29,426.44 to live on that year. Had we purchased the $30,000.00 medical malpractice premium that year, we would have had a fat *minus* $573.44. To be perfectly honest, there would have been a hell of a deduction that would have brought us up to the poverty level.

I couldn't meet the insurance levy. I had questions.

Who would get the $30,000.00? Deserving patients injured by doctors?

How much of the $30,000.00 will the insurance companies keep?

How much will the lawyers get of the $30,000.00?

Why the sudden, astronomical increase in the premium that year?

Has a new source of wealth been tapped? By whom?

Is this new enterprise good for the ill and injured?

Is malpractice battery?

Why isn't malpractice a criminal offense?

Why is the contingency-fee system permitted?

Doesn't this crowd the courts?

Doesn't this cause nuisance suits?

Why isn't the successful defendant of a malpractice suit recompensed for legal fees and inconvenience by the unsuccessful plaintiff? Isn't this the British system? This would surely ease the courts' dockets.

Why should the deserving victim of malpractice bear the uncertainty of recompense? The extravagant legal expense? Since most of the bad outcomes are no one's fault, why not have a "no-fault compensation system" to assure recompense and defray legal expense?

Is society so cynical that this is impossible?

Why not put more rotten doctors and lawyers in jail?

So Olive and I continued our life unprotected against malpractice suits. Our naive, our free, and our happy way of doing "our thing"—trying to fix dislocated shoulders, fractured limbs, slipping knees—had been spoiled by a vague uncertainty. We continued to practice uninsured, happily, but with niggling worry—until the hassle we'd been dreading commenced on January 3, 1985, the beginning of my sixty-fifth year, when most American geezers get their social security check.

"Woe Unto You, Lawyers!"

IN OUR SOCIETY of happy plaintiffs' lawyers, the day came when one of them delivered me a message initiating a lawsuit.

A malpractice suit, when uninsured, meant the threat of the loss of our home and all means of our future support. At sixty-five, the prospect of poverty is disturbing because, by then, we had become used to indoor toilets and running water. Also, we had run out of energy. So, the human protective instincts, as strong as thirst, forced defensive tactics. What had initiated the legal action against us?

Seven years previously, a Helena orthopaedist had referred his patient to see if I could help remedy a troublesome ankle. Three previous ankle operations had failed to satisfy his patient. After examination, it was my judgment that all I could offer was an ankle solidification operation (arthrodesis). I did my best to inform the patient of the seriousness of an ankle arthrodesis. I stressed that the ankle would never hinge again. I exhorted there would be, forever, no further tapping time with the music after the ankle was solidified! This permanent stiffness would be the payment for alleviating the pain of the imperfect joint. I think I even put the patient in a stout plaster walking cast for two weeks to emphasize this point. Yes, there's risk: death from anesthesia, amputation following bone infection, reoperations for failures, and special shoes. Absolutely! Let the patient understand and balance the risks and realistic expectations. Let the patient, not the doctor, say "go" to elective surgery.

I did the ankle arthrodesis. After the operation, the referring surgeon continued the patient's care. Soon after the operation, the patient walked in the woods, still wearing the cast, and stepped on an upright stick. The stick thrust its way through the cast deeply into the bottom of the foot in front of the heel. The dirty stick infected and scarred the deep tissues, causing contractures that dipped the forefoot downward. A higher-heeled shoe was in order, but the patient described being comfortable both barefooted and in a flat shoe at the last visit to my office.

A thousand miles away and seven years later, the patient complained that the foot pained her during bowling. The patient's orthopaedist tried to help with another operation. He wedged the tibia, just above the old ankle-solidification site to tilt the front of the foot up. This curved the bottom of the leg bone forward, just above the solid ankle, forward like a comma. Although the forefoot would not tend to tiptoe so much now, the new forward curve made the heel hit the ground harder with each step. This pounding overloaded the little "subtalar" joint still functioning between the old, solidified ankle joint and the top of the heel bone. (This remnant joint allowed useful side-to-side foot motion.) In no time this little joint ground down and became so painful, that it, too, need solidification. That made five operations! No wonder the person lashed out!

Who got the ax? Me! Why? Because the surgeon who had made the wedge implied I had goofed and had solidified the old ankle with too much of a downward direction of the foot.

Had I mistakenly fused the ankle in a tiptoe position? No! Am I perfect? No! Hell, no! Who is? It is possible to fuse the ankle in too severe a tiptoe position, but I *didn't*. It was easy to see that my arthrodesis on this person was correct when the X-rays were studied. The *forefoot* ahead of the ankle joint had contracted downward and this had nothing to do with my fusion. The tiptoeing was caused by the stick injury after my operation. The X-rays showed a proper arthrodesis.

How to defend? I learned—the doctor-defendant must do the scut-work or he is going to be in deep shit. The doctor knows the technicalities. His attorney does not. His attorney knows the law, the great mystery! The doctor does not. I sent copies of X-rays to great surgeons from Seattle to London. My friend Dr. Wayne Southwick wrote that there was no merit to the allegation. The great ankle authority, Josiah Grant Bonnin of London, studied the X-rays of the plaintiff, then stressed the harm done to the plaintiff by the surgeon who wedged the tibia. We all knew this operation ruined the subtalar joint and necessitated the final operation. The lawsuit never materialized. The complaint was settled "with prejudice." (That sounded bad, but believe me, I learned; it's good!)

Why tell such a dreary story? I do this to protest a wrong.

Bad scene! Outrage! Mental rape! I've never hated. It was close. Is this what lawsuits do to people? The event implied stinging disgrace. Within a week, Olive's sister May asked what I had done wrong. I want to be the one to say, "I'm not perfect," rather than hear over and over, "Nobody's perfect, Doc, don't worry, the trial will come out okay!" Office appointments were canceled. "What'd ja do, Doc?" forced tiresome repetitious explanations.

The event was a hassle. I never want another one.

This defense occupied Olive's thinking and mine and robbed our life from January to sometime in late May. We gathered evidence. Copied X-rays. I'm lucky I had them. I sent them to an authority on the ankle. When would he answer? What would he say? We saw the lawyer. We waited again. We sought witnesses who wanted nothing to do with it. Even old friends balked.

We were embarrassed by financial offers to help pay the legal expense! We read, filled out, and replied to endless documents from the State Malpractice Board that always ended with "Have a nice day!" Enough said.

Such activity devours time which is life! It corrodes the desire to innovate. Why bother to learn new ideas, new techniques? The trial lawyers are waiting for failure.

Twenty years ago at the New York meeting of the American Academy of Orthopaedic Surgeons, a New York orthopaedist asked me what I did if I mistakenly removed a meniscus from the knee? My answer was loud. "Jesus, man, I hurt the patient. I meant no harm. Let's stand true. I tell the patient. I tell the father. I tell the mother. I tell the nurses. I tell my doctor friends. I tell and talk. Let's learn from the booboo; that's our duty. I don't want to do that again! Tell the world!"

The little man smirked and asked, "Where do you live?"

I answered, "Montana, why?"

The little man said, "You wouldn't last a minute in New York. They'd sue the bejesus out of you."

Malpractice insurance protects the doctor against a financial disaster but may tempt the initiation of a malpractice action without merit because of the attraction of a large money pool. Defensive medicine is costly to the nation. It can postpone an urgent operation because the fear of a possible malpractice suit can force the surgeon to waste valuable time obtaining "defensive" tests and consultations until it is too late to avert a fatality.

The threat of malpractice suits has destroyed the practice of medicine in many small Montana towns. The income of many of the general practitioners in these little towns is insufficient to maintain a malpractice premium, especially the coverage for obstetrics. Can uninsured doctors deliver the ranchers' wives, their hired men's wives, storekeepers' wives, or the waitresses any more? Yes, but with terror. Many have quit delivering babies because the birth of a defective child or an unforeseen obstetrical accident would ruin them. The small-town physicians have been displaced by the midwives and physician's assistants. Economic efficiency? Perhaps. However, these small communities may have lost a valuable asset. They were highly educated physicians who served these communities. These are the physicians able to *teach* the midwives and assistants who now replace them. These were the physicians like Dave Rossiter who became proficient in X-ray technology, like Phil Pallister who has genetic syndromes named after him.

A new age has dawned.

Just after midday of January 3, 1985, I received notification that I was to be sued. I deliberately walked out the entrance door to the clinic with no boots, or hat, or coat. I was considering a long walk to the west and to my death. Who wants to live in a world like this if this is society's reward for my life's efforts? I crossed the highway. I passed the rodeo grounds. I approached a new road I hadn't been on before. It was the road to the new golf course. Elmer Hotvedt, my old pharmacist friend, drove his vehicle past me. He stopped. He tried to talk to me. He tried to get me to get in his car. I said nothing to the good man. I kept walking toward the west. I climbed the foothills. I didn't know I was as strong as I seemed to be and I feared it would take longer than I wanted. I kept going and going, thinking that when the sun went down it would get colder and I would get sleepy and freeze. After a couple of hours I must have been in the area that our kids used to talk about, "the Rockies." To my right were caves. At my feet were bobcat tracks. Go to sleep? That would be all right. Have a bobcat come tearing out of one of those caves and claw my balls off? I grabbed up a big club, got mad, and took one hell of a walk. After a while I could see pickup trucks roaming the hills. They had formed a search party for this old man. That made me kind of proud. I sat for a while in a snowbank and marveled at how close they came without seeing me. I then boldly struck out for a long, detoured walk home. The moon came up. By then there were dozens of pickup trucks with their tiny lights to be seen, crawling over the foothills like ants, but now far away from me. After a seven-hour walk, I saw the full moon well up in the sky. The wind came up. Hypothermia threatened. I pushed the front door of our house wide open. Olive threw her arms around me. Our old friend Rita Gress, who had operated with us for so many years, was there keeping Olive company on that bad night.

Brandy never tasted so good. I sat there in my chair in a half-trance until two AM. When I stood up to go to bed, my right iliopsoas muscle contracted, and there I stood by the bedroom door on one foot. The opposite contracted thigh was fixedly flexed at a right angle at the hip, with the knee bent 90° and my foot pointing toward the floor. I stood there like the crowing cock. I had the rigor of the "rooster syndrome." I passed out. I woke up to see Ron Handlos, my good physician's-assistant friend, who came to help. Every muscle was cramping, and I learned how well a shot of potassium works when Olive poured out a teaspoonful of the stuff and said, "Take this. You old fool!"

Times Are Different

I QUIT WORKING in the operating room October of 1992. No one is going to say to me, "Doc, you're getting too old to operate. You're going to kill somebody if you keep it up!" If that ever happened, *that* would be relying upon the law. How many times have I said, "Law is not enough"? By the time one waits for the law to fix it, it's too late!

"Did you quit operating?" I am asked.

"Yes."

"Did you quit practicing altogether?"

"No. I still consult with patients once a week."

A typical day of consultations is quite different from the old days. It is defensive medicine in action.

A dozen years ago the hospital expanded and stuck a lab wing to the east, which wrecked my view of the mountains. When Harker Dale, the contractor, finished the building and heard me bitching, he laughed at me and told me to stick a picture of the mountains in the window. There's some black humor to that. Later they added a building to the north. This killed the view of the Tobacco Roots. Then I had a conniption fit, I confess. I am still offended by the insensitivity. If I can't see the mountains, why am I here? They did fix up a little room here to calm me down *a bit*. You still can't see the Tobacco Roots, but you *can* see the Beehive in the Madison Range.

On my new office wall hangs an old Hogarth reprint that Squee Gerard gave me years ago. The engraving is called "The Company of Undertakers." I call it my "anti-hypocrisy/ role-playing" picture, my "I-don't-want-to-be-like-that" picture. It displays a cluster of fat and pompous physicians of the eighteenth century who are amply furnished with wigs and warts. Every doctor should study this beauty. If my bedside manner ever got too thick, one look at those old boys fixed that problem.

Also hanging on the wall is an ancient hospital scene. In it is my granddad when he was a young doctor. He's watching the surgeon take a boy's leg off. The man at the head of the table is pouring ether over a gauze-covered sieve just the way we used to do it. The picture is over a hundred years old. Doctors operated with their bare hands then!

My grandma's old slate hangs near the photo. She used

it in the 1860s and 1870s before they had pencils and tablets available for the kids. If my words get too raunchy and I think of Grandma, I taper off a bit—for a while.

A sketch of Winternitz, my old pathology professor, looks down with the rest.

And there is Gordon Petrie ready to give me hell.

I'm "going beyond." An eight-inch-high model of a backhouse sits on my big desk. It's hard for a person with an active mind to resist opening the door to the little privy. When they do, the whole shebang springs apart because it has a mouse trap mechanism waiting to be sprung! Each occasion merits a little pencil mark on the back of it.

Charles Brozovich from Butte rewarded me with the little backhouse. He did so when we finished a reconstruction job on his kneecap. He had fractured his patella. An orthopaedic surgeon had operated. As with all of us who operate, "You can't win 'em all." It failed. The two halves of the patella had remained separated for a couple of years. Each time Charles bore weight on the injured side with that knee bent, it would fold. He dropped to the floor like an ox. And, he'd land right on it. When he first arrived he was so drunk his wife had to tell me his story. He was yellow with jaundice. I thought then, *the hell with operating on his knee. He's dying from alcoholism*! I scared the bejesus out of him, and insisted upon a detoxification program. He sweat it out, beat the horror, and returned to live again, with pride! I'm proud too (of both of us), and to be his friend! I operated and the surgery succeeded. When he could hunt mushrooms again, he came in all smiles and gave me my backhouse treasure. Every time Mr. Brozovich returns, he wants to know the score. It's a hundred and sixty-five.

On another typical day, my secretary, Mrs. Danette Clark, tells me a patient with an elbow problem is ready. I meet the patient. He is a merchant from Butte. I remind him that Butte is my favorite city and we get down to business.

"How do you know you have a tennis elbow?"

"I don't know, Doc; that's what they told me."

"Which elbow?"

"The left one."

"Are you left-handed?"

"No."

"How'd it start?"

The patient answers, "My wife had me painting our guest house last summer when it started. I must have been holding heavy pails of paint in my left hand. I'm not sure. I thought it would go away, but it never did."

"Did they give you a cortisone shot?"

"Yes."

"Did it work?"

"After the pain went away, it felt so good I thought it did. For a week."

"Let me see it."

The man rolls up the sleeve of his left arm. A proper examination of his elbow continues. He has full range of motion. There is no deformity, swelling, or other irregularity. I ask him to point to and touch the area of his elbow that bothers him. He places the forefinger of his right hand on the skin of his left elbow just below the lateral epicondyle.

I clasp his left hand and wrist and ask him to extend his wrist against resistance. He winces a bit and again points to the same spot. I then poke an area a bit lower down the arm to make sure the interosseous nerve is not involved. I do Gary Crawford's test for this also. I search the inner side of his joint and his opposite elbow. Some patients have bilateral problems.

I have him sit by my desk. I tell him he has a "tennis elbow."

He answers, "Yes, Doc. That's what they told me I had. They said I would have to have an operation. My friend had that done successfully but he has a four-inch scar over his elbow. I heard that you fix these in your office."

He then asks, "How come the doctors don't do it like you do?"

I tell him, "I don't know."

He wants to know what I'm going to do. I tell him the protocol, then say, "I want you to listen carefully. If you don't like what I say, you can go back to Butte right now and we'll still be friends. Listen to me!"

I go on, "I had tennis elbow when I was forty. It went away, untreated, after a couple of years. Yours could too."

Then I ramble, "Ten years ago, we made a survey of the patients I had operated on over a twenty-year period. Mrs. Losee helped me obtain the data and we got a good database, not just twenty or thirty patients. This is what we found: Eighty-five of a hundred will be over their symptoms by eight weeks after their operation. Ten will take a season to get over it. It seems as though every patient who lives in Livingston takes that long. If the operation takes a season to work, the symptoms could have disappeared by then! And the operation fails its mission in five out of a hundred."

And I ramble, "Listen carefully. What can go wrong? Ten years ago I operated on Mary Hauser from Whitehall. The wound leaked joint fluid when I finished her operation. I didn't think a thing about it. That happens frequently. Mary's dripping elbow became infected. *I infected her elbow*. We had her in the hospital for a few days. She had to take antibiotics, and after three weeks her elbow was pretty stiff. It took her *eight* weeks to get over it! She could have had a permanent elbow stiffness, but she didn't. Another possibility is to have a numb spot on the back of your arm. Two of the folks we studied did, but the numbness left. About one in five or six will have a temporary cyst over the spot where we operate. A fellow from Lincoln whom I operated on twenty years ago took twelve weeks for his cyst to go away. I don't know of any cysts that remained. If you still have the sore elbow after four months, I'll do it again. A 'redo' is more likely to fail. I had two brothers who needed a redo seventeen years after I first operated on them. It's unlikely I'll be doing any redo's seventeen years from now!"

I hate this part, but I continue, "Remember! I don't carry

malpractice insurance. The insurance people want more than I make. That's because my practice is different. If something goes wrong, and you want to sue me, I'll have to fight like hell to keep our home, and you and your lawyer won't get much, so now is the time to think of this. If you want this kind of 'protection' "—I quietly think, "revenge" is a better word—"I'll send you to Dr. Johnson in Billings. He does this operation and he carries malpractice insurance. Do you want me to do it?"

"Yeah, Doc; that's what I came here for. I already heard you don't have malpractice."

And I wonder if the patient heard half of my words.

Then I dictate my orders to him. He writes them. These pertain to his aftercare. We swap chairs so he can write comfortably on my desk. I provide him with a prescription for an antibiotic if he needs it. I provide him with what I call a "poison sheet," data about the drug. I preach to him that the decision to take a drug is as important as the decision to have an operation and to tell his friends that.

When we're through writing the orders, I tell him, "Wait here. I'll be back. I have to set it up. It takes lots more time to get ready than it does to do the job. I'll come and get you when I'm ready."

"Can my wife watch? She's been waiting out in the car with our dog. Just a minute. I'll go get her."

I am introduced to his wife and I repeat many, many, many words. In the treatment room I start to prepare the patient's left elbow. I dry-shave the area and scrub the skin with surgical soap. Ten-twenty-nine, Mrs. Clark, could kill me, she's so sick of the story, but the dry shave always reminds me of it. As I shave, I begin:

"A couple of years ago a man came here from Plevna, Montana, to have this done. That's way over by Broadus, I think. That day, I offered him some salty licorice I had picked up in Canada when I was visiting our kids. He didn't like it and he spit it out. I must have had a dull razor blade that day. It took a lot of scraping to get the hair off. Two weeks later—it was near Christmas—the patient sent me a package. Within it, were his words: 'Merry Christmas, Doc. Here is some proper candy and a new package of razor blades!' "

The story is finished and the patient with the tennis elbow is seated with his left arm flexed and resting on the end of the table. At that moment our big physician's assistant, Ron Handlos, sticks his head in the door to ask, with a devilish smile, if anybody has fainted yet. Whenever he says that, some of my patients start to turn green. But, I've figured an antidote. I put the patient to work. I order the patient to help me by extending the wrist when I ask. This tightens the cords that I sever.

So we do the little tennis-elbow operation with a number-fifteen blade. There's nothing to suture. We wrap the elbow in an Ace bandage and our patient walks down the hall. We say good-bye and that's that. Not operating any more? That's right! The tennis-elbow operation really isn't an *operation*. It's like paring fingernails. It's an "office procedure"! That whole five-minute process must have taken an hour and a half. That amount of time spent on such a minor procedure wouldn't fare very well with a modern, business-oriented health maintenance organization, would it? How in the hell do these businesses "maintain" health?

The first tennis-elbow operation I did was thirty years ago. The woman from the Ruby Valley asked me about her aching elbow. She developed it during the winter bowling season. She was the last patient of the day. I examined her and rapidly diagnosed a tennis elbow. She asked me to help her. I told her that my friend, Dr. Igor Bitenc, in Montreal, had told me that he had seen his old professor in Vienna make a cut over the sore area. I emphasized that I had never done it. She asked me to try. I painted her elbow with tincture of iodine, injected xylocaine into the sore area, and cut the aponeurosis just below the epicondyle. I put a Band-Aid over the cut. She went home right away. I went home too. It succeeded. Everybody was innocent. Everybody was happy after a fifteen-minute affair. Those were the days when my heart was young and gay!

Some Patients Need Time with Their Doctor

MY RETIRED ORTHOPAEDIC friend, Dr. Perry Berg from Billings, and I lose our minds when we get together. On these occasions we nearly stroke out from laughter. During dinner we hurl anecdotes at each other in loud voices as we lean forward over our plates making sure our messages (with occasional moistened tidbits of cake) reach each other's ears. Why is it that the more *painful* the experience was for us, the *funnier* it now seems to both of us? We recall our roles, our dignities, our prides, our fantasies, our frustrations, the revelation of orthopaedic crap that once besmudged our young brains.

As the laughter dies down, from exhaustion and social necessity, we soberly admit to each other, in more quiet voices, that in our later years we both tended to approach surgical nihilism, and that is to say, and I think Perry would agree, we turned toward *the direction of caution*, not from fear but from lifelong observation and orthopaedic disappointments.

As a way of bowing out of my beloved practice, I have appointed myself to the role of consultant, a Montana definition of which is "a castrated tomcat." My area of expertise is very limited, and people seem to know what it is. I know and remember a lot about knees, less about shoulders, some about feet, and a hell of a lot about tennis elbows! Many of these present-day consultations are not from other physicians nor from other orthopaedists but are sought by the patients themselves.

My French friend Dr. Guy Liorzou says *listen* is the first commandment of the clinician.

The thirty-three-year-old lady ruptured her anterior cruciate ligament on a Sunday when skiing with her boyfriend at Big Sky, Montana. The ski patrol brought her down the hill in a toboggan. Her boyfriend transported her to the emergency room, where she was seen by an orthopaedist and was told to have her knee operated on within five days or it would be too late.

Ten-twenty-nine, my secretary, respected her urgent request for consultation and arranged a priority appointment. The patient came to the office and started to weep. She made her living as a waitress, and had neither insurance nor money. Most of all, she was terrified that if she did not have the operation done she would have a crippled knee. I listened.

The next commandment for the clinician to obey is to *look at the function.* Let's see what this lady can do. She wore one of those awkward canvas straight-leg braces. She had not yet removed it for four days. No one had told her how long to wear it, how to manage a shower, what to do when it slipped down, how to relieve its itching, or whether to wear it in bed. She actually thought something would come apart if she took it off. Why not? Doctors frighten people at times. I asked her if she would like to get rid of the damned thing. She breathed a sigh of approval. When it was removed she spent four or five minutes itching and rubbing her extremity. I quickly checked its stability. She slowly extended and flexed her knee with great satisfaction. There was no swelling and no tenderness about her knee. She could painlessly stomp her leg on the floor when she stood. She carefully tested a first step on the leg with no trouble. I told her how to stiffen her knee, then asked her to walk across the office floor while keeping her injured knee stiffly straightened. No problem.

I interrupted the functional exam to carry out the third

commandment. *Examine the patient.* An examination of the knee is more fun than going fishing for me. This lady had a slightly positive Lachman's sign and anterior-drawer sign. These positive tests show abnormal movement when the examiner attempts to slide the upper tibia forward relative to the lower femur at the knee joint. She also had a suggestion of a pivot shift, the giving-way dysfunction of the knee. I tested and obtained a little slide to the joint without a jolt or jamming. If there is jamming when the knee is tested, the injury is usually serious enough to indicate an operation. She brought X-ray pictures that did not help me improve my diagnosis.

From this examination, I now knew she had ruptured or stretched the anterior cruciate ligament of her knee. I knew a lot about that. Now I felt safe in looking at her function again. It was time to take a walk with the lady. She did very well. We walked down the hall and tried the stairs. She did very well one step at a time. We walked out doors. We tried a little trot. It was more of a gallop, but after twenty yards it smoothed out. We talked about twists and sudden stops and how they would make her knee go out. I actually taught her how to carefully make her knee "go out" by showing her how to twist and lean on the injured leg while supporting herself, leaning forward, and grasping the side of the examination table. I taught her to practice this, daily, *to learn what maneuvers to avoid.*

We then listened again. This lady clearly did not want an operation at this time. I saw no urgency and asked her to return in two or three weeks for more instruction. It was all right for her to return to work when she felt able, but I cautioned her that giving way on twists, turns, or sudden stops would occur until she mastered her new impairment.

The crying was over. She returned to work and a year later doesn't give a damn about skiing! She had but three slight giving-way episodes all year. When asked if she was ready for an operation yet, her answer was, "Hell no, not me!" She was told her knee was at an increased risk. She well understood that an operation on her knee was a possible eventuality.

The old fellow came to Ennis from a couple of hundred miles away. "I'm a car salesman. I stand around a lot in the cold and in parking lots. I'm okay walking, but my knees hurt if I lift heavy stuff. I'm a little stiff in the morning and when I get out of my car after a long ride. My family doc sent me to the orthopaedist and he told me I need a new knee. I'm afraid *not* to go through an operation after his recommendation. He did not give me an alternative. I want to know what you think. Can I let it go too long? I've decided to do what you tell me. You operated on my neighbor's shoulder years ago."

"Did I wreck him?" I ask.

"No." He laughed.

I prod, "Come with me. We're going outside. Put your jacket on."

He walks down the hall with an ever-so-slight side-to-side motion that we call crabbing. He reciprocates as he walks down stairs, advancing first one leg, then the other. He runs up the stairs for me. He jumps down the last two steps and lands on both feet without complaint. We take a walk together. I point to downtown Ennis below the alluvial terrace and ask if he would have trouble walking there.

"No," is his answer.

We walk a hundred yards on the flat. I don't see him crab from side to side now. Let's see you hop on your right foot. Hop toward me and stop on the first painful hop. He gave ten hops on the right foot but stopped after six on the left.

"Could you walk to the tree line there?" I point a quarter of a mile away. He responds, "I can walk all I want, Doctor. I'm just stiff at times, and my left knee hurts if I stand on it for any length of time. I can relieve it by shifting my weight."

I conclude that his function is slightly limited. It is not bad today. I'm not asking him. I'm watching him.

Back inside, I examine him: The left knee is ever-so-slightly bowed. It doesn't wobble as if it has worn away substance. It didn't settle or perceptibly bow with each step. I squeeze the inside knuckles together while I flex and extend his knee and I get no squeak of bone on bone, nor does the test hurt him. He deserves an X-ray study. I want to see the films he brought along with him. His X-ray confirms my thought. He had narrowed a bit on the inside of his left knee from joint wear.

I asked him again, "You told me you didn't want an operation, didn't you?

"Don't have your knee operated on until *you want it operated on*. There are risks to those operations. *I* don't know of harm in waiting too long. If you died, it'd be too late to operate, that's for sure! Maybe a serious illness would make an operation not advisable in the future. And if your back doesn't bother you, don't worry about rocking from side to side as your walk, keep doing it. It's nature's way of taking the load off your knee."

I concluded the patient had been offered a serious operation before it was really needed. I thought that this man's first consultation had been hurried and the conclusion had been formed without benefit of the patient's contribution to the study. But these consultations take time—I can't do more than five or six a day.

A woman comes to consult and volunteers, "I'm thirty-five-years old. I teach dancing four times a week. I twisted my knee and my surgeon took out my outside cartilage. He did this last March. It's July and I'm still on crutches and in a lot of pain."

I look at her function and realize that this lady is in trouble. She can only ambulate by hopping on her uninjured extremity.

I examine her and am shocked to see that in four months, the operated side is beginning to look knock-kneed. The joint is swollen and stiff. The X-ray confirms bone rubbing on bone over the outside knuckles.

"What has your orthopaedist recommended?" I asked.

"He wants me to wait a while before putting in an artificial joint. I was supposed to be able to walk in a week or two after the cartilage operation. They did the operation through the arthroscope. They say football players go back to playing in a couple of weeks after the arthroscope. Mine is taking an awfully long time getting over it. What do you think, Doctor?"

"I don't operate any more. I think I'm going to send you to another orthopaedic surgeon a long ways from here. And, I'm going to send you to him as quickly as you can arrange and as quickly as we can get an appointment."

A year later the patient was off her crutches following a formidable wedge operation performed above her knee joint. Her knees no longer "knocked," but she still limped. Her pain was alleviated, but dancing was history!

My thesis is that these difficult problems need *unhurried*, thoughtful, caring study and analysis. They need *unhurried*, proper, and well-contemplated supervision—something that the orthopaedic surgeon in the full swing of his or her practice should find the time for. The service is possible, necessary, and fulfilling. It's a bit like old fashioned "doctoring"!

Epilogue

I'm So Damned Glad!
Now, I'm So Damned Glad!

AT THIS MOMENT I have placed the receiver back on its hook and I heave a happy sigh. Olive had handed me the phone indicating that it was Gus Hassock calling me from Great Falls, Montana.

"Doc, this is Gus Hassock."

"Yes, Gus, the last time I saw you was when Phil Pallister and I talked to your students at M.S.U. (Montana State University) about some ethical problems that frequently faced us. That was a few years ago."

"Yes, Doc, at least seventeen years ago."

"What's on your mind, Gus?"

"Next Friday, April fifteenth, that baby you delivered, Kim, will be forty years old, and I want to tell you how proud I am of her and I want to remind you of your part. She is a director of special education in a school in Golden Valley outside of Minneapolis."

We brought each other up to date, and he reminded me that, after I had delivered his daughter, his wife, Corinne, wanted a cold beer. He continued, "You went down to Oscar Clark's bar and brought up a six-pack. You, Madeline Flowers, and I had a cold beer in your office. Even though Corinne had asked for one, after you got it, Corinne changed her mind. She wasn't feeling so well."

I responded, "Gus, Madeline Flowers was a master nurse. She kept me in line."

"And Doc, do you remember her husband, Johnny Flowers?"

I certainly did. He was a cowboy legend. He met his

240

boss, Mr. Anceny, with a team of horses drawing a buck-board. This was at the end of a branch line of the Northern Pacific Railroad. It was called *Anceny*. (Ted Turner owns the spread now.) They both were seated and Johnny Flow-ers was driving his boss in the outfit back to the home place. Anceny asked Flowers, "John, show me how they drive on the reservation?" (Reportedly and proudly, John Flowers was part Cherokee.) John stood up in the buck-board. With his left hand, he whirled his big hat about his head while yelling some obscenity of the day. He threw the reins as far as he could above and in front of the horses' heads. With his now-free right hand, he shot his six-shooter into the air. There was a run-away and Anceny was taught.

We joshed some more and hung up.

Gus Hassock was talking about his daughter, Kim. Kim's mother had advised at the conclusion of her delivery, "Doc, what you need is a long-handled spoon!"

Now, I initiate a phone call to my secretary at her home today.

"Danette?"

No answer. She's not organized yet. She's making some-thing in her kitchen.

I try again, "Ten-twenty-nine?"

Danette's got the phone in her hand. She spouts back to me, "Yes, Ten-twenty-nine." We call each other "Ten-twenty-nine" because I delivered Danette on October the twenty-ninth on my thirty-third birthday. Her mom, Ginny Segota, did all the work that night. Ginny didn't even take time to use the rickety old delivery table in the adjoining little room where we kept the babies. Baby Danette plowed her way, head first, belly down, out across the bottom sheet of Ginny's hospital bed that rested beneath the big east win-dow, the window that revealed the entire view of the Mad-ison Range, the view which reminded Mrs. Orr of God.

I then tell Danette, "Dr. Leslie is being operated by Dr. Sim at the Mayo's right now. Dr. Sim is only going to op-erate to replace his left knee and Dr. Leslie will be ready

to come home Tuesday or Wednesday. It will take Olive
and me three days to get there in our camper so that we can
bring him home as we promised. We're taking the puppy.
I won't be able to see any patients Monday and you said
you could head 'em off."

"Okay."

Hugh, Dr. Leslie, our veterinarian, came to Ennis in the
mid-1950s. After he came I never again had to pull
through, cut off, and "circum-suture" back a protruding rectum of a calf (that was subsequently named "Fannie") on
the manure-soaked, garden-hose-strewn, wet basement floor
of Otis Crooker's Sportsman's Lodge. (Calf survived. I was
promised, but never received, a steak from the same animal
at harvest time!) Hugh Leslie and his wife, Arlene, are all
alone and Olive and I love them and want to help. When
we get to Rochester, maybe I can visit about some orthopaedics with the great Mayo doctors! No matter.

These two little occurrences of the moment to me carry
the joy of the little things of life. I am so damned glad Olive and I chose to do our thing the way we did and where
we did it. I'm so damned glad we weren't fooled by the
gods of power, of money, of fear, of hate, of fame. I'm so
damned glad we're human, imperfect, and know those
things. I'm so damned glad we needed so little law, that we
never sued. I'm so damned glad we could dream, we could
think, we could pray, we could work, we could play, and
that Olive is my wife and we are parents and grandparents.
I'm so damned glad I was a doctor, that I learned so much
about life and creativity, and so little of killing and destruc-
tion. I'm so damned glad that Olive and I were taught to
love people, and that we did love people. Like all people,
we need our privacy for rest and repose. And, as life is
given to us, we shall always come forth to love some more!